Praise for **CAREERS** *in Student Affairs*

"*Careers in Student Affairs* arrives at precisely the right moment for our profession. Each chapter brings research to life, illuminating how best to decipher institutional cultures. Readers will be asked to think deeply about complex and difficult subjects in fresh, new ways, and will be rewarded with enhanced confidence in their decision making. I can envision those new to the field engaging with their supervisors and colleagues around this book as a welcome, shared experience. This book is a must-read for all of us who seek to build a community of next generation student affairs thinkers and doers."

—**Felice Dublon,** Vice President and Dean of Student Affairs, School of the Art Institute of Chicago

"This text is a fabulous next step for the existing literature on student affairs career practice and advancement, as it takes into account a wide spectrum of career stages and pathways. The authors adeptly ameliorate critical issues relevant to a range of higher education administrators both theoretically and practically, which increases understanding and skill development in essential career areas."

—**Brett Perozzi,** Associate Vice President for Student Affairs, Weber State University

"*Careers in Student Affairs* provides a valuable insider's look at many important areas of the profession that are rarely discussed in such detail. The authors use theoretical frameworks to understand and inform practical issues, which brings the classroom closer to the field. Faculty, new professionals, mid-level professionals, and senior-level professionals will all benefit from reading it."

—**Timothy Ecklund,** Chair, NASPA Faculty Council

"This book clearly articulates the advice and career guidance student affairs professionals commonly seek. The knowledge and insights the authors have gained from decades of experience are woven together in a manner that promotes immediate application to the myriad of issues that challenge student affairs professionals on a daily basis. Individuals in early stages of their career development as well as experienced professionals will find this book to be an essential reference that 'demystifies' the unwritten operating rules for professionals in higher education. Each topic is addressed with a perfect blend of theory, research, and real-world application."

—**Kathryn T. Hutchinson,** Vice President of Student Affairs, St. John's University

CAREERS
in Student Affairs

Student Affairs Administrators
in Higher Education

CAREERS
in Student Affairs

A Holistic Guide to
Professional Development
in Higher Education

EDITORS
PEGGY C. HOLZWEISS & KELLI PECK PARROTT

Careers in Student Affairs: A Holistic Guide to Professional Development in Higher Education

Copyright © 2017 by the National Association of Student Personnel Administrators (NASPA), Inc. All rights reserved.

Published by
NASPA–Student Affairs Administrators in Higher Education
111 K Street, NE
10th Floor
Washington, DC 20002
www.naspa.org

No part of this publication may be reproduced, stored in a retrieval system, or transmitted in any form or by any means, now known or hereafter invented, including electronic, mechanical, photocopying, recording, scanning, information storage and retrieval, or otherwise, except as permitted under Section 107 of the 1976 United States Copyright Act, without the prior written permission of the Publisher.

Additional copies may be purchased by contacting the NASPA publications department at 202-265-7500 or visiting http://bookstore.naspa.org.

NASPA does not discriminate on the basis of race, color, national origin, religion, sex, age, gender identity, gender expression, affectional or sexual orientation, or disability in any of its policies, programs, and services.

Library of Congress Cataloging-in-Publication Data

Names: Holzweiss, Peggy C., editor. | Parrott, Kelli Peck, editor.
Title: Careers in student affairs : a holistic guide to professional development in higher education / Peggy C. Holzweiss and Kelli Peck Parrott, Editors.
Description: Washington, DC : NASPA, [2017] | Includes bibliographical references and index.
Identifiers: LCCN 2016054092 (print) | LCCN 2016058941 (ebook) | ISBN 9780931654640 (pbk.) | ISBN 9780931654657 (ePub) | ISBN 9780931654763 (Mobi)
Subjects: LCSH: Student affairs services--United States. | Student affairs administrators--Training of--United States. | Student affairs administrators--In-service training--United States. | Student affairs administrators--Professional relationships--United States.
Classification: LCC LB2342.92 .C37 2017 (print) | LCC LB2342.92 (ebook) | DDC 378.1/97--dc23
LC record available at https://lccn.loc.gov/2016054092

Printed and bound in the United States of America

FIRST EDITION

CONTENTS

Preface   ix

PART I: PROFESSIONAL PERFORMANCE

Chapter 1   Contemporary Challenges in Higher Education Administration   3
Amelia Noël-Elkins

Chapter 2   Understanding Campus Cultures   25
Rebecca McBride Bustamante

Chapter 3   Practicing and Developing Professionalism   45
William Smedick

Chapter 4   Building a Support Network   67
Kevin W. Bailey and Mikia Carter

Chapter 5   Practicing Politics: The Art of the Possible in the Milieu of the Maddening   91
David W. Parrott

Chapter 6   Conflict and Resolution in the Workplace   117
Merna Jacobsen

Chapter 7   Ethics and Ethical Decision Making   141
Peggy C. Holzweiss

PART II: PROFESSIONAL DEVELOPMENT

Chapter 8 Authoring Personal and Professional Success 167
Peggy C. Holzweiss

Chapter 9 Taking the Job Search to the Next Level 195
Lesley-Ann Brown-Henderson and Shelia Higgs Burkhalter

Chapter 10 Accepting and Starting a New Position 225
Peggy A. Crowe

Chapter 11 Becoming a Faculty Member 245
Mimi Benjamin and John Wesley Lowery

Chapter 12 Strategies for Effective Supervision 267
Kelli Peck Parrott

Chapter 13 Advancing to Leadership Levels: Changing Rules 293
Dean Bresciani

Chapter 14 The Keepers of the Profession 313
Donald D. Gehring

The Authors *327*
Index *333*

PREFACE

IN THE EARLY days of master's preparation programs in student affairs, faculty could expect students to be in their 20s, attend graduate school full-time, and come to the programs with minimal or no work experience in the field. Yet as the demographics of the undergraduate populations on college and university campuses have changed, so too has the composition of the students in graduate programs. Master's students are now of varying ages, may have experience with full-time employment either in higher education or other types of organizations, come from diverse backgrounds with a wide array of expectations and needs, and require a variety of educational options, from part-time attendance to online course delivery.

ORIGINS OF THE BOOK

Most books on professional development in higher education have prioritized the needs of one specific audience, such as new professionals or mid-level managers. Books for new professionals match the demographic and descriptive characteristics of graduate students entering the field, and books targeted to mid-level professionals assume that a graduate degree has already been earned and foundational knowledge mastered. Neither type of book meets the needs, for example, of the graduate student who worked for 5 years in industry before deciding to pursue a career in higher education. He is not a new professional. He has full-time work experience, knows how to conduct a job search, and has supervised others. Nor does either type of book address the needs of the 40-year-old who started working at a college without a graduate degree, advanced due to experience and performance, and now needs a master's degree to obtain a management position. She fits the description of a mid-level manager who is ready to assume more leadership responsibilities but does not yet have the required foundational background.

In addition, existing books on professional development in higher education often focus on personal journeys. Although these stories can be quite powerful for communicating messages, they run the risk of being dismissed because readers must be able to connect the contexts in the stories to their individual circumstances before they can internalize the messages. The stories also often lack links to theory and research that could help make them more relevant to a broader audience.

The idea for *Careers in Students Affairs: A Holistic Guide to Professional Development in Higher Education* was generated by two higher education faculty members reflecting on the challenges of finding relevant textbooks on professional development to use during practicum courses. We would assign one book only to find that our students resonated with pieces of it but dismissed the rest as too basic for their needs. We would switch to a different book and encounter the same problem. After some trial and error, we found ourselves foregoing textbooks altogether and finding relevant material elsewhere. This book was born from a need to address a broader cross section of topics at various levels of experience and bring in theory and research to complement practical advice.

THREE INTENTIONS

Careers in Student Affairs: A Holistic Guide to Professional Development in Higher Education is written with three primary intentions. The first intention is to pick up from the point that texts for new student affairs professionals end. Most of these texts focus on the needs of first-time professionals and are useful resources with relevant insights. This book assumes that readers are familiar with the topics covered in such publications and need information on transitioning from their first positions to further levels of leadership.

The second intention is to address contemporary issues in the higher education environment that are not covered in the graduate curriculum but that employers expect student affairs professionals to be prepared for from their first position and beyond. This book discusses "soft skills" related to these issues, including conducting organizational culture audits, navigating the political environment, and applying conflict management techniques. Each of these topics is addressed from the perspective of theory, research, and practice.

The final intention of this book is to review supervisory skills. Many graduate students feel underprepared to supervise others when they enter the profession, but in their first positions, they are often asked to supervise paraprofessionals, administrative support staff, or colleagues. Even professionals who work for a few years before taking on supervisory roles are not well trained for supervisory responsibilities, and they often struggle to develop good strategies.

AUDIENCE

This book is intended for several audiences: Graduate students in higher education and student affairs graduate programs who need knowledge about professional development; graduate preparation faculty who teach professional development topics; professionals who are working in their first positions and need to know more about transitioning into more advanced roles; professionals who supervise others and want to improve their skills; and professionals who want to build their competencies and plan for various career paths to senior-level positions, executive leadership, and faculty roles.

HOW TO READ THIS BOOK

The book is organized into two parts. Part I discusses professional performance and covers contemporary challenges in the higher education field, developing professionalism and support networks, and ways to navigate important issues such as organizational cultures, politics, conflicts, and ethics. Chapter 1, "Contemporary Challenges in Higher Education Administration," provides an overview of trends in contemporary higher education, including trends that affect the job market, institutional resources, and organizational structures. Chapter 2, "Understanding Campus Cultures," highlights the importance of understanding organizational culture and discusses how to conduct a personal culture audit to determine "fit." Chapter 3, "Practicing and Developing Professionalism," defines professionalism and describes what professionalism looks like in practice and how it can be developed. Chapter 4, "Building a Support Network," highlights the importance of networking and obtaining mentors and provides strategies for both. Chapter 5, "Practicing Politics: The Art of the Possible in the Milieu of the Maddening," describes the political environment in higher education and reviews ways to navigate it effectively. Chapter 6, "Conflict and Resolution in the Workplace," discusses common types of conflicts and explores key competencies in conflict resolution. Chapter 7, "Ethics and Ethical Decision Making," reviews ethics and ways to make effective decisions when faced with competing values.

Part II addresses professional development, such as defining personal and professional success, advancing a career in student affairs, becoming an effective supervisor, transitioning to faculty roles, and giving back to the profession. Chapter 8, "Authoring Personal and Professional Success," highlights the importance of planning one's professional development and considering issues such as obtaining additional experience, getting an advanced degree, and creating a work–life balance. Chapter 9, "Taking the Job Search to the Next Level," provides guidance on career searches and covers challenging topics such as searching while unemployed, conducting a dual career search with a partner, and seeking positions in an international setting. Chapter 10, "Accepting and Starting a New Position," delves into what happens after a job offer is extended, from negotiations to the first few months on the job. Chapter 11, "Becoming a Faculty Member," offers guidance to those who wish to transition into part-time or full-time faculty roles. Chapter 12, "Strategies for Effective Supervision," provides strategies for building good relationships, working with different generations, and providing critical feedback for improvement. Chapter 13, "Advancing to Leadership Levels: Changing Rules," reviews senior- and executive-level leadership and the responsibilities and challenges of these positions. Finally, Chapter 14, "The Keepers of the Profession," concludes the book by discussing the importance of giving back to the profession and the various ways in which that can be accomplished.

Careers in Student Affairs: A Holistic Guide to Professional Development in Higher Education is a comprehensive look at being a student affairs professional in higher education. The book's purpose is to provide practitioners with the information they need to be successful in their careers.

ACKNOWLEDGMENTS

Writing a book requires a team of people, and this book is no exception. We would first like to thank NASPA–Student Affairs Administrators in Higher Education for recognizing the need for this book and providing an opportunity to see the vision come to life.

The book would not exist without the amazing authors who contributed their wisdom and perspectives to each chapter. They represent the full range of experiences in the higher education field, from faculty to new professionals to seasoned administrators. All had very busy schedules and even some campus crises and personal challenges during the writing process, but they always answered the call for outlines, drafts, and reviews. Their primary purpose in participating in the book was to give back to the profession in a meaningful way, and they accomplished that goal successfully. A personal debt of gratitude is extended to Amelia Noël-Elkins, Kevin Bailey, Mikia Carter, Lesley-Ann Brown-Henderson, Shelia Higgs Burkhalter, Peggy Crowe, Bill Smedick, Merna Jacobsen, Dave Parrott, Rebecca Bustamante, Dean Bresciani, Mimi Benjamin, John Lowry, and Don Gehring. They were all wonderful to work with and truly exhibit what it means to be a professional in the field.

On a personal level, we would like to thank our family and friends for supporting us through this process. Their encouragement kept us going and gave us confidence. Our partners in life provided a listening ear when we encountered challenges, and we would not have been able to complete the book if they had not taken on some of the burdens on the home front. We thank them for always being in our corners. And our beautiful children remind us every day how important it is to have balance in our lives. We are so proud of you!

Finally, we would like to thank all the graduate students who chose higher education as their career path and honored us with the opportunity to teach them in their master's preparation programs. Through their stories of triumph and challenge, they showed us what they needed to know. They inspired this book, and we dedicate it to them.

November 2016

Peggy C. Holzweiss
College Station, Texas

Kelli Peck Parrott
Gainesville, Florida

PART I

PROFESSIONAL PERFORMANCE

CONTEMPORARY CHALLENGES IN HIGHER EDUCATION ADMINISTRATION

Amelia Noël-Elkins

HIGHER EDUCATION HAS frequently come under attack. In 1934, Walter Crosby Eells wrote an entertaining commentary in the *Journal of Higher Education* in which he described higher education as "a curriculum that is a mass of inherited rubbish" (p. 188) and "serving as everything from a reformatory to an amusement park" (p. 187). Although criticisms of higher education are not new, the rhetoric attacking higher education has increased in volume and intensity in the contemporary era (Williams, 2012). For example, in the midst of an unprecedented budget crisis in the state of Illinois, the Illinois Policy Institute published a special report arguing that the higher education crisis was caused not by the lack of a state budget 7 months into the fiscal year, but rather by the exorbitant administrative salaries and generous pensions that made tuition skyrocket (Dabrowski & Klingner, 2015). These types of attacks directed at the personnel in higher education administration are of particular concern to those considering a career in student affairs.

To make informed decisions about careers and job opportunities, student affairs professionals must understand the challenges facing higher education, the demands made of the profession, and the ways in which those challenges and demands affect individual careers. Recent wholesale cuts of staff and faculty at large institutions (Huckabee, 2015; Magaw, 2015) make a career in higher education administration less secure than in the past. No one can predict who or what will be cut during difficult financial times, but it does seem likely that early- and mid-career professionals could be a target. It is imperative that those entering into or occupying student affairs positions do all in their power to make themselves knowledgeable, marketable, and, as much as possible, indispensable.

This chapter will explore:

- the emergence of the student affairs profession,
- modern trends influencing higher education administration,
- ways to remain relevant within the field, and
- ways that supervisors can help student affairs professionals respond to challenges and remain relevant.

EMERGENCE OF THE PROFESSION

Student affairs as an organized profession within higher education in the United States is relatively new, but its roots can be traced to the emergence of colonial colleges in the 1600s (Rudolph, 1990). Colonial colleges primarily educated young male students around the age of 15 whose parents sent them to school because of disciplinary problems at home. The students lived in dormitories, and the tutors who lived with the students monitored them quite closely. Rudolph (1990) described the colonial college tutor as "a young man just out of college . . . probably interested merely in earning a few dollars shortly before going on to theological school or before definitely committing himself to a career" (p. 161).

With roots in the tutor roles played by the college-educated men of those times, student affairs began to take shape as a distinct profession during the late nineteenth century with the naming of deans of men and women (Rhatigan, 2009). These administrative positions were distinct from academic deans and provided oversight for the students' behavior and activities outside the classroom. However, as college student populations grew, deans of men and women saw their responsibilities become more challenging. In an effort to help each other address these challenges, the deans began meeting to discuss issues and exchange ideas. These meetings developed into the first professional associations in the field and began the process of formalizing the various roles and responsibilities held by these early administrators.

Although the functions of student affairs were addressed in some manner throughout the history of higher education, the publication of *The Student Personnel Point of View* in 1937 by the American Council on Education (ACE) marked the first effort to standardize professional practice. Considered by many to be a foundational document, *The Student Personnel Point of View* formally articulated the philosophy behind the student affairs profession. Student affairs professionals were to view students holistically and tend to all aspects of their development—intellectual, physical, emotional, and social. The document also called for coordinated efforts in 23 functional areas as well as national leadership for the profession.

Today, two national associations, NASPA–Student Affairs Administrators in Higher Education and ACPA–College Student Educators International represent the primary interests of and research about the profession. Yet even these organizations are relatively young. ACPA became a stand-alone organization in 1991 (Caple, 2009). NASPA (2015) was founded as early as 1918 but assumed its current form in the 1960s and 1970s. Other professional associations, representing the large variety of functional areas now existing in higher education, share a similar history, and they continue to evolve as well.

MODERN TRENDS IN HIGHER EDUCATION

Although the student affairs profession now has associations, philosophies, standards, theories, and research to guide practice, a complex interplay of social trends and shifting institution needs also shapes the changes that occur within the field, and student affairs professionals must understand the way in which these trends and changes affect their roles on campus if they are to prepare themselves to meet employers' needs and have longevity in the field.

Recruiting Executive Leadership from Industry

Today, as the responsibilities of the presidency shift from running the institution to acquiring and managing resources, governing boards are increasingly looking to industry leaders rather than academic administrators to manage the business side of the institution (Cook & Kim, 2012). The ACE American College President Study (Cook & Kim, 2012) found that 20% of the presidents they surveyed came from careers outside of education. Traditionally, academic administrators have risen through the ranks to the presidency and other executive leadership positions (Cohen & Kisker, 2010). Leaders who rose through the ranks understood the institution and the effects of higher education on students.

Industry leaders can have a positive effect on certain aspects of a higher education institution, but they can have a negative effect if they do not prioritize student learning and development when they make decisions that require balancing a variety of competing demands. Constituents of higher education (e.g., students, parents, donors) have legitimate concerns about the costs of college, yet they also often demand individualized attention and high-quality facilities (e.g., state-of-the-art recreation centers, luxury residence halls, etc.) as well as discounted rates for tuition and fees (Rivard, 2014). Employers demand graduates who have experience working with the technology and software found in the modern work environment (National Association of Colleges and Employers, 2014), and to meet this demand, institutions must acquire and continually upgrade technological tools so that students develop the required competencies before entering the workforce. Meanwhile, critics (including legislators, politicians, and pundits) condemn what they view as lavish and exorbitant spending on nonfaculty positions. Students and their parents consider these positions essential, but critics consider them superfluous and believe they increase administrative costs (Pearlstein, 2011). When the president comes from outside the academy and does not prioritize learning over business efficiencies and meeting consumer expectations, balancing these demands can become more complicated.

Some high-profile presidents with a corporate or business background have caused consternation and criticism because they did not understand the academy and the learning environment (Jaschik, 2016; Miller, 2015). Executive leaders from outside the academy who apply traditional business strategies may make resource decisions based on where most of the funds are being spent without fully understanding the consequences of those decisions. Some studies indicate that the expansion of student services has been a significant driver of increasing college costs (Desrochers & Hurlburt, 2016; Descrochers & Kirshstein, 2014). Executives with a corporate or business background may curtail spending on student services without realizing that it is important not to.

Getting to know new leaders and trying to understand their views on the cocurricular environment can help student affairs professionals discover ways to educate these leaders about the value of student affairs. As part of this educational effort, professionals can refer to data on the positive effect of student service programs and resources on student learning, and in so doing, they can help leaders understand how their management decisions may affect student success.

Growing Competition for Students

This trend has changed the landscape of higher education by putting pressure on all parts of higher education to continually meet the needs and demands of students and their families. In response to the increased pressure, institutional priorities have shifted from student learning and development to student satisfaction, to the detriment of the learning environment. The trend is likely to continue, and competition for students will likely increase, since the number and percent of U.S. high school graduates is expected to drop through 2023 (Hussar & Bailey, 2014), with the largest declines expected in the Northeast and the Midwest.

Changing Organizational Structures

To address declining enrollment and revenue flows and meet the demands of consumers, employers, and critics, a growing number of institutions are making changes to their organizational structures. Leaders may reduce personnel, reorganize various areas of the institution, or eliminate student resources. Those who work as student affairs administrators are affected by these decisions because leaders may not view the cocurricular experience as critical to the academic mission.

To improve institutional effectiveness, leaders may reorganize reporting lines; for example, they may move academic advising or career services from a division of student affairs to a division of academic affairs. In 2015, the National Association of Colleges and Employers found that although more than half of career services offices were housed in student affairs, a significant number were no longer located there.

Some organizational changes are more extensive. For example, in 2001, in an effort to implement cost-saving measures, Texas Tech University leaders eliminated the division of student affairs (Grassgreen, 2011). A less drastic organizational strategy is to maintain what is offered but merge student and academic affairs to increase efficiency (Cook & Lewis, 2007).

Changes to organizational structures at some institutions illustrate how important a flexible understanding and definition of the term "student affairs" needs to be in the context of a higher education institution. While some functional areas may shift to academic affairs management, services for students are still considered part of the broader student affairs practice. Professionals should have a good understanding of the variety of environments for student affairs operations and prepare themselves to work within those environments by developing strong relationships across the institution. In this way, they equip themselves to adjust to various kinds of structural changes.

Using New Technologies

Massive Open Online Courses (otherwise known as MOOCs), hybrid course delivery, and online institutions have significantly changed higher education's model of content delivery, providing more access to higher education content and knowledge (Kamenetz, 2010). Yet because of this increased access, students have additional expectations that institutions must fulfill. At residential campuses with young adult populations, the traditional face-to-face model of student development and programming are largely successful; however, students taking online courses are not able to access the delivery of student services in the same manner. This population, consisting primarily of older adults (Fetzner, 2013), may even value different student services that require additional resources.

No less challenging is the dependence on new technology to

communicate. This dependence is particularly challenging for student affairs professionals who rely on quality face-to-face contact with students to enhance engagement. Yet students are increasingly technologically savvy and willing to try new communication methods, often without thinking about the consequences. For example, the emergence of Yik Yak and other social media platforms can turn an incident or issue into a viral sensation (Gardner, 2016) perhaps more quickly than professionals are able to respond to if they are not knowledgeable about effective ways to use these technologies.

To meet these challenges, student affairs professionals should understand how to use technology to deliver services and communicate effectively. They can take an online course to experience what a classroom feels like in the virtual environment and thereby gain insight into what services distance education students may need. If they join social media sites to find out what students are sharing there, they are better able to educate students about the consequences of not carefully considering messages before sharing them.

Student affairs professionals also need to make conscious and informed decisions about the degree to which they and their organization will engage. Once an office or organization chooses to have a Facebook page, for example, many other decisions must be made about who will maintain the page, who will be allowed to post items, how often items will be posted, whether negative items published by students will be removed, and so on. Although technology can expand opportunities for engaging and informing students, professionals need to plan and think before they engage.

HOW TO REMAIN RELEVANT AS A PROFESSIONAL

Student affairs professionals who overlook trends and fail to improve their skills and knowledge as required run the risk of being passed over for promotions or other advancement opportunities, whereas professionals who are aware of and responsive to current trends in the field can plan more effectively for their own development and careers. To remain relevant, professionals must make a conscious choice to follow current events in the field and begin adapting to the trends or foreseeable changes.

Major institutional shifts such as changes in presidential leadership may not affect early career professionals in day-to-day work the way they might affect those in mid-level or upper-management positions. Leadership changes may not affect some professionals at all if their specific work function is not on the agenda of the new leadership. However, institutional characteristics can make a difference in how different professionals experience institutional shifts. In smaller institutions, for example, shifts at the presidential level are more likely to have a major impact on the work of early career and mid-level professionals because there are usually fewer administrative layers between those positions and the president.

Other changes can effect student affairs professionals on a more practical level. Financial constraints and budget cuts can have an immediate effect on salaries, career advancement opportunities, and program budgets. Many institutions have implemented furlough days to weather cutbacks (Egger, 2015), and other institutions have eliminated or reduced operating, programming, or travel expenditures to address tight budgets. Individual reactions to these changes may differ depending on the stage of the professional's career. For example, a seasoned professional who has spent several years at a university and who is heavily invested in a retirement system may decide it is wise to ride out the institution's financial difficulties because of his or her long-term investment in that job or community. On the other hand, a younger professional who has been at an institution for a shorter time and who has less invested in retirement or fewer community connections may have more flexibility and may wish to consider a move to another institution or another position. However, the age-old warning that the "grass is not always greener" must be heeded. An institution that is struggling financially now may recover quickly, whereas another institution that appears financially healthy may experience fiscal woes in the near future. Careful investigation and thought must be given before making a career move based on even these most practical of issues.

The following section reviews several topics professionals may wish to consider as they align their own competencies with changes they may encounter in the higher education environment.

Review Professional Competencies

As a good starting point for remaining relevant in the field, student affairs practitioners of all levels should review their résumé or professional portfolio for gaps in knowledge or skills. Although there is no perfect checklist of skills required to move to the next job opportunity, the joint ACPA and NASPA (2015) publication *Professional Competency Areas for Student Affairs Educators* reviews 10 areas of competency that span virtually all student and academic affairs units. The technology competency, for example, includes skills such as being able to adapt to the rapid changes in technology in the field and being able to critically analyze the quality of information gathered through digital tools. To grow and develop competency in technology, student affairs professionals should consider how these skills connect with departmental and institutional priorities and mission and how they can be used to advance the needs of students and build relationships across the institution.

Although no one can be an expert on every topic, a résumé or portfolio does need to outline a breadth and depth of knowledge that demonstrates a student affairs professional's ability to contribute effectively to the work environment. Sheryl Sandberg's (2013) "lean in" concept can help in determining when that threshold has been achieved. When a student affairs practitioner knows enough about the majority of the responsibilities in a position to be able to fulfill those responsibilities effectively and has enough administrative experience to be able to meet the learning curve required for other areas (e.g., basic understanding of resource management) then he or she has demonstrated the mastery and cross-functionality essential for that position.

Know Institutional Types

Student affairs professionals who want to remain relevant in the field also need to understand how current trends affect different types of institutions. The United States is home to more than four thousand 2- and 4-year degree-granting institutions of higher education (Snyder & Dillow, 2015) with a staggering amount of diversity in institutional types, from community colleges to private institutions to large research universities. Various trends in higher education will produce different kinds of changes at each institutional type. For instance, when state funds are reduced, large research universities may increase tuition or aggressively pursue private donations to make up the difference. These institutions benefit from strong enrollment and support from a vast pool of alumni and are thus able to use both methods to replenish the lost funds. Community colleges, on the other hand, must keep tuition low to attract students and typically do not have the benefactors needed to overcome funding gaps. A reduction in state funds for these institutions often means that resources, services, programs, and even staff positions must be eliminated. Professionals who learn more about the different institutional types and how they operate can prepare themselves for working on these campuses and develop the competencies they need to be effective.

Understand Specialization versus Generalization

Student affairs professionals who understand institutional types will also have insight into what student affairs roles may look like at those institutions. For example, community colleges often have limited staff positions, so professionals may have multiple student affairs responsibilities such as advising student government, managing the student center facility, serving as a student conduct officer, and coordinating student orientation. These student affairs professionals are considered *generalists* because they work across multiple functional areas in the field. As institutional size increases, so does the opportunity for more focused roles. In midsize regional institutions, for example, one person may be hired to coordinate new student orientation. These professionals are considered *specialists* because they become experts in one functional area in the field.

Although institutional size and type can affect whether student affairs professionals are generalists or specialists, roles of both types can be found on any campus, and professionals must make conscious choices about which type of role to pursue. New hires with a high degree of specialization may require less training, and they can begin fulfilling needs quickly—a valuable trait to the employer. In addition, in some areas of higher education (financial aid, athletics compliance, etc.), a professional with a high degree of specialized knowledge is of immense value to the office and institution because of the complex and challenging set of rules the office and institution must follow. However, some of the best ideas of most benefit to the office and institution can come from an employee who has experience in a different area of higher education. And having broad knowledge and experience in diverse areas such as campus police, career services, housing, and student activities can provide a professional whose career goal is to become an executive leader, such as a vice president for student affairs, with excellent preparation for the demands of the role. With a broad foundation of that kind, the professional can give the organization well-informed leadership.

Moving between generalist and specialist roles can be challenging. Someone with a high degree of specialization in one functional area may be viewed as not understanding other functional areas and could be overlooked when applying for those positions. On the other hand, someone with a high degree of generalization could be seen as not having the depth of knowledge needed to perform the responsibilities of one functional area. By focusing on transferrable skills and learning about various functional areas, professionals can prepare themselves for working in different types of roles and make valuable contributions within each area.

Identify Professional Development Opportunities

Once student affairs professionals identify gaps in competencies, knowledge, and experience, they should identify professional development opportunities to help close those gaps. Many professionals choose conference attendance as a primary means of development, but it may be difficult to rely on this activity in leaner economic times because travel funds are often among the first things eliminated in many budgets. In addition, many professionals who attend conferences gather small bits of knowledge and interesting ideas only to return to their campus and take no action. For reasons such as these, it is inadvisable to focus only on conferences as a means of professional development and career advancement.

Other options such as involvement in professional organizations and interaction with colleagues across campus are particularly important in developing a professional identity (Hirschy, Wilson, Liddell, Boyle, & Pasquei, 2015). Opportunities for interaction in state or regional professional associations often cost significantly less than those at the national level, and the chance to sit down with a colleague from across campus costs nothing at all. Furthermore, developing a new program or project on campus provides student affairs professionals with valuable administrative experiences and knowledge. In pursuing these kinds of experiential learning opportunities, professionals can increase their knowledge and skills, become more valuable to their current employer, and improve their professional identity (Hirschy et al., 2015).

Student affairs professionals should also take advantage of unplanned opportunities to adapt to change and build new competencies. For example, reorganizations, whether desired or not, may provide an opportunity for new skill development, collaborative projects, new positions, or even a promotion. Krumboltz's (2009) happenstance learning theory posited that "human behavior is the product of countless numbers of learning experiences made available by both planned and unplanned situations in which individuals find themselves" (p. 135). To help maintain a positive perspective and become more proficient at adapting to new situations, think of each change in higher education as an opportunity to develop professionally.

Identify Personal Priorities

As student affairs professionals make decisions about development opportunities that can help them remain relevant in the field, they must also consider their priorities and lifestyle choices while keeping in mind that their priorities may change over time. At all stages of their careers, professionals should have conversations with supervisors, peers, and mentors about aspects of career growth that are most important to them, such as time commitment, depth of student contact, and professional experience in areas that are not listed in their current position descriptions. Super's (1980) self-concept theory stated that a person's life at any given moment is the aggregate of the various roles that person assumes at that time. If that is so, early career professionals without personal commitments such as children or life partners may want to devote themselves to their career and soak up every professional opportunity that presents itself. In this early career stage, professionals have exceptional opportunities to gain experience by volunteering for activities such as alternative spring break trips, evening student activities, or study abroad supervision. Mid-career professionals, on the other hand, may make career and professional development choices based on different priorities. Partners, children, or aging parents can limit the types of responsibilities they can consider. Ideally, mid-career professionals have obtained a variety of experiences early in their careers and can be more selective in choosing development opportunities that best enhance their current skills and knowledge. Options include focusing on professional organization leadership or volunteering to lead an institutional task force.

It is not necessary for every student affairs administrator to define professional development as career advancement or to adopt career advancement as the goal of development. By choice, some professionals may wish to spend their entire careers in one type of support position, and they may have no desire to advance to leadership or management positions. These professionals provide value to the work environment through mentoring younger professionals, providing historical continuity, and using their extensive, in-depth knowledge to strengthen their unit. Professional development for these individuals is necessary, worthwhile, and desired, but it may occur in a different way. For instance, they can take on challenging projects, such as managing partnerships with other offices, to stay engaged with the work environment while also improving their skills and better defining their roles.

Understand Different Career Paths

Student affairs professionals also need to determine what type of career path will benefit them most: (a) longevity at one institution or

(b) working at a variety of institutions. Both paths benefit and challenge professionals who are building their professional identities. Professionals who choose longevity at one institution gain an in-depth perspective on processes and procedures, are likely to have numerous connections across the campus, and acquire a deep understanding of institutional culture. Yet a long career at one institution can limit their ability to obtain needed experiences and control the timing of their career advancement. Professionals who choose to work at a variety of institutions, on the other hand, can better manage career transitions and can target positions that will build specific competencies. Professionals who take this path come to understand different institutional types and realize that effective solutions to problems at one campus may not be effective at another. However, changing institutions takes a considerable amount of time, and professionals can spend the first year at a new institution just trying to understand their responsibilities and the institution's culture. Professionals who choose this path also do not gain an extensive knowledge of organizational functions and networks that can be beneficial in future leadership roles. Professionals who are aware of the benefits and limitations of each path, whether they consciously choose one path over another or whether they find themselves following a path because of personal circumstances, are better able to plan their development and create meaningful development opportunities.

Consider Nontraditional Career Opportunities

Student affairs professionals who make an effort to remain relevant can encounter unexpected career opportunities. For example, they may find that their skills and talents match positions in industries outside of higher education, which may come with a significant salary increase and offer new types of career challenges. However, professionals should give considerable thought to making the transition to a new environment. Although industry positions will leverage transferrable skills and abilities, making this type of transition is equivalent to starting a new career. Professionals will need to adapt to and learn the organizational culture and expectations, develop mentors and trusting relationships, and create an entirely different plan for career development. In addition, professionals who move to a position outside of higher education may find that it is more difficult to return to the higher education field at a later point. They need to assess the benefits and challenges to determine whether transitioning to an industry position is a good career decision.

Within the field of student affairs administration, consulting may be an appealing option for those who have enough specialized knowledge and experience. Consulting allows student affairs professionals to use their expertise to help other institutions build capacity on needed topics. Consulting opportunities may initially take the form of invitations to speak at training events, and an increase in invitations may signal that there is a growing need for that expertise, which a professional can then leverage to build a consulting career. The career may be either full-time or part-time depending on need. Professionals who develop a full-time career in consulting have control over when and where they work, but they do not have institutional benefits, such as health care, and as market forces ebb and flow, they may experience periods of financial instability. Consulting part-time may be more attractive to some professionals because they can continue working at an institution while sharing their expertise with other institutions. However, ethical and legal aspects of this situation must be considered, and professionals should seek supervisor approval as well as abide by any institutional policies and processes covering outside employment.

Finally, the demand for greater accountability in higher education outcomes has created a demand for staff competency and programmatic effectiveness certification, including everything from athletics advising certification to program evaluation. Private organizations, such as accreditation and compliance-based groups, may hire professionals with these skills to become members of site-visit teams to review individual institutions. Professionals who serve as reviewers on these assessment teams gain knowledge of the certification process, expand networking opportunities, and develop competencies that are useful in a variety of work environments. As with part-time consulting, the ethical and legal ramifications of working outside of the institution must be considered.

ADVICE FOR SUPERVISORS

Student affairs professionals in supervisory roles should regularly discuss trends in higher education with their staff members. These discussions can help identify potential challenges to office functioning as well as opportunities for professional development. Early career professionals may not easily make connections between trends and competencies, so being explicit about the ways the two are linked can improve their awareness and understanding. More seasoned professionals who may be ready for additional responsibilities can benefit from a supervisor who encourages them to attend training courses or lead change efforts on relevant topics. Supervisors who take these steps can help their staff members consider what they need to do to remain relevant in the field. Supervisors have a critical role to play in generating that awareness.

When trends affect the institution directly, it is important for supervisors to address the changes openly and maintain a positive attitude. For instance, if budgets must be cut, the supervisor should share the details with staff members and emphasize that the team has the opportunity to identify creative solutions. If organizational changes will occur, the supervisor should have the staff brainstorm about what they may need to learn to be more effective in the new structure, and then provide as much support as possible for that learning. If supervisors see the possibilities, staff members are likely to see them too and embrace the coming changes rather than fight against them.

Finally, supervisors can establish a partnership initiative in which staff members identify opportunities to build relationships across the institution and develop strategies for creating projects with other units. This initiative can help the student affairs office accomplish goals and increase awareness while also encouraging staff members to expand their professional network and build cross-functional competencies. An initiative of this kind also allows professionals to discuss the importance of the cocurricular environment with colleagues who may not fully understand the purpose of student affairs administration.

CONCLUSION

Student affairs professionals work in a complex, evolving environment. Criticisms of higher education continue to influence the ways in which institutions adapt to economic and social change. Adaptations may involve institutional leaders selecting presidents who come from outside the academy, altering organizational structures to increase efficiencies, or investing in technology to meet the demands of constituents. It is imperative that those pursuing or developing careers in higher education be aware of and responsive to the trends as they emerge. Paying close attention to what is happening in higher education allows student affairs professionals to be more deliberate about the skills and knowledge they acquire as they plan their development, seek career opportunities and experiences, and make wise decisions regarding their individual needs.

QUESTIONS FOR REFLECTION

- What trends are affecting my institution right now, and what does it mean for my professional development?

- What connections do I have across the campus, and how can I develop new ones?

- What career opportunities interest me, and how can I become more deliberate about developing competencies for these opportunities?

- In what ways do I currently obtain professional development, and what other methods do I need to consider to improve my professional competencies?

REFERENCES

ACPA–College Student Educators International & NASPA–Student Affairs Administrators in Higher Education. (2015). *Professional competency areas for student affairs educators.* Retrieved from https://www.naspa.org/images/uploads/main/Professional_Competencies.pdf

American Council on Education. (1937). *The student personnel point of view* (American Council on Education Studies, Series 1, No. 3). Washington, DC: Author.

Caple, R. B. (2009). Reflections on 1989–1994. *Journal of College Student Development, 50*(6), 710–711. doi: 10.1353/csd.0.0103

Cohen, A. M., & Kisker, C. B. (2010). *The shaping of American higher education: Emergence and growth of the contemporary system* (2nd ed.). San Francisco, CA: Jossey-Bass.

Cook, B., & Kim, Y. (2012). *The American college president—2012.* Washington, DC: American Council on Education.

Cook, J. H., & Lewis, C. A. (2007). *Student and academic affairs collaboration: The divine comity.* Washington, DC: NASPA–Student Affairs Administrators in Higher Education.

Dabrowski, T., & Klingner, J. (2015). *Pensions v. higher education: Skyrocketing pensions, bloated administrations are pricing students out of college degrees.* Retrieved from https://d2dv7hze646xr.cloudfront.net/wp-content/uploads/2016/02/PensionvsHigherEd_Report_web.pdf

Desrochers, D. M., & Hurlburt, S. (2016). *Trends in college spending: 2003–2013.* Retrieved from American Institutes for Research Delta Cost Project website: http://www.deltacostproject.org

Descrochers, D. M., & Kirshstein, R. (2014). *Labor intensive or labor expensive? Changing staffing and compensation patterns in higher education.* Retrieved from American Institutes for Research website: http://www.air.org/resource/labor-intensive-or-labor-expensive-changing-staffing-and-compensation-patterns-higher

Eells, W. C. (1934). Criticisms of higher education. *The Journal of Higher Education, 5*(4), 187–189. doi: 10.2307/1975149

Egger, R. (2015, December 9). At Western Illinois University, cutting 50 faculty won't be enough. *WNIJ and WNIU Northern Public Radio.* Retrieved from http://northernpublicradio.org/post/western-illinois-university-cutting-50-faculty-wont-be-enough

Fetzner, M. (2013). What do unsuccessful online students want us to know? *Journal of Asynchronous Learning Networks, 17*(1), 13–27. Retrieved from http://sloanconsortium.org/publications/olj_main

Gardner, L. (2016, February 29). The reactive leader. *The Chronicle of Higher Education.* Retrieved from http://www.chronicle.com/article/The-Reactive-Leader/235439

Grassgreen, A. (2011, March 31). Challenging the role of student affairs. *Inside Higher Ed.* Retrieved from https://www.insidehighered.com/news/2011/03/31/texas_tech_university_dismantles_student_affairs_and_eliminates_administrative_positions

Hirschy, A. S., Wilson, M. E., Liddell, D. L., Boyle, K. M., & Pasquei, K. (2015). Socialization to student affairs: Early career experiences associated with professional identity development. *Journal of College Student Development, 56*(8), 777–793. doi: 10.1353/csd.2015.0087

Huckabee, C. (2015, December 14). Western Illinois U. says it needs to eliminate 50 faculty jobs. *The Chronicle of Higher Education.* Retrieved from http://chronicle.com/blogs/ticker/western-illinois-u-says-it-needs-to-eliminate-50-faculty-jobs/107379

Hussar, W. J., & Bailey, T. M. (2014). *Projections of education statistics to 2022* (41st ed.). Retrieved from http://nces.ed.gov/pubs2014/2014051.pdf

Jaschik, S. (2016, March 2). Last nonacademic president? Not a chance. *Inside Higher Ed.* Retrieved from https://www.insidehighered.com/news/2016/03/02/experts-doubt-debacle-mount-st-marys-will-diminish-board-interest-nontraditional

Kamenetz, A. (2010). *DIY U: Edupunks, eduprenuers, and the coming transformation of higher education.* White River Junction, VT: Chelsea Green.

Krumboltz, J. A. (2009). The happenstance learning theory. *Journal of Career Assessment, 17*(2), 135–154. doi: 10.1177/1069072708328861

Magaw, T. (2015, July 10). University of Akron to slice budget by $40M, cut 215 jobs. *Crain's Cleveland Business*. Retrieved from http://www.crainscleveland.com

Miller, V. (2015, December 10). Regents acted "in bad faith" in University of Iowa president search, AAUP concludes. *The Gazette*. Retrieved from http://www.thegazette.com

NASPA–Student Affairs Administrators in Higher Education. (2015). The history of NASPA. Retrieved from http://www.naspa.org/about/history

National Association of Colleges and Employers. (2014). Career readiness competencies: Employer survey results. Retrieved from https://www.naceweb.org

National Association of Colleges and Employers. (2015). *NACE 2014–15 career services benchmark survey for colleges and universities*. Bethlehem, PA: Author.

Pearlstein, S. (2011, November 25). Four tough things a university should do to rein in costs. *The Washington Post*. Retrieved from https://www.washingtonpost.com

Rhatigan, J. J. (2009). From the people up: A brief history of student affairs administration. In G. S. McClellan & J. Stringer (Eds.), *The handbook of student affairs administration* (3rd edition) (pp. 3–18). San Francisco, CA: Jossey-Bass.

Rivard, R. (2014, July 2). Discount escalation. *Inside Higher Ed*. Retrieved from https://www.insidehighered.com/news/2014/07/02/prices-rise-colleges-are-offering-students-steeper-discounts-again

Rudolph, F. (1990). *The American college and university: A history*. Athens, GA: The University of Georgia Press.

Sandberg, S. (2013) *Lean in: Women, work, and the will to lead*. New York, NY: Knopf.

Snyder, T. D., & Dillow, S. A. (2015). *Digest of education statistics 2013* (NCES 2015–011). Retrieved from http://nces.ed.gov/pubs2015/2015011.pdf

Super, D. E. (1980). A life-span, life-space approach to career development. *Journal of Vocational Behavior, 16*, 282–298. doi: 10.1016/0001-8791(80)90056-1

Williams, J. J. (2012, February 19). Deconstructing academe: The birth of critical university studies. *The Chronicle of Higher Education*. Retrieved from http://chronicle.com/article/An-Emerging-Field-Deconstructs/130791

2

UNDERSTANDING CAMPUS CULTURES

Rebecca McBride Bustamante

Cultural understanding is desirable for all of us, but it is essential to leaders if they are to lead. (Schein, 1992, p. 15)

COLLEGES AND UNIVERSITIES are complex organizations. Student affairs professionals who wish to have a successful career need to develop the ability to observe and describe elements of an institutional campus culture. To develop this ability, student affairs professionals need to understand general characteristics of culture and theories of organizational culture. They also need a set of tools to help them identify subcultures within the campus culture and conduct culture audits as well as personal culture audits. Professionals can use these tools to determine whether they fit a particular campus culture, and they can apply these tools when supervising others.

This chapter will review:

- the terms *culture* and *organizational culture*,
- theories of culture and organizational culture,
- the role of subcultures within campus cultures,
- institutional and personal culture audits,

- culturally aware supervision, and
- change leadership.

THE IDEA OF CULTURE

Although the term *culture* is frequently used on college and university campuses to refer to a student affairs culture, a culture of assessment, or a college-going culture, the term is rarely defined or contextualized in ways that reflect the academic literature on culture. What does culture really mean?

The idea of culture has roots in the discipline of anthropology (Hall, 1976; Kluckhohn & Strodbeck, 1961). Traditionally, *culture* has been defined as a learned meaning system consisting of shared beliefs, values, norms, symbols, customs, behaviors, and artifacts—all of which are used by members of a group to make sense of their experiences and to foster a sense of identity and community (Geertz, 1973; Samovar & Porter, 1995). This meaning system is transmitted over time and across generations (Ting-Toomey, 1999) and tends to be more unconsciously experienced than learned (Ting-Toomey & Oetzal, 2001). A culture includes symbols and behaviors that can be observed, as well as norms, values, and beliefs that might not be readily evident, particularly to people from outside the culture. Figure 2.1 displays culture as an iceberg, only part of which is visible above the water's surface.

Figure 2.1. **The Visible and Invisible Elements of Culture**

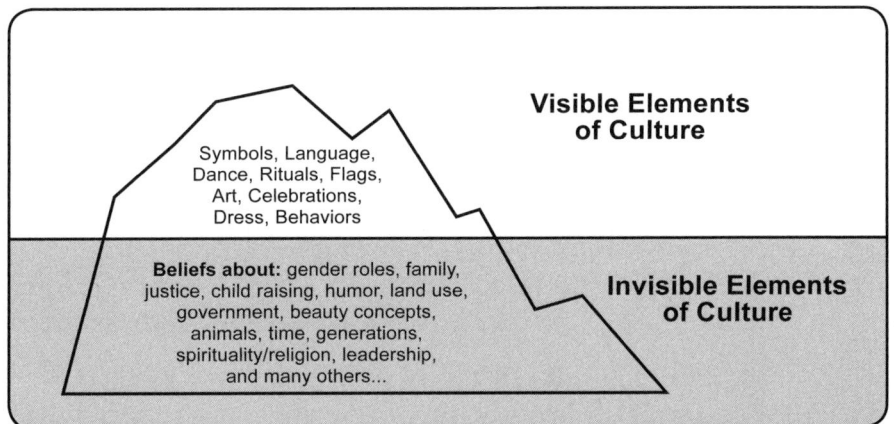

Note. Copyright © 2015 by R. M. Bustamante. Reprinted with permission.

Cultures are generally not homogeneous—that is, the people who belong to cultures usually exhibit individual characteristics in behavior and personality; and subgroups or subcultures exist within larger cultures because people typically identify with more than one group within the culture (Brislin, 1993). Crenshaw (1989) referred to people's identification with various cultures simultaneously as *intersectionality*. Some contemporary authors have gone further and described people's multidimensional identities as *pluri-identities* (Eaton, Bustamante, Ates, & Berg, 2016; Mahdavi & Knight, 2012).

THEORIES OF ORGANIZATIONAL CULTURE

The idea of *organizational culture* emerged from the classic anthropological definition of culture described above. The term specifically refers to the cultures and subcultures exhibited and experienced within organizations. Bolman and Deal (1997) described organizational culture as "beliefs, values, practices, and artifacts that define for members who they are and how they do things at work" (p. 250).

Although the concepts of organizational culture and organizational climate are often confused, some organizational theory scholars have attempted to distinguish them (see Schneider, Ehrhart, & Macey, 2013). In general, organizational culture is considered deeply entrenched and difficult to change—it involves meaning, language, symbols, and norms transmitted over time and across generations and is characterized by shared narratives and traditions (Ting-Toomey, 1999). Organizational climate is considered more ephemeral or temporary—it is something that changes in response to current events, happenings in the external environment, and incidents within the organization. Organizational climate research typically involves the use of surveys, whereas studies of organizational culture are best conducted using qualitative approaches such as ethnography or case studies. Nevertheless, the terms are often used synonymously in higher education environments.

In his popular text *Organizational Culture and Leadership*, Edgar Schein (1992), one of the most renowned scholars of organizational culture, presented a model of organizational culture that has been used across many academic disciplines. His model (see Figure 2.2) consists of three levels:

- *Artifacts* are considered observable and may include signs, logos, architecture, websites, written documents, symbols, mascots, sayings, mission statements, and a myriad of observable formal and informal behaviors, including language that describes accepted norms, which Deal and Kennedy (1982) described as signaling "the way we do things around here" (p. 4).
- *Basic values* are often overtly espoused by organizational members and leaders, but they are sometimes covert and assumed.
- *Underlying assumptions* are generally not overtly expressed and might be identified only through sustained analytical inquiry (e.g., through surveys or interviews).

Figure 2.2. **Schein's Levels of Organizational Culture**

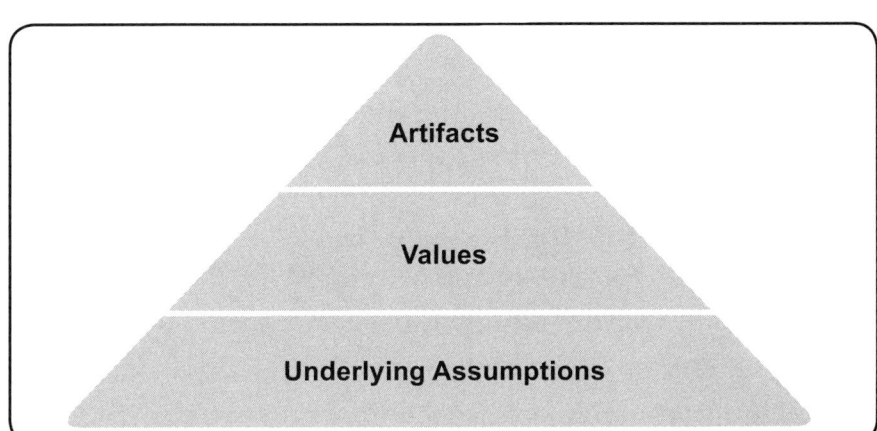

Schein (1992) assumed that the model could be generalized to most institutions and that applications of the model would enhance organizational effectiveness. He also assumed that administrators or leaders enact cultural changes using their authority and influence (Bess & Dee, 2012).

Although campus administrators may find Schein's (1992) model helps them assess or plan for changes in campus cultures, critics question the model's restrictiveness and overreliance on defined cultural descriptors—that is, definitions intended to be a one-size-fits-all model. These cultural descriptors cannot account for the unique cultural contexts of all college campuses and tend to be too broad. For instance, critics claim that positivist approaches like Schein's may exclude the perspectives of actual members of an organization and therefore exclude the voices of diverse groups on a campus.

Manning (2013) observed that there are two basic approaches common to many organizational culture theories:

- The *corporate culture* approach is based on the idea that cultures can be managed by upper-level administrators, who are assumed to be responsible for controlling messages and meaning.

- The more egalitarian *anthropological* approach accounts for the roles all organizational members play in shaping culture and constructing meaning from individual and collective experiences.

The two approaches reflect a positivist view and a social constructivist view, respectively, and both are apparent in various applications of organizational culture theory to campus contexts. Anthropologists tend to be social constructivists; they believe that people construct and recreate their own meaning through interactions with others. They would likely insist that each organizational (or campus) culture has unique characteristics and that to understand these characteristics, observers have to carefully explore or study members' interpretations of artifacts, experiences, messages, and behaviors.

THEORIES OF INSTITUTIONAL OR CAMPUS CULTURE

Scholars of higher education have tried to apply theories of organizational culture to complex higher education organizations. Initially, they focused on developing typologies of higher education organizational cultures (Birnbaum, 1988; Smart & Hamm, 1993). For example, Cohen and March (1974) classified higher education organizations as *organized anarchies* because organizational goals often seemed vague or in conflict. Birnbaum (1988) added three other types of higher education organizations:

- a *collegial* type, which shares power and decision making across an institution;
- a *bureaucratic* type, which depends on a hierarchical structure to define where power and decision making resides; and
- a *political* type, which consists of interest groups competing for power and decision-making authority.

Although simple typological theories like these can be used for general classification purposes, many scholars consider them static and reductionist and argue that they do not adequately account for the unique characteristics of individual campuses, including the individual institution's mission, student demographics, governance and funding structures, and other internal and external characteristics. Tierney (1988) proposed a more focused approach that includes observing the meaning of ceremonies, events, and language used by multiple groups and constituencies on a campus. This approach is less structural, and it represents a more social constructivist and anthropological view of campus cultures. Martin (1992) emphasized that campus leaders must also take an integrative approach to understanding campus cultures; that is, they must review a variety of perspectives from organizational entities and members.

Contemporary models of organizational culture and leadership in higher education tend to stress the importance of accounting for multiple lenses, perspectives, and subcultures (see Ibarra, 2001; Kezar & Eckel, 2002; Manning, 2013). Current theorizing focuses on the fact that people on college campuses generally belong to more than one subculture, and students have multiple identities (see Winkle-Wagner & Locks, 2014). Current theorizing also focuses on emerging models of leadership: transformational leadership, inclusive leadership, grass roots leadership, servant leadership, and socially responsive leadership (see Kezar & Lester, 2011; Kezar, Carducci, & Contreras-McGowan, 2006).

SUBCULTURES IN HIGHER EDUCATION ORGANIZATIONS

Subcultures in higher education organizations can be identified and described. Subcultures are dynamic and constantly changing, but they tend to maintain distinct characteristics. They manifest in different campus structures such as divisions, departments, disciplines, and formal student organizations, and they manifest in less formal social group affiliations based on race, ethnicity, religion, sexual orientation, nationality, physical ability, age/generation, and other identities or characteristics. Typically, subcultures define campus diversity, and administrators make efforts to ensure that diverse subcultures are equally represented in decision making.

Division Subcultures

Subcultures exist within departments in the form of different divisions. For example, within student affairs, the division of residence life and recreational sports may have different cultures, and within academics, the chemistry department and fine arts department may have different cultures. In these cases, student affairs administrators can apply a cultural frame to understand the values, underlying assumptions, and drivers of departments and divisions and develop their knowledge of how to collaborate effectively across campus.

Group Identity Subcultures

Some subcultures are brought to the campus by students, faculty, and administrators of various nationalities, races, ethnicities, religions, sexual orientations, and levels of ability. These group identity subcultures are often related to each other in complex ways because people generally do not belong to only one subculture. Their identity is shaped by many different factors, and they typically have more than one social group affiliation or identity. For example, people might describe themselves as belonging to or identifying with several subcultures related to region, marital status, religion, race, ethnicity, gender, sorority, alma mater, and so on. One person might describe herself as an *Irish, Catholic, single, straight, White, woman, tiger, Chi Omega, from the Midwestern United*

States. Another person might describe himself as a *gay, Black, Latino, Puerto Rican, Methodist, college administrator.* In the academic literature, these multiple identities have been referred to as *intersectionality* (Crenshaw, 1989) and, more recently, as *pluri-identities* (Eaton et al., 2016). Theorists use the newer and more complex idea of pluri-identities to describe the multifaceted, multidimensional, ever-evolving nature of identities, which change as people develop and interact with people from other cultures and with other cultural identities.

Some subcultures are unique to higher education in the United States. For example, in U.S. college and university settings, many higher education professionals distinguish between the culture of student affairs and the culture of academia or the professoriate. Manning (2013) called the professoriate a collegium culture and noted that in this culture, academic freedom is prized and expert power is valued over positional authority. According to Manning (2013), this kind of power is frequently disconcerting to administrators because its underlying assumptions are different from those of administrators: "Where administrators (even those who begin their years as faculty) value efficiency, decisiveness, and expedience, faculty prefer thorough explication of a topic, consideration of long-term implications, and adherence to tradition" (p. 38).

Student affairs professionals can take the first steps toward connecting the very different cultures of academic and student affairs by exploring subcultural differences, attending to the underlying assumptions and motivations of faculty members, learning more about what motivates faculty to be involved in collaborative efforts, and identifying areas of overlap. To establish relationships with faculty members, student affairs professionals can invite faculty to participate in campus activities related to their research or teaching interests. For example, a student affairs professional could ask a few policy professors to help plan a guest speaker series on Title IX programming, or ask a few science professors to provide input on key considerations in advising science, technology, engineering, and math (STEM) majors. In taking such actions, student affairs professionals are better able to meet student needs and develop innovative campus programs.

Relations Among Cultures and Subcultures

Student affairs professionals should take note of subcultures when analyzing or discussing campus culture because to do less ignores the complexity of the institutional culture. As Bess and Dee (2012) pointed out, "A single subcultural category is unlikely to capture the richness and diversity of organizational life in a college or university" (p. 387). Subcultures within organizations are nested, embedded, and overlapping, and one subculture should not be viewed as superior or more valid than another (Manning, Kinzie, & Schuh, 2006). Campus members, including students, administrators, staff, and faculty, often identify openly with various subcultures, and these subcultures intersect with the culture of the institution. Student affairs professionals must therefore consider how the larger organizational cultures and subcultures intersect and reflect the pluri-identities of the people who are part of the higher education organization.

CULTURAL COMPETENCE AND CULTURE AUDITS

Cross, Bazron, Dennis, and Isaacs (1989) originally proposed a developmental model of cultural competence for mental health organizations, and Sue (2001) and Sue and Constantine (2005) applied the model to higher education organizations. Bustamante, Nelson, and Onwuegbuzie (2009) defined organizational cultural competence in educational organizations as how well an institution's policies, programs, and practices reflect the values, perspectives, and experiences of culturally diverse groups (subcultures) of people, particularly student groups. An institution must have culturally competent and responsive practices to cultivate a campus culture that responds caringly and appropriately to students' needs in a culturally diverse world.

One way student affairs professionals can assess organizational cultural competence is by performing culture audits, which typically involve a team effort and multiple methods of exploring the characteristics of a college or university. Elements of campus culture might be manifest in an institution's traditions, artifacts, messages, ceremonies, language, traditions, espoused values, and overt subcultures (see Bustamante et al., 2009; Kezar & Eckel, 2002; Tierney, 1988). The team collects data using a variety of methods, including: organizational climate surveys of various campus groups; focus group interviews and town hall meetings; observations of artifacts and websites; field observations of various campus groups' behaviors; and individual interviews with key stakeholders, such as administrators, campus leaders, students, faculty members, staff, alumni, and community members.

Tierney (1988) first proposed a framework for using culture audits in higher education that includes observing institutional rituals, meetings, and events, and interviewing individuals to examine cultural meaning. Tierney's (1988) framework focuses on six elements:

- mission,
- environment (stable, changing, accommodating),
- socialization of newcomers,
- information (value and control),
- strategy (who makes decisions), and
- leadership (formal and informal).

Similar methods of assessing campus inclusion and equity include Bensimon's (2004) equity scorecard, Bustamante et al.'s (2009) culture audit, and climate surveys (see Harper & Hurtado, 2007). In general, these tools have proven to be valuable to administrators in assessing campus cultures. Higher education professionals benefit by becoming good organizational analysts (Amey, Jessup-Anger, & Tingson-Gatuz, 2015), and culture audits are an effective means by which they can analyze and understand campus cultures.

Personal Culture Audits

A campus culture audit is usually part of a strategic assessment plan to collect data for campus improvement purposes, and a team of people usually implements the plan over time. However, student affairs professionals can use audit strategies to carry out a *personal* culture audit. In career searches, the term *fit* is frequently used to describe the extent to which a candidate either fits within a specific organizational niche or might blend into the current campus or department culture. Conducting a personal culture audit can help professionals determine whether a campus's cultural environment is a right fit for them and matches their career goals.

The following are steps student affairs professionals can to take to collect data for a personal culture audit:

1. **Conduct a thorough environmental scan.** Student affairs professionals should obtain information about how the college or university, student affairs division, and the department of interest might be perceived by those outside the organization. Typically, an environmental scan involves gathering outside information about the campus through media sources such as social media, periodicals, and websites, as well as from professional organizations such as NASPA–Student Affairs Administrators in Higher Education and ACPA–College Student Educators International. When conducting an environmental scan, student

affairs professionals should give keen attention to current legal, social, cultural, and political issues as well as technological and demographic trends affecting the campus. Important information can also be gathered by searching state-level higher education sources.

2. **Examine campus artifacts.** Artifacts are considered manifestations of a campus culture and often provide clues about what is valued and considered meaningful at a particular campus, division, or department. Artifacts often indicate the role tradition plays and how conservative, progressive, or innovative a campus culture is. Many artifacts can be found on campus, division, and department websites. Particular attention should be paid to photos, links, events, articles, and the backgrounds of department members. Student affairs professionals should reflect upon the meaning and values behind these artifacts, and compare them to their own career needs and goals. For example, after reviewing and noting various artifacts, a student affairs professional might ask the following questions: How does this culture appear to align with my values? Do these traditions and practices appeal to me? Is this a place that is on the cusp of change, and is it what I am looking for?

3. **Take time to visit and observe interactions and behaviors.** To get a feel for a an institution and determine whether it is a good fit, student affairs professionals should try to visit the institution to observe artifacts, language, behaviors, and messages on campus. They should walk around, conduct a field study, and observe the building structures. Where are various buildings located? Where are various departments housed? Is there new construction? What statues are placed in prominent places? What messages, mission statements, and art are displayed on

campus? Where do students, staff, and faculty gather? What special events are advertised? What are people talking about? Student affairs professionals should take field notes that can be referred to later when deciding whether to work at the institution.

4. **Informally interview people from the campus.** Student affairs professionals should reach out to a few people in their area of interest who work or have worked on that campus. They should ask these individuals open-ended questions about their experiences, such as: How would you describe the campus culture? What do/did you most like about working there? What do/did you dislike? Professionals should take notes during the interviews but keep any information gathered completely confidential, and they should not share it or post it on social media websites. Professionals should remember that they are doing a culture audit for personal use only in making an important career decision.

Culture Reviews

Sometimes, particularly when a student affairs professional has worked in a position for a while, a campus culture might begin to feel toxic or suffocating. Perhaps the professional no longer feels motivated to push for change in the department or within the existing campus culture. In that case, it might be time for the professional to consider leaving. In *The 7 Hidden Reasons Employees Leave*, Branham (2012) noted that the need to disengage is culture-related if it involves a mismatch of expectations or a mismatch between an employee's values and beliefs and what is expected of the employee in that working environment. Branham (2012) described employee disengagement as a gradual process, not a process triggered by a single event.

To monitor the level of their engagement or disengagement, student affairs professionals may find it helpful to occasionally take the pulse of their department and campus culture. Taking the pulse of a department or culture is similar to conducting a personal culture audit. A professional should review a campus culture to determine if the work environment is still a good fit and aligns with his or her personal values and career aspirations. If the professional determines that a campus culture is not the kind of culture in which he or she will thrive, the professional should begin investigating other employment options.

However, student affairs professionals should bear in mind that there might be opportunities to reinvent themselves within the current culture of their campus. Professionals should pay particular attention to indications that positive change is imminent or possible. These indications may be communicated through messages and artifacts and may come from new leadership, strategic plan initiatives, emerging groups on campus, and active responses to higher education trends. If indications of potential positive change are present, professionals can find ways to reinvent themselves and create coalitions with others who share similar interests.

ADVICE FOR SUPERVISORS

When beginning a leadership or supervisory position in a new campus culture, it is essential to take time to observe and learn about the new culture *before* making any substantial changes or modifications. Not doing this is a common mistake that new leaders make. Supervisors must first obtain the trust, acceptance, and respect of the people they will be working with in the new cultural setting, and to do this, supervisors must first understand the culture and become accustomed or acculturated to it. Supervisors should use a modified personal culture audit approach, ask questions, and observe to learn more about norms, beliefs, expectations, and behaviors shared by group members. Then find ways to adapt to the new culture and begin to make needed changes slowly.

Supervisors should also consider the organizational culture and various subcultures when making leadership decisions and communicating with colleagues. Culture is often considered the elephant in the room and is not discussed, but it is important to metacommunicate or talk openly about cultural conditions and influences. One way to do this is to have open discussions about beliefs and values and how they manifest in artifacts or language and other observable behaviors on campus.

Most supervisors tend to manage employees via policies, procedures, and explicated job roles—in other words, they use structural methods—because those methods seem easy to comprehend and manipulate. But policies and procedures and explicated job rules are often generated from unwritten rules and expectations or shared assumptions concerning cultural affiliation. Typically, employees learn about these unwritten rules when they do not adhere to them and commit a faux pas. Supervisors can manage best if they communicate with new employees about these cultural expectations and in that way help them acculturate to the organization. For example, by discussing how communication should be handled, a supervisor can address both structural aspects (e.g., the supervisor will review all reports before they are published) as well as cultural norms (e.g., e-mail messages need to have a formal tone even when written to office colleagues). Supervisors may also wish to highlight any general practices regarding how employees should interact with each other (e.g., office staff should use the break room to eat their lunches). In this way, they can help new employees understand unwritten expectations.

Finally, supervisors should take time to consider what employees bring to the organization in terms of intersectionality or pluri-identities and how those different identities may affect the organizational environment. When there is an important decision to be made, supervisors should allow each employee to provide feedback and ask each employee to consider the decision from a variety of perspectives associated with various subcultures so that issues can be identified and addressed. After obtaining feedback individually, supervisors should bring the discussion to the group and highlight subculture influences that may need to be considered. This will demonstrate that it is important to consider culture when making decisions, and it allows the group to find relevant ways of addressing various cultural influences.

CONCLUSION

Organizational change is a dynamic, constantly shifting process, but it is not necessarily a fast one: Researchers have suggested that it can take 3 to 7 years for an organizational change to become institutionalized and reflected in organizational practices (Alvesson, 2013). However, the change process can be accelerated if those involved recognize an organizational culture's underlying assumptions and beliefs (Cameron & Quinn, 2011; Schein, 2010). Steps for initiating organizational culture change include obtaining consensus on the meaning of various campus traditions and artifacts, communicating changes through stories, identifying shared values, and strategizing for cultural change (Cameron & Quinn, 2011; Holzweiss, Bustamante, & Fuller, 2016; Mills, Bettis, Miller, & Nolan, 2005).

True change leadership, which involves influencing rather than coercing others, can take many forms, from emergent grass roots leadership to campus coalitions, and it can come from many levels and areas (subcultures) within a campus—it is not contingent on positional power (a position or title). For those reasons, all student affairs practitioners can benefit from having a cultural assessment tool in their professional toolbox and from using it to understand their campus cultures.

QUESTIONS FOR REFLECTION

- How might you apply Schein's (1992) organizational culture model (artifacts, basic values, and underlying assumptions) to the culture of your institution or the institution that interests you?

- Reflect on the results of your personal culture audit. What do you think some of the artifacts (e.g., statues, artwork, architecture, symbols) you observed say about the campus culture? Which messages provide cultural clues?

- What intersections do you see between your personal values and pluri-identities and those of the campus where you hope to work?

- What potential cultural changes or shifts might be occurring or are likely to occur at your institution? How might those shifts provide you with opportunities to develop your career?

- As a student affairs professional, how might you integrate a cultural frame of reference into your leadership approach?

REFERENCES

Alvesson, M. (2013). *Understanding organizational culture* (2nd ed.). London, England: Sage.

Amey, M. J., Jessup-Anger, E. R., & Tingson-Gatuz, C. (2015). Unwritten rules: Organizational and political realities. In M. J. Amey & L. M. Reesor (Eds.), *Beginning your journey* (4th ed.), 17–41. Washington, DC: NASPA–Student Affairs Administrators in Higher Education.

Bensimon, E. M. (2004). The diversity scorecard: A learning approach to institutional change. *Change, 36*(1), 45–52. doi: 10.1080/00091380409605083

Bess, J. L., & Dee, J. R. (2012). *Understanding college and university organization: Theories for effective policy and practice. Volume 1–State of the System*. Sterling, VA: Stylus.

Birnbaum, R. (1988). *How colleges work: The cybernetics of academic organization and leadership*. San Francisco, CA: Jossey-Bass.

Bolman, L. G., & Deal, T. E. (1997). *Reframing organizations: Artistry, choice, and leadership* (2nd ed.). New York, NY: Wiley & Sons.

Branham, L. (2012). *The 7 hidden reasons employees leave: How to recognize subtle signs and act before it's too late*. Washington, DC: Amacon.

Brislin, R. (1993). *Understanding culture's influence on behavior*. New York, NY: Harcourt Brace Jovanovich.

Bustamante, R. M., Nelson, J. A., & Onwuegbuzie, A. J. (2009). Assessing school-wide cultural competence: Implications for school leadership preparation. *Educational Administration Quarterly, 45*(5), 793–827. doi: 10.1177/0013161X09347277

Cameron, K. S., & Quinn, R. E. (2011). *Diagnosing and changing organizational culture: Based on the competing values framework* (3rd ed.). San Francisco, CA: Jossey-Bass.

Cohen, M., & March, J. (1974). *Leadership and ambiguity: The American college president*. New York, NY: McGraw Hill.

Crenshaw, K. (1989). Demarginalizing the intersection of race and sex: A black feminist critique of antidiscrimination doctrine, feminist theory and antiracist politics. *University of Chicago Legal Forum, 1989*(1), 139–167. Retrieved from http://chicagounbound.uchicago.edu/uclf/vol1989/iss1/8

Cross, T. L., Bazron, B. J., Dennis, K. W., & Isaacs, M. R. (1989). *Towards a culturally competent system of care: A monograph on effective services for minority children who are severely emotionally disturbed*. Washington, DC: Georgetown University Child Development Center, Child and Adolescent Services System Program Technical Assistance Center.

Deal, T. E., & Kennedy, A. A. (1982). *Corporate cultures: The rites and rituals of corporate life*. New York, NY: Harper Collins.

Eaton, P., Bustamante, R. M., Ates, B., & Berg, H. (2016). *Tracing faculty privilege(s): Be(com)ing through dialogic cartographic narratives*. Unpublished manuscript. College of Education, Sam Houston State University, Huntsville, Texas.

Geertz, C. (1973). *The interpretation of cultures*. New York, NY: Jossey-Bass.

Hall, E. T. (1976). *Beyond culture*. Garden City, NY: Doubleday.

Harper, S. R., & Hurtado, S. (2007). Nine themes in campus racial climates and implications for institutional transformation. In S. R. Harper & L. D. Patton (Eds.), *Special issue: Responding to realities of race on campus* (New Directions for Student Services, No. 120, pp. 7–24). San Francisco, CA: Jossey-Bass.

Holzweiss, P., Bustamante, R. M., & Fuller, M. B. (2016). Institutional cultures of assessment: A qualitative study of administrator perspectives. *Journal of Assessment and Institutional Research, 6*(1), 1–27. doi: 10.5325/jasseinsteffe.6.1.0001

Ibarra, R. (2001). *Beyond affirmative action: Reframing the context of higher education*. Madison, WI: University of Wisconsin Press.

Kezar, A. J., Carducci, R., & Contreras-McGowan, M. (2006). *Rethinking the "L" word in higher education: The revolution of research on leadership* (ASHE Higher Education Report, Vol. 31, No. 6). San Francisco, CA: Jossey-Bass.

Kezar, A. J., & Eckel, P. (2002). The effects of institutional culture on change strategies in higher education: Universal principles or culturally responsive concepts. *Journal of Higher Education, 73*(4), 443–460. doi: 10.1353/jhe.2002.0038

Kezar, A. J., & Lester, J. (2011). *Enhancing campus capacity for leadership*. Stanford, CA: Stanford University Press.

Kluckhohn, F., & Strodbeck, F. (1961). *Variations in value orientations*. New York, NY: Row Peterson.

Mahdavi, M., & Knight, W. A. (2012). *Towards the dignity of difference? Neither 'end of history' nor 'clash of civilizations.'* New York, NY: Routledge.

Manning, K. (2013). *Organizational theory in higher education*. New York, NY: Routledge.

Manning, K., Kinzie, J., & Schuh, J. (2006). *One size does not fit all: Traditional and innovative models of student affairs practice*. New York, NY: Routledge.

Martin, J. (1992). *Cultures in organizations: Three perspectives*. New York, NY: Oxford University Press.

Mills, M., Bettis, P., Miller, J. W., & Nolan, R. (2005). Experiences of academic unit reorganization: Organizational identity and identification in organizational change. *The Review of Higher Education, 28*(4), 597–619. doi: 10.1353/rhe.2005.0046

Samovar, L. A., & Porter, R. E. (1995). *Communicating between cultures* (2nd ed.). Belmont, CA: Wadsworth.

Schein, E. (1992). *Organizational culture and leadership* (2nd ed.). San Francisco, CA: Jossey-Bass.

Schein, E. (2010). *Organizational culture and leadership* (4th ed.). San Francisco, CA: Jossey-Bass.

Schneider, B., Ehrhart, M. G., & Macey, W. H. (2013). Organizational climate and culture. *Annual Review of Psychology, 64*, 361–388. doi: 10.1146/annurev-psych-113011-143809

Smart, J. C., & Hamm, R. E. (1993). Organizational culture and effectiveness in two-year colleges. *Research in Higher Education, 34*(1), 95–106. Retrieved from www.jstor.org/stable/40196098

Sue, D. W. (2001). Multidimensional facets of multicultural competence. *The Counseling Psychologist, 29*, 790–821. doi: 10.1177/0011000001296002

Sue, D. W., & Constantine, M. G. (2005). Effective multicultural consultation and organizational development. In M. G. Constantine & D. W. Sue (Eds.), *Strategies for building multicultural competence in mental health settings* (pp. 212–226). Hoboken, NJ: Wiley & Sons.

Tierney, W. (1988). Organizational culture in higher education: Defining the essentials. *Journal of Higher Education, 59*(1), 2–21. doi: 10.2307/1981868

Ting-Toomey, S. (1999). *Communicating across cultures*. New York, NY: McGraw Hill.

Ting-Toomey, S., & Oetzel, J. (2001). *Managing intercultural conflict effectively*. Thousand Oaks, CA: Sage.

Winkle-Wagner, R., & Locks, A. M. (2014). *Diversity and inclusion on campus: Supporting racially and ethnically underrepresented students*. New York, NY: Routledge.

3

PRACTICING AND DEVELOPING PROFESSIONALISM

William Smedick

WHAT IT MEANS to be a professional can be learned (Lund, 2014), but where do individuals acquire the skills and knowledge to become professionals, and what does it look like in practice? Wilson et al. (2013) found that neither undergraduate nor graduate students fully understood the meaning and significance of professionalism or professional behavior. Some students defined being professional as having expertise or competence for the work environment; others noted that professionalism meant working hard and behaving appropriately but associated it with a way of dressing or meeting a supervisor's expectations. Although these findings focus only on undergraduate and graduate students who have not yet been employed or who have not yet moved through the phases of maturation, they highlight the fact that when graduates enter the work environment, they do not understand professionalism and what it looks like in practice (McCafferty, 2014; Wagner, 2012).

If college students or young workers do not understand professionalism, perhaps professionalism is learned through sustained experience within the work environment. In higher education settings, student affairs practitioners learn about professionalism by joining a community of practice (Wenger, 2000), paying attention to cultural norms and expectations, and engaging with others who can assist in their development.

This chapter will examine:

- defining professionalism in the field of higher education,
- the ways in which professionalism is learned,
- the community of practice framework, and
- professionalism in practice in higher education environments.

DEFINING HIGHER EDUCATION PROFESSIONALISM

The National Education Association (2015), which considers higher education faculty and staff among its constituencies, provided a good starting point for defining professionalism in higher education: "We believe that the expertise and judgment of education professionals are critical to student success. We maintain the highest professional standards, and we expect the status, compensation, and respect due all professionals" (para. 7). This statement implies that professional respect is earned by seeing oneself as a professional and behaving accordingly. In higher education, student affairs professionals are expected to put student success first and focus on the goal of education throughout their practice.

The Council for the Advancement of Standards in Higher Education (CAS; 2015) publishes standards and guidelines that look at professionalism in student affairs in terms of divisional, functional, and individual levels. At the divisional level, professionalism begins with administrators' relationship to the programs and services for which they have direct responsibility. For example, intentionally designed programs require that administrators first decide upon outcomes and goals and then develop plans and strategies. The outcome category includes learning outcomes for students as well as prioritized institutional outcomes, such as enhancing the sense of community or engaging diverse populations effectively. Beyond the divisional level, each functional area has its own set of standards that further define professional practice. For example, providing assessment data regarding the effectiveness of advising programs may be a functional area standard for those working in academic advising. At the individual level, areas of professionalism include general knowledge, skills, and interactive competencies. CAS (2015) also provides guidelines for self-mastery that can serve as a useful, though not an exhaustive, checklist for student affairs practitioners.

In the seminal book *Learning Reconsidered*, Keeling (2004) defined higher education professionalism by the degree of attentiveness directed toward the student learning mission of institutions. Keeling emphasized that student affairs practitioners should regularly assess student learning and form partnerships across the institution to create a seamless learning environment. Whitt (2006) stressed the importance of engaging students outside of the classroom, teaching them what educational success requires, advocating for diversity in all aspects of the educational environment, and using assessment data to identify and expand learning activities in the cocurricular setting.

These descriptions of what educators must do and how they should act provide student affairs practitioners with a general set of guidelines, but a list of standard competencies provides additional details to help practitioners understand and develop professionalism in student affairs. ACPA–College Student Educators International and NASPA–Student Affairs Administrators in Higher Education (2015) developed a list of competencies for the field that highlights the skills, attitudes, and values that student affairs educators must have to work effectively with students and enhance student success within any area of higher education. Competencies are grouped by category (e.g., personal and ethical foundations) and are divided into foundational, intermediate, and advanced levels.

In sum, professionalism in higher education is the use and development of skills and competencies that contribute to quality practice and that enable student affairs practitioners to contribute significantly to the educational mission of their institutions. Although this definition makes individual development a key component of professionalism, the entire student affairs community has a responsibility to demonstrate what professionalism looks like in the higher education environment.

LEARNING PROFESSIONALISM

Student affairs practitioners who wish to identify areas where they may need to improve or develop their professionalism must do more than rely solely on their own perspectives; they must shape their behavior through interactions with other practitioners. Wenger's (2000) communities of practice model describes how this process occurs. Practitioners can use the model to guide their personal and collective learning communities and purposefully enhance professionalism.

Wenger (2000) defined a community of practice as a group of people who share common interests and learn from each other through social interaction. The community can be thought of as a series of concentric circles, with new members of the group on the outer circles and more seasoned members within the inner circle. As new members learn more about shared goals and gain the knowledge, skills, and expertise needed to address those goals, they begin moving closer to the inner circle. The more advanced members of the group assist the newer members by providing opportunities for development and by sharing expertise and knowledge. When new members of the community do something that violates the norms or expectations of the community, they encounter a natural boundary and receive negative feedback or supportive correction from more experienced members of the community.

These communities of practice exist in several contexts within higher education. Consider the following example. An academic advising office hires a new graduate of a higher education master's program to join its staff. This new graduate comes to the office with foundational knowledge of academic advising and one internship experience that helped define the graduate's practice of advising at a beginning level. As the new graduate begins full-time work in the office, colleagues and the graduate's supervisor contribute to the graduate's advising knowledge by sharing case studies of individual student situations, institutional policies and practices, and expectations for what advising should accomplish. If the graduate makes a mistake while advising, the supervisor may request a one-on-one meeting to review the situation, correct the error, and suggest better practices. Through regular conversations and interactions with the community of practice in the advising office, the new graduate begins to develop an in-depth understanding of how to be an advisor and how to improve professionalism.

The new graduate may also attend a professional conference sponsored by an academic advising association. With its many resources and services, the association is another community of practice. The conference is an opportunity for more advanced members of the community to present educational sessions on the knowledge and skills required for academic advising. Association members may also informally exchange advising experiences or share best practices from their home institutions. The social exchange of both formal and informal learning at the conference can help the new graduate gain an improved understanding of academic advising and perform better in his or her institutional role. The graduate can also pass on lessons learned to other professionals.

Using the communities of practice model, Wenger (2000) highlighted two components of professionalism: competence and experience. *Competence*, gained through training and practice, includes the types of skills and behaviors widely accepted in the field. For example, higher education is governed by federal guidelines related to student privacy rights more commonly known as the Family Educational Rights and Privacy Act (FERPA). Graduate preparation programs often introduce these guidelines to new professionals and teach them what FERPA means in the professional environment. As new professionals move into full-time employment, they begin to apply that knowledge to their daily practice. The more decisions they make regarding FERPA guidelines, the more their competency in this area increases. When FERPA competency is achieved, experienced professionals then contribute to the community of practice by sharing their wisdom with other practitioners.

The *experience* component of the model views professionalism in terms of particular institutional contexts. For example, a 4-year institution on the East Coast of the United States may approach new-student orientation activities in a different manner from a 2-year community college on the West Coast. Those same new-student orientation activities may consist of 3 days of events at one institution and only 1 day at an institution across town. In other words, professionalism may be viewed differently at each institution based on cultural norms and expected practices. Wenger (2000) encouraged administrators who were moving from one cultural experience to another to ask, "What definitions of roles, norms, codes of behavior, shared principles, and negotiated commitments and expectations hold the community together?" (p. 231). Considering the answers to this question helps student affairs professionals align their personal values with an institution's norms and practices. As a result, professionals will be more successful in the working environment. (See Chapter 2 for further discussion of organizational culture.)

Wenger (2000) also discussed three key aspects of establishing an identity within a community of practice. Individuals must have a *home base* where they learn from opportunities in a primary community of practice. In higher education, student affairs practitioners may share ideas with work colleagues or take classes, workshops, and seminars offered through their institution. Individuals also need *trajectories*; that is, they should seek additional communities of practice that help them learn from established members of the community. Student affairs practitioners may join professional associations and participate in conferences, conventions, webinars, and volunteer experiences. *Multimembership* moves professionals beyond traditional community boundaries so that they can enhance their competencies and creativity. In higher education, student affairs practitioners may find these boundary-breaking opportunities through designing and leading corporate training programs or consulting with entrepreneurial organizations and nonprofit entities (Wenger, 2000). They may even find these opportunities at the same institution. For example, student affairs professionals have been at the forefront of providing inclusive environments that enhance student success, and they are well positioned to lead institutions in these efforts.

The communities of practice model explains how student affairs practitioners learn professionalism. The process involves both individual and group components. On an individual level, practitioners are expected to take an interest in becoming professionals and to work to improve themselves. At the group level, members of the community are expected to shape practitioners' behaviors through observation and feedback. Both the individual and group components of this process are important. As professionals gain experience within various communities of practice in higher education, they increase their professional competencies and reach a point when they can pass their knowledge on, thereby perpetuating the community cycle.

PRACTICING PROFESSIONALISM

Communities of practice often use the formal competencies all professionals work toward to shape professional behavior. Competencies such as those identified in *Professional Competency Areas for Student Affairs Educators* (ACPA & NASPA, 2015) represent the shared goals and expectations of student affairs communities of practice, and they define what it means to be a member of the higher education field. However, the publication neglects to fully define the more nuanced or "soft" skills needed for professionalism. Burkard, Cole, Ott, and Stoflet (2005) identified several competencies needed for entry-level positions in higher education, including communication, collaboration, and group facilitation; but because they are not defined in the ACPA and NASPA (2015) publication, practitioners must guess what those skills look like. For example, a foundational competency for the Organizational and Human Resources category is "communicate with others using effective verbal and non-verbal strategies" (ACPA & NASPA, 2015, p. 24), but there is no explanation of what effective communication means or what types of strategies may be adopted.

This section seeks to explain specific norms and skills applicable to the higher education work environment that formal competencies do not directly address. Student affairs practitioners need to understand norms and skills that apply to meeting behavior, professional communication, respectful relationships in the workplace, and general office etiquette (e.g., meeting deadlines, following institutional policies). By understanding expectations, practitioners can improve their professionalism at the point of entry into the field and refine their skills as they gain more experience.

Meeting Behavior

Meetings are a part of a student affairs practitioner's daily work schedule and present regular opportunities to build or negate a professional reputation. The ways in which practitioners conduct themselves in meetings, whether as a leader or participant, can affect the degree of respect they earn.

The purpose of meetings is to enhance communication and to collaborate on important issues or activities. When these two primary goals are accomplished, professional respect is established. Meeting participants are expected to arrive on time to the meeting, put away cell phones or other distracting items, read all information for the meeting ahead of time, listen attentively to others in the meeting, ask clarifying questions, offer feedback on ideas, allow others to share feedback, and stay until the meeting has concluded. Participants observe proper etiquette by communicating in a timely way with the meeting organizer; for example, to share that they will be late to the meeting or that they are expecting an important call and will step out of the meeting when it occurs. Practitioners who are present, attentive, and prepared show their meeting leader and the others present that they take their professional responsibilities seriously.

Meeting leaders should behave in a professional way. They need to plan the agenda and desired outcomes, invite colleagues to participate (and provide as much notice of the meeting as possible), start and end the meeting on time, follow the agenda, keep everyone on topic, close the meeting with a summary of what was accomplished and what still needs to be done, and follow up with participants concerning any lingering issues or tasks (Meiring, 2015). Although taking each of these steps may appear to be simple, mastering each step takes practice.

For example, meeting leaders must stay focused on the relevant information and desired outcomes. It is easy for the discussion to take various turns away from the stated purpose. Meeting leaders must control the direction of meetings while still communicating with everyone respectfully. In addition, those invited to the meeting are likely participating because the topic affects their work in some way. Meeting leaders must make sure that all participants have an opportunity to share concerns and ideas—this is a critical part of leading a meeting. Quieter participants may be overlooked unless the leader provides those individuals with an opportunity to voice their opinions. Even concluding the meeting requires skill: leaders must ensure that everyone leaves the meeting clearly understanding their responsibilities for moving forward.

All meetings present opportunities to build relationships and networks. Arriving before the meeting or staying after the meeting can provide professionals with informal opportunities to get to know a colleague or student better.

Professional Communication

The way in which student affairs practitioners communicate in reports, memorandums, e-mail messages, or social media also affects how others view their professionalism. Practitioners need to communicate effectively and use good judgment with language.

Practitioners should first discuss expectations with their supervisors. For instance, if a practitioner is required to provide a written report, he should ask about the expected deadline as well as the level of detail needed. He should find out whether the document should be a draft or a finished product with citations and whether he should leave room for others to add parts of it. He should pay close attention to the stated deadline and make sure the report is submitted on time. If he must go past the deadline, he should let his supervisor know as soon as possible and be honest about what has happened and when he will submit the report. Clarifying expectations in the beginning and acknowledging problems quickly demonstrates to a supervisor that the practitioner is someone who takes responsibility and works through challenges.

Practitioners should also give careful attention to electronic and paper correspondence. Using the proper letterhead for letters of recommendation or official business is a common practice, and failure to follow this practice can be perceived as unprofessional. Practitioners should review their letters for typographical errors or grammatical and punctuation mistakes before printing them. Communicating via an error-free document demonstrates that a practitioner is detail-oriented and cares about quality communication.

Although formal correspondence is still used in the workplace, it is much more common to communicate through e-mail. It is important to keep in mind that e-mail is not a private form of communication. It is wise for professionals to treat e-mail as they would formal correspondence. E-mail messages should begin with a salutation such as "Dear Mr. Jones" or "Good Morning, Aisha." The message should also have a formal closing expression such as "Sincerely" or "Best Regards" followed by the sender's name. Once the recipient has responded to the initial message and there is additional e-mail communication, the salutation and closing expression are no longer needed, but the sender's name should continue to be included at the bottom of subsequent messages to maintain a formal tone. It is also wise for professionals to refrain from sharing personal information about themselves or others and to think twice before sending any negative information through e-mail. In both cases, it is best to request a face-to-face meeting rather than risk the e-mail message being shared with an unintended recipient.

Since social media platforms are increasingly being used in higher education to maintain informal relationships with students and colleagues as well as to increase formal communication with various constituent groups (Graham, 2014), student affairs practitioners need to develop a set of best practices in this area also. Whether using Facebook, Twitter, Instagram, LinkedIn, or other social media platforms, practitioners should always consider how their presence, what they share, and what is shared with them might be perceived by others. In addition, it is important for practitioners to consider any additional responsibilities they might have when obtaining certain kinds of information through social media.

When communicating via social media, student affairs practitioners should know their audience and the intentions for the communication. Even if a practitioner's personal Facebook posts are thoughtful and appropriate for public viewing, those with whom the practitioner has connected can also post items on that practitioner's profile page, which can lead to unintended consequences. For example, if a student whom a practitioner has allowed to be a Facebook friend shares a picture of underage individuals consuming alcohol at a student organization party, the practitioner may face an ethical dilemma and have to decide to report a policy violation to the institution's student conduct office. Someone viewing the picture on the practitioner's Facebook page may assume the practitioner attended the party and participated in some way. Having current students as Facebook friends can be very damaging to a professional's reputation.

However, it is still possible to create social connections with students in a professional manner. Instead of connecting through a personal account, there are options on Facebook for creating private groups for a class or student organization. Or a Facebook page can be created for a student affairs office to share information and post pictures of official activities. Students can follow the office page and stay connected that way.

It is important for student affairs practitioners to discuss expectations regarding social media use and professional electronic identity with their supervisors. There may be cultural norms that encourage electronic engagement with students, or practitioners may be discouraged from reaching out in this way. Seeking guidance from a supervisor can help practitioners define where the boundaries should be.

In general, when using electronic forms of communication, student affairs practitioners should consider several basic practices.

- **Consider how the communication will be viewed by others and who might view it.** Practitioners should think carefully about what and with whom they share before hitting the send button on an e-mail or before posting a comment to social media. A practitioner's reputation can be affected by how others perceive his or her communication.
- **Be mindful of personal privacy and the privacy of others.** Social media sites have privacy settings that can limit what is shared and with whom. In addition, e-mail communication can often contain both business and personal communication within the same message or series of messages. Editing out personal information before forwarding, or deleting messages altogether, can help practitioners keep private information private.
- **Delete inappropriate comments or photos.** For example, if an individual posts an inappropriate comment or photo on a practitioner's social media page, the practitioner should delete the material so it does not reflect unfavorably on him or someone else. As a member of the community of practice, the practitioner should let the individual know that the material was inappropriate and why. This will assist in the development of the individual's professionalism.
- **Consider developing a personal policy for social media use.** Practitioners can share a personal policy for social media use

with students and colleagues who wish to connect via social media. For example, a practitioner's policy could be that she will only accept an invitation to connect after a student has graduated or that she maintains separate personal and professional social media accounts.

- **Monitor electronic identity.** Practitioners should conduct periodic Internet searches of their names to see what results are generated. It is not uncommon for a potential employer or even students and colleagues to conduct a similar search. Finding problems early and addressing them quickly can help practitioners avoid a marred professional reputation.

Respectful Relationships in the Workplace

Face-to-face interactions within the work environment also affect how practitioners are perceived by their colleagues. It is critical for practitioners to establish positive relationships with their supervisors, as supervisors help practitioners achieve success on the job. Respectful relationships should also be cultivated with colleagues who perform similar responsibilities; administrative support staff who help the office run smoothly; and paraprofessional staff, such as student workers or residence advisors who work on a part-time basis but make significant contributions to the functionality of the office. Each of these relationships requires attention, respect, and regular care.

How practitioners establish and manage these relationships affects whether others see them as being easy to work with and enjoyable to be around. A good starting point is for a practitioner to express genuine interest in a colleague while not moving too fast or becoming too personal. One suggestion is to look around the colleague's immediate workspace and note any photos or other materials that he or she may have posted. The practitioner should ask questions about these items, and find out why they are important. Even if the practitioner discovers that there are few shared interests, these posted items can provide an opportunity to connect on a regular basis. For example, if one of the photos is of the colleague's children, the practitioner can periodically ask what the children are working on in school or doing for afterschool activities. The small gesture of taking an interest in what is important to that colleague can help build a good working relationship that lasts over the long term.

It is important for practitioners to respect any boundaries or areas of discomfort each individual may have. For instance, a paraprofessional staff member may refer to a practitioner as "Ma'am" or "Sir," even if the practitioner indicates that it is acceptable to be addressed by first name. Even if a practitioner prefers a less formal style of communication within the relationship or being called by first name, the practitioner should refrain from correcting the language. Allowing the staff member to do what feels comfortable builds trust and leads to a positive work partnership. Similarly, if a colleague seems uncomfortable when a practitioner inquires about the staff member's children, it is best to stop asking, since it is likely that a boundary has been encountered.

Boundaries may stem from cultural differences. Taras and Rowney (2007) identified different cultural norms concerning communication styles and expectations, word selection and meaning, degree of directness, and the use of nonverbal cues as several factors that can lead to misperceptions, misunderstandings, and mistrust. For example, some colleagues may expect a degree of formality when relationships are forming. Using informal language or calling them by their first names can be interpreted as showing disrespect. Using sustained eye contact may be a way of demonstrating attentiveness, but a colleague may perceive the eye contact as intimidating. The best way to navigate cultural differences in the work environment is to clarify expectations for each relationship. Making an effort to ask colleagues about their preferred name and communication style demonstrates sensitivity to their individual needs. If unanticipated challenges arise, having a conversation about what happened and what can be done in the future can improve understanding and build trust.

When establishing work relationships, practitioners should consider where to set their boundaries. Practitioners should ask questions such as, How much of my personal life am I willing to share within the work environment? Will I discuss romantic relationships or what I did over the weekend? Will I socialize with my colleagues outside of work? If so, which colleagues will I select to socialize with, and how will that socializing affect my working relationships? Work relationships can become complicated when they move beyond the professional environment, especially if there is a power difference between the colleagues, such as between supervisors and administrative support staff. Work relationships can also be complicated if information that is shared in a personal setting crosses over into the professional environment—such information might include a health condition or a new job offer. It is best for practitioners to set boundaries between their professional and personal lives; doing so creates a positive work–life balance and builds a foundation for making decisions about workplace relationships.

General Office Etiquette

Behaviors such as overpromising on outcomes, failing to meet established deadlines, and not following institutional policies can diminish a practitioner's professional reputation and cast doubt on the practitioner's ability to perform job responsibilities. Regardless of whether these behaviors were the result of the administrator being unaware of personal limits, not fully understanding the responsibilities involved, or desiring to sidestep burdensome bureaucracy, such conduct will diminish a practitioner's professional reputation and cast doubt on the practitioner's ability to perform job responsibilities.

Student affairs practitioners can incorporate several practices to increase effective performance on the job and build a positive professional reputation.

- **Seek additional information about an assigned project.** A practitioner should ask questions about how long the project may take, who else may need to be involved, and what outcomes should result. Once all questions have been answered, the practitioner can share a tentative plan with her supervisor so that details can be reviewed and expectations can be clarified.
- **Engage campus experts.** When unsure of a policy or process, practitioners can consult experts such as admissions and human resources personnel, lawyers, purchasing agents, campus security officers, and others. Taking this step may increase the time it takes to verify the information, but it will help the practitioner avoid making errors in judgment.
- **Follow the chain of command, and respect the organizational structure.** Although going straight to the vice president for student affairs with a concern may help a practitioner address a situation quickly, the practitioner's supervisor is not likely to appreciate being excluded from the communication. In addition, the supervisor may be able to provide the practitioner with insights that can help the practitioner avoid barriers or mistakes. As a rule, if someone has a stake in the outcome of a policy, procedure, or program, it is wise to keep that person informed before moving on to another member of the organization.
- **Understand leaders' communication preferences.** Practitioners should adjust their practices to meet the expectations of their supervisors. For example, some supervisors may want their employees to copy them on all official business, whereas others may prefer a more selective approach. Clarifying expectations

about things like this can help practitioners and their supervisors establish a positive working relationship. If it is not clear what the supervisor wants, it is best to err on the side of communicating frequently and in detail until told otherwise.

- **Develop a transition document.** Practitioners should develop a transition document so that someone else can perform their responsibilities in their absence. For instance, if a practitioner is out of the office for a significant amount of time because of a health or family crisis, or if a practitioner obtains a new position at another institution and has not had time to train someone to fill the role. A transition document is a detailed report of a practitioner's responsibilities and how those responsibilities are performed. Such reports can assist others in making a smooth and effective transition, and can increase a practitioner's professional reputation for being prepared, organized, and considerate.

ADVICE FOR SUPERVISORS

Supervisors play a significant role in helping staff members develop professionalism. These leaders have direct responsibility for identifying practitioners' strengths, providing corrective action and feedback, and connecting practitioners to resources for continued growth. As part of the community of practice within student affairs, supervisors have an obligation to both model professionalism and ensure practitioners have an opportunity to improve their own professionalism.

Haley, Jaeger, Hawes, and Johnson (2015) provided the following recommendations for supervisors:

- **Be clear about expectations and desired job and project outcomes.** Sharing this information provides practitioners with needed context as they define what professionalism

means within the organization and what good performance looks like (Haley et al., 2015).
- **Align job expectations and outcomes with professional competencies.** In discussions with employees, supervisors should be explicit in making the connection between professional competencies and job expectations and outcomes (Haley et al., 2015). This may include setting specific goals during an annual performance evaluation process, identifying competencies to develop through those goals, and revisiting progress throughout the year.
- **Discuss professional development with employees, and provide feedback for performance.** Traditional practices such as evaluating an event after it has been completed or compiling monthly reports can provide supervisors with opportunities to praise employees for the competencies they have developed and identify additional behaviors they may need to work on to enhance their professionalism (Haley et al., 2015).
- **Encourage employees to seek mentors from outside the office or institution.** These mentors can provide additional guidance from a broader perspective and serve a valuable function in the development of the employee's professionalism. Supervisors can go a step further and connect employees to possible mentors; they can also let employees know that within the mentoring relationship, they should work on developing a specific competency (Haley et al., 2015).

CONCLUSION

Carpenter and Stimpson (2007) linked behavior, thought, intention, and actualization: "If the practitioners in the field act professionally, think professionally, and hold themselves out to be administrators, then they will go a long way toward making their preferred social construct 'actual'" (p. 269). This perspective connects professionalism to practitioners who value being professional and who behave in ways that are expected in the field. Yet they may not fully understand professionalism or what norms they are expected to observe (Wilson et al., 2013). It is necessary for the entire community of student affairs practitioners to help shape professional behavior with and for each other. This involves discussing expectations and acceptable behavior with those in the home base environment and sharing expertise across the field through involvement in professional associations and mentoring other professionals. By actively contributing to the definition and development of professionalism in themselves and others, practitioners can continue the cycle of social learning and ensure that the field of higher education contributes to students' success.

> **QUESTIONS FOR REFLECTION**
>
> - How am I participating in communities of practice in higher education to advance my knowledge and skills?
> - How do others perceive my professionalism in meetings and various communications?
> - Are there ways in which I am compromising or enhancing my professional reputation in my use of social media?
> - What professional boundaries have I set for students, colleagues, and supervisors?
> - In what ways do I model the kind of professionalism I would like students to learn from and emulate?
> - How am I contributing to the development of other student affairs practitioners' professionalism?

REFERENCES

ACPA–College Student Educators International & NASPA–Student Affairs Administrators in Higher Education. (2015). *Professional competency areas for student affairs educators.* Retrieved from https://www.naspa.org/images/uploads/main/Professional_Competencies.pdf

Burkard, A., Cole, D. C., Ott, M., & Stoflet, T. (2005). Entry-level competencies of new student affairs professionals: A Delphi study. *NASPA Journal, 42*(3), 283–309. doi: 10.2202/1949-6605.1509

Carpenter, D. S., & Stimpson, M. T. (2007). Professionalism, scholarly practice, and professional development in student affairs. *NASPA Journal, 44*(2), 265–285. doi: 10.2202/0027-6014.1795

Council for the Advancement of Standards in Higher Education. (2015). *Standards and guidelines for student services development programs.* Washington, DC: Author.

Graham, M. (2014). Social media as a tool for increased participation and engagement outside the classroom in higher education. *Journal of Perspectives in Applied Academic Practice, 2*(3), 16–24. doi: 10.14297/jpaap.v2i3.113

Haley, K., Jaeger, A., Hawes, C., & Johnson, J. (2015). Going beyond conference registration: Creating intentional professional development for student affairs educators. *Journal of Student Affairs Research and Practice, 52*(3), 313–326. doi: 10.1080/19496591.2015.1050034

Keeling, R. P. (Ed.). (2004). *Learning reconsidered: A campus-wide focus on the student experience.* Washington, DC: ACPA–College Student Educators International & NASPA–Student Affairs Administrators in Higher Education.

Lund, B. (2014, Fall). Spending time with talent to better prepare students for workplace realities. *Proceedings of the Marketing Management Association,* 197–201. Retrieved from http://www.mmaglobal.org/publications/Proceedings/2014-MMA-Fall-Educators-Conference-Proceedings.pdf

McCafferty, D. (2014, May 19). Millennials unprepared for workplace challenges [Web slide show]. Retrieved from http://www.cioinsight.com/it-management/workplace/slideshows/millennials-unprepared-for-workplace-challenges.html

Meiring, A. (2015). Just another meeting? Eight steps to an effective meeting. *Professional Nursing Today, 19*(4), 17–19. Retrieved from http://reference.sabinet.co.za/document/EJC181167

National Education Association. (2015). NEA's vision, mission, and values. Retrieved from http://www.nea.org/home/19583.htm

Taras, V., & Rowney, J. (2007). Effects of cultural diversity on in-class communication and student project team dynamics: Creating synergy in the diverse classroom. *International Studies in Educational Administration, 35*(2), 66–81. Retrieved from http://www.cceam.org/index.php?id=214

Wagner, T. (2012). *Creating innovators: The making of young people who will change the world.* New York, NY: Scribner.

Wenger, E. (2000). Communities of practice and social learning systems. *Organization, 7*(2), 225–246. doi: 10.1177/135050840072002

Whitt, E. J. (2006). Are all of your educators educating? *About Campus, 10*(6), 2–9. doi: 10.1002/abc.148

Wilson, A., Akerlind, G., Walsh, B., Stevens, B., Turner, B., & Shield, A. (2013). Making 'professionalism' meaningful to students in higher education. *Studies in Higher Education, 38*(8), 1222–1238. doi: 10.1080/03075079.2013.833035

4

BUILDING A SUPPORT NETWORK

Kevin W. Bailey and Mikia Carter

IN THE BESTSELLING book *The Tipping Point*, Malcolm Gladwell (2002) used the term *connectors* to describe people who introduce others to various social circles. He defined connectors as people who have an "extraordinary knack of making friends and acquaintances" (p. 41). Colleagues in higher education often comment about how small the student affairs field feels, since everyone seemingly knows countless others through graduate school, places of employment, professional association involvement, presentations, or social media activities. Because of these connections, or *networks*, it seems that there are only a few degrees of separation between thousands of colleagues in the profession.

This chapter will review:

- networking behaviors, or how student affairs professionals can connect with others;
- social media's influence on networking;
- ways to build and maintain a mentoring relationship;
- the difference between mentorship and sponsorship;
- steps to take to create and maintain the two-way relationship between mentor and mentee; and

- actions to take if the relationship no longer meets the needs of the mentee.

Gladwell did not intend for everyone to be a connector or to have a connector's extraordinary knack for meeting people—that ability is not inherent in everyone. However, all student affairs professionals must have or must cultivate a modicum of the connector spirit or ability because connecting is a vital part of personal and professional success. Connections support us, believe in us, guide us, challenge us, and help us grow (Reesor, Bagunu & Gregory, 2015). Having more connections leads to greater opportunities for professional and personal success.

NETWORKING

For some individuals, *networking* conjures images of building relationships for the purpose of deceit, manipulation, or personal gain (Reesor et al., 2015). However, in the professional world, networking usually entails the natural process of meeting new colleagues, building support structures for professional responsibilities, and being effective in a job at any level in the organization. The process of networking can improve boundary-spanning skills, and these skills help student affairs professionals create relationships outside of the primary unit or department and accomplish needed tasks (Forret & Dougherty, 2001). Stenken and Zajicek (2010) suggested that networks provide professionals with (a) opportunities to learn about job expectations and the culture of the organization and (b) opportunities to transfer information about organizational procedures and best practices. Networks can even provide support in a time of need or crisis (Dulworth, 2008; Stenken & Zajicek, 2010).

Networks and networking are also helpful in the context of job progression because "a large network of contacts provides information about current events within or outside of the organization that may affect the manager's job performance and career" (Yukl, 2002, p. 23). Professionals who have colleagues to consult with when they are considering important decisions, employment conundrums, courses of action, career moves, or workplace crises have access to varying perspectives that they might not consider otherwise.

Forret and Dougherty (2001) defined *networking behaviors* as "individuals' attempts to develop and maintain relationships with others who have the potential to assist them in their work or career" (p. 284). Their research yielded five dimensions of networking behaviors:

- Maintaining contacts
- Socializing
- Engaging in professional activities
- Participating in church and community organizations
- Increasing internal visibility

A professional's place in an organization influences networking behaviors. Those in positions higher up in an organization's hierarchy require a greater need for networking behaviors. Within higher education, networking may include institutional activities such as joining planning committees, advising a student organization, and volunteering at large-scale student events (Kelly, 1984). Outside the campus environment, networking may include assisting with community organizations, such as Rotary and Lions clubs, or issue-based nonprofit groups, such as March of Dimes or Big Brothers Big Sisters. These organizations often have a need for volunteers and can provide invaluable community connections.

Networking can be perceived as intimidating or fake, yet is neither when done for the right reasons. As Reesor et al. (2015) noted, "If you're sincerely interested in someone's background, values, thoughts, and opinions, this is a different type of relationship" (p. 181). Networking must be genuine and not forced.

Examples of networking include talking to someone while standing in line at a university sporting event or talking to a colleague while working out at the recreation center (Reesor et al., 2015). Meeting a presenter at a conference, a leader in a professional association, or someone who works at the institution can spark genuine interest. Start the conversation by expressing interest in the information shared, the background disclosed, or the professional journey discussed. Be mindful that the first conversation is just an introduction, not an interview. Be sensitive to the time spent on the introduction, and ask for a business card, Twitter handle, or phone number as a way to continue the conversation.

Introverts and those with shy personalities may struggle with networking because they fear rejection, are uncomfortable in the presence of strangers or new acquaintances, or experience energy drain in social encounters that involve perceived small talk (Gelberg, 2008). Gelberg (2008) and Zack (2010) suggested that individuals reduce their discomfort or anxiety with networking by adopting a different mind-set and nomenclature and thinking of networking as a process of building relationships. Gelberg (2008) noted that "a mutual exchange is at the core of all relationships, and when you place your attention on serving others or learning from others, you will find this process both more interesting and less daunting" (p. 46).

When building relationships and connecting, it is important to focus on the other person. A skilled networker asks questions and lets the other person's answers guide the conversation. A natural conversation allows both individuals to learn more about one another, and the discussion will provide a lead-in for future conversations. Professionals should practice such discussions to decrease feelings of discomfort and inadequacy.

Social Media

In today's technological world, social media sites offer convenient networking spaces. As Bagunu and Quiñones-Ortega (2015) noted, "Online engagements, in most cases, are a way to follow up and maintain relationships with colleagues you meet through various professional development opportunities" (p. 165). Social media outlets can be helpful when face-to-face interactions are not possible because of distance. (See the mentoring section of this chapter for a more in-depth conversation about connecting through social media.)

One of the pitfalls of networking through social media is the potential for inauthentic interactions (Bagunu & Quiñones-Ortega, 2015). Privacy settings on most platforms allow individuals to hide aspects of who they are or limit the information others can view. Some professionals may even take on a persona in an online environment that is not indicative of their true beliefs. Although doing so can allow professionals to express controversial opinions while protecting their online reputations, the lack of alignment between true personality and electronic identity affects networking authenticity. As Bagunu and Quiñones-Ortega (2015) noted, "The more authentic and personal you can be, while maintaining your professionalism in your online interactions with others, the more you'll have meaningful interactions and authentic networking relationships" (p. 170).

It is important to carefully consider the use and purpose of various social media platforms. Determine which accounts will be used for personal and professional purposes, what will be posted on those accounts, and how posts align with the intended purpose of the accounts. Many student affairs practitioners use LinkedIn for business purposes, such as posting and finding jobs and maintaining relationships within a network. Facebook may be used to share personal interests as well as professional opinions. Some practitioners have separate Twitter accounts for personal and professional use. Others regularly monitor their social media accounts and block others whose profiles or posts do not align with the purpose of their account. Practitioners must be mindful of what they share through social media networks as it can affect how others perceive them. An inadvertent comment or inappropriate photo can lead to unintended consequences.

Networking Preferences: Generational Differences

Professionals from different generations seem to have different networking preferences. Cardon and Marshall (2015) suggested that Generation X and Generation Y (millennial) business professionals are driving the use of social networking platforms in the workplace. Professionals from earlier generations are generally newer to electronic communication and social networking (Hahn, 2011), and as a result may favor or default to more traditional networking options.

We, the authors of this chapter, are a case in point. Mikia is a new professional, and Kevin is a vice president for student affairs (VPSA). In our conversations about networking, it was evident that we approached the process very differently. Kevin prefers to collect business cards and interact with people face-to-face; communication, typically via e-mail, is sporadic, and business cards are stored for later reference. He is less likely to build relationships via Twitter or LinkedIn or to respond immediately to text messages. Conversely, Mikia prefers to ask for a phone number and place contact information in her smart phone. She may hand out a business card, but it is not the first thing she requests from a new contact. She uses GroupMe and other social media apps to network with professionals who share similar experiences or interests. For Mikia and many other new professionals, relationships are built organically through social media. When developing a cross-generational networking relationship, a conversation about preferred communication methods and frequency should happen early in the relationship.

Network Maintenance and Growth

Student affairs professionals should be intentional about maintaining and developing their networks, and this means attending to issues of quantity and quality. Networks require time and attention to keep the relationships worthwhile and valuable (Dulworth, 2008). Yukl (2002) explained that "old relationships need to be maintained and new ones established as people in key positions change, the organization changes, and the external environment changes" (p. 24). Keeping up with these changes is a function of a professional's place in the organization and job role. A mentor can be helpful in thinking through organizational and environmental changes and creating strategies regarding who needs to be approached and the appropriate networking behaviors to be employed.

A student affairs professional's network should increase with career growth—someone at the dean or director level should have a much more extensive network than a graduate student or new professional. With such growth comes more opportunities. As Dulworth (2008) noted, "The more people you have in your network, the more opportunities you have open up to you, the more knowledge you can access, and the more talent you can tap" (p. 19). However, professionals often do not spend much time analyzing the quality of their network and identifying people at various professional levels and from a variety of backgrounds with whom to build relationships; they often meet people in a random fashion and make arbitrary decisions about both making and maintaining connections.

Dulworth (2008) posited the concept of a networking quotient (NQ) that is expressed as part of an equation:

$$IQ + EQ + NQ = success$$

IQ is the capacity to learn, whereas EQ is emotional intelligence, as described by Goleman (2005). If IQ is set and if there is very little that can be done to control EQ, then NQ is the place where professionals have the most control in order to achieve the level of success that they desire. Dulworth (2008) described three primary types of networks—personal, professional, and virtual—and provided a quiz that quantifies NQ on a scale of below average (need to be much more intentional about developing and maintaining your network) to networking genius.

A simpler way for professionals to assess the quality of their network is to do the following. First, they should give some thought to their career goals and current job quality. Second, they should list the people currently in their network. This list need not be exhaustive. New professionals may have a shorter list of connections, and seasoned professionals may not remember everyone they know or have met and networked with. This activity is designed to assist with visualizing areas of strength and areas for improvement within a network. The list can be divided in one of three ways:

- by *level* (e.g., graduate student, new professional, senior-level, etc.);
- by *title* (e.g., director, dean, vice president); or
- by *function* (e.g., housing, career services, international programs).

Once professionals have drafted their list, they should review it for gender and ethnicity and assess how frequently interactions occur. Professionals should ask questions about when they last saw or interacted virtually with a person, whether a type of professional is missing from the list, and whether one functional area or institution is overrepresented. Asking such questions, especially in light of their career goals and current job needs, helps to evaluate the quality of the network and to identify ways to strengthen it. Sharing the list with a mentor for feedback can be helpful in improving the quality of the network.

Networks develop as student affairs practitioners gain experience and interact more often with colleagues both within and outside of their institutions as well as in professional associations. Virtual and face-to-face networks can assist professionals with:

- vetting potential doctoral programs,
- obtaining résumé critiques,
- preparing for the next job,
- seeking advice for dealing with a challenging supervisor or employee,
- identifying candidates for an open positions, and
- identifying volunteer opportunities at the state, regional or national level.

The purpose and use of the network is limited only by the skill set and knowledge of the people in it.

MENTORING

A logical and natural next step in developing a network is to establish a *mentoring relationship*. Mentoring relationships can be described in several ways. Zachary and Fischler (2009) defined a *mentor* as a guide who helps professionals understand goals and ways to navigate them. Salimbene (1981) described a mentor as a more experienced individual who serves as a guide, advisor, and assistant to someone who is less experienced. Peddy (1998) explained that a mentor is a role model or counselor focused on the best interest of a *mentee*. All of these descriptions refer to the multiple roles that mentors fulfill. As student affairs professionals continue their journey in higher education, they will find mentors who can fulfill one or more professional (and personal) roles in their lives. Unlike a teacher or a coach, a mentor will be able to provide guidance by discussing the mentee's future career plans (Zachary & Fischler, 2009) and sharing how to achieve a certain position or level of success within an institution.

Kelly (1984) identified two types of mentoring relationships formed in different ways: those consisting of an employee and supervisor formed through an existing relationship in the workplace, and those consisting of a mentor and mentee who find each other through other means. Graduate students or new professionals may assume that a supervisor is the best mentor option because the supervisor is aligned with their chosen career path and shares the same professional interests; they spend a significant amount of time with the supervisor, and the supervisor knows the student's or employee's skills, capabilities, and deficiencies better than anyone else. However, supervisors may not be a good choice for various reasons. The supervisor may want to confine the relationship to stated job roles, or the supervisor may see mentoring responsibilities as conflicting with job duties and requiring extra work and time. The relationship can be further complicated if the employee is searching for a new job—which could be viewed as evidence of disloyalty or a lack of commitment to the organization—and wants to have a conversation with the mentor about the job search. Supervisors also may not be good candidates for a mentoring relationship because they may not have knowledge and experience that matches the mentee's goals.

In the second type of mentoring relationship, a mentee connects with a mentor more naturally; the two "fall into" their relationship or develop a relationship over time that evolves into a mentoring relationship even though that was not their expressed purpose in the beginning. This type of mentor-mentee relationship develops naturally when a professional needs advice or guidance and consistently seeks out one person to answer questions or to provide support. A professional may select a supervisor as a mentor or may develop a relationship with another professional over time—both approaches can produce the same level of satisfaction. The effectiveness of the relationship depends on what is being sought and how it is fulfilled within the mentor-mentee relationship.

Proactive approaches to finding a mentor include becoming familiar with mentoring concepts and defining goals. Kelly (1984) suggested that professionals interview colleagues to gain insight into their background and goals. Student affairs professionals should think about their career goals and talk to colleagues who have attained those goals to learn more about career paths and challenges. They should select impressive professionals as mentors.

Professionals should not be afraid to approach speakers, award winners, authors, directors, or senior-level student affairs practitioners and start a conversation. Instead, professionals should prepare an introduction and be ready to start a dialogue. As with networking, finding a mentor is about building relationships. If a conversation between a professional and a potential mentor goes well, the professional should ask the individual if he or she has time to meet for coffee, or send the individual an e-mail to continue the conversation. A few questions student affairs professionals can ask to learn more about the potential mentor include the following:

- What do you do?
- What are the duties/functions/responsibilities of your job?
- What kinds of problems do you deal with?
- What kinds of decisions do you make?
- How did this type of work interest you, and how did you get started?
- How did you prepare for this work?
- If you were entering this career today, would you change your

preparation in any way?

The Functions and Phases of a Mentoring Relationship

Kram (1983) introduced two mentoring functions: the career function and the psychological function. When performing the career function, the mentor guides the mentee through career advancement. The mentor helps the mentee identify job opportunities, review application materials, and practice interview skills, and the mentor provides insight regarding institution type. Through sponsorship, coaching, protection, and exposure, the mentor helps the mentee learn "the ropes of organizational life" and prepare for career advancement opportunities (Kram, 1983, p. 614). When performing the psychological function, the mentor helps the mentee gain a sense of competence and helps clarify the mentee's career identity. Activities derived from the psychological function include role modeling, acceptance, counseling, and friendship. When performing this function, the mentor provides emotional and personal support to the mentee outside of job acquisition and career progression. Mentor and mentee learn more about each other's values and what drives them, and they share information on a personal level (Kram, 1983).

In addition to describing the two functions of mentoring, Kram (1983) described four phases of a mentor-mentee relationship:

- initiation,
- cultivation,
- separation, and
- redefinition.

Although the phases are sequential, the time it takes to move from one phase to the next depends upon the mentoring relationship.

The first phase, *initiation*, occurs when a mentee admires and respects the sought-after mentor (Kram, 1983). Connections begin to form through informal interactions, common work tasks, or a colleague's suggestion that the professional reach out to a certain leader. Once the introductions have concluded, a mentee will begin asking career-related questions, and a mentor will begin guiding the mentee. For example, once a professional secures a position in career services, she may decide that her ultimate goal is to be a director. She may begin a conversation with the director in her office that initiates a mentoring relationship. They may have biweekly meetings to discuss the mentor's journey and the mentee's goals.

Cultivation is the next phase in the mentor-mentee relationship (Kram, 1983). During this phase, a mentor begins challenging, coaching, and exposing a mentee to things beyond the mentee's comfort zone. The mentor might encourage the career services professional mentioned above to give a presentation at a national conference or to take the lead in a new career initiative that requires collaboration among faculty and others across the campus—neither are in the current job description of the employee and are considered stretching assignments. In this phase, a mentor takes the time to understand what a mentee needs and creates opportunities for the mentee to overcome fears that may be hindering the mentee's growth. The mentee begins to find a confidence that strengthens the relationship. During this phase, mentees will know whether they should continue to seek opportunities to develop the relationship or whether they should disengage if they believe that the relationship no longer meets their developmental needs (Kram, 1983).

The *separation* phase is more difficult for mentees (Kram, 1983). Mentees who have advanced in their careers may feel that they no longer need the mentor, and Kram (1983) explained that "some turmoil, anxiety and feelings of loss generally categorize this period as the equilibrium of the cultivation phase is disrupted" (p. 618). However, the mentor does not face as much turmoil. The mentor has done the work of preparing the mentee for set goals and may enjoy knowing that he or she was able to help the mentee.

Redefinition is the final phase in the mentor-mentee relationship (Kram, 1983). In this phase, mentor and mentee have redefined their relationship as one of mutual friendship. The mentor continues to support the mentee, and the mentee is grateful for the mentor's time and guidance. The mentee no longer needs the mentor's assistance to achieve the goal, but the relationship never dissolves; it evolves into a peer relationship.

Over the course of their careers, mentees generally have two to three mentors (Henderson, 1985). One mentor may have multiple mentees simultaneously (Scandura & Pellegrini, 2007). Sometimes, mentoring relationships involve team mentoring; in this case, each mentee is responsible to the mentor and to the rest of the team.

Whatever form the relationship takes or however many mentors or mentees may be involved, mentoring relationships are crucial aspects of professional development. A workplace mentor can help solve problems, assist with career progression within the office, guide advancement into higher levels of leadership, and advise on issues of organizational navigation. As Langdon and Gordon (2007) noted, "As individuals rise through the ranks, they need help and support in making career decisions and juggling them with other life choices" (p. 212). Mentoring relationships provide professionals with this help.

Sponsor Relationships

Mentors should not be confused with sponsors. Langdon and Gordon (2007) explained that sponsorship is a limited relationship focused on the student affairs professional's goal of gaining a specific career position or opportunity. Porter (2014) distinguished between a mentor and a sponsor in this way: "Mentoring is a gift. A sponsor, on the other hand, is more transactional" (para. 3). A senior-level sponsor, according to Porter (2014), is not going to make an extra effort on behalf of a professional "unless they have proven their worth" (para. 3). Before a sponsor can advocate for a student affairs professional, the sponsor must trust the professional's abilities, feel that the professional is loyal, and know that the professional will be a great asset in the future position. Porter suggested that to obtain sponsors, professionals should join networks filled with influential people such as association leaders, senior-level student affairs professionals, or key staff in the president's office. Professionals can also meet influential people in the region by becoming a member of a nonprofit community board. Anyone who is willing to speak to the abilities of a professional or be an advocate for a potential job can be a sponsor (Porter, 2014).

A successful transition from mentorship to sponsorship requires a strong mentor-mentee relationship. The relationship may become a sponsorship dynamic if the mentor is in a position of power, and it may lead to access to a coveted job. At times, a professional may not know the sponsor on a personal level; he or she may be someone in the professional's corner who advocates from a distance (Pentland, 2015).

Mentoring Millennials

Members of the millennial generation—those born between 1980 and 1995—are digital natives and social learners who work best in teams (Meister & Willyerd, 2010). They are currently being supervised by baby boomers—those born between 1946 and 1961—and Generation Xers—those born between 1962 and 1979 (Cennamo & Gardner, 2008). Baby boomers are focused on achievements and prefer to speak openly and in a direct style. Generation Xers are risk takers and prefer things to be summarized and to the point. Tech-savvy millennials have a communication style that differs from the style of both the other generational groups.

Mentoring millennials can be challenging for baby boomers and Generation Xers. Millennials believe that they can make informed decisions after quickly searching a website or an application, and they do not always realize that they might overlook important information or fail to gain a full understanding of the situation by taking this approach. When millennials have a question, they often search the Internet for an answer, but they should be guided to seek the input of colleagues.

Millennials should be mindful of colleagues' communication preferences. Since baby boomers tend to prefer in-person conversations, scheduling a meeting or conversation may be the best way to connect, and the baby boomer colleague will appreciate that the professional made an effort and took time to learn more. On the other hand, since Generation Xers tend to appreciate both e-mail and informal communication, millennials should ask specific questions and keep the exchange brief and direct when seeking information from a Generation X colleague. By engaging colleagues through their preferred communication methods, millennials are more likely to build relationships within their work environment, which in turn can grow their professional networks.

Generational differences also exist in the way baby boomers, Generation Xers, and millennials view the world and define success. Brack (2012) noted that millennials seek employability and flexibility, whereas baby boomers and Generation Xers want job security and structure. Millennials who want to be successful in today's diverse workforce must learn to adapt, slow down, communicate effectively about their needs, and realize that not all their achievements will be recognized. Mentors can help millennials negotiate for needs such as flexible work schedules and professional development opportunities and provide sponsorship as well as advice regarding enrichment, fulfillment, and trust in work relationships (Meister & Willyerd, 2010).

Millennials need mentors to be flexible. It may be beneficial for the mentor to adopt a coaching role. This role will allow the mentor to offer advice, and then, once the advice is followed, to extend praise and affirm the mentee. Baby boomer or Generation X mentors should not seek out or expect formal mentor-mentee relationships with millennials. Instead, both millennial mentees and their elder mentors need to collaboratively define the mentoring relationship and adapt it to their own styles, so that the relationship is beneficial for both parties.

E-Mentoring

In student affairs, professionals often connect with each other at conferences. But using technology may be the easiest way for a mentor and mentee to stay connected if they do not work for the same institution. Scandura and Pellegrini (2007) called this use of technology *network mentoring*. This form of mentoring allows a mentee to have greater access to several mentors at one time, is less intimidating for introverted professionals, and can provide a record of the interaction in the event that a conversation needs to be recalled. Disadvantages to e-mentoring include the increased likelihood of miscommunication, a longer time frame needed to develop a trusting relationship, and concerns about confidentiality (Scandura & Pellegrini, 2007). Although online interactions are quick and convenient, and most professionals are used to the various formats available (Brack & Kelly, 2012), tone in written language and body language observed via video calls can easily be misconstrued. Participants may also be less committed to the relationship because it lacks face-to-face interaction (Ensher, Heun, & Blanchard, 2003).

Professionals who are interested in developing e-mentoring relationships should first engage potential mentors in person, such as when attending presentations at a conference. For example, following a presentation, a professional can request the presenter's e-mail address in order to start a virtual conversation after the conference. Questions can be exchanged through periodic e-mails or text messages. As the e-mentoring relationship develops, they can plan periodic phone conversations or video calls, which afford more personal opportunities to discuss issues.

Mentors can help mentees by sharing resources or inspirational messages every few weeks to remind the mentee of available support. Ensher et al. (2003) explained that "while mentoring relationships vary in the degree of psychosocial support they provide, informal counseling is usually a key element that enhances most effective mentor–protégé relationships" (p. 271). As long as an e-mentoring relationship provides support and regular communication, it can be just as successful as a face-to-face mentoring relationship.

Mentoring Introverts

Developing a mentoring relationship with introverts presents unique challenges. Introverts tend to be reflective, focused, and self-reliant (Zack, 2010). At times, they are shy and fearful of being judged, criticized, or evaluated. In situations that they find stressful, introverts may experience a racing heart, find it difficult to concentrate or understand, or become distressed by an increase in negative self-talk (Gelberg, 2008). Introverts gain energy away from social encounters. To gather the energy to sustain the mentoring relationship and feel comfortable, introverts should take time to reflect on their goals before seeking out a mentor (Gelberg, 2008). For example, if shyness is a problem when presenting, an introvert can identify professionals with admirable presentation styles and select one to be a mentor. To initiate the conversation, the introvert should come to the meeting with a list of questions, thoughts, or ideas about the potential mentor's observed presentation style. Outlining items to share and practicing will help the introvert stay engaged during the meeting (Gelberg, 2008). Although introverts may find the process of developing a relationship draining, they tend to often prefer the one-on-one interactions that mentoring provides and grow to appreciate the deeper relationships that develop (Zack, 2010).

Introverts sometimes find it difficult to form mentoring relationships because they fear rejection. Some potential mentors may decline to engage in a mentoring relationship because they do not have enough time or are not a good fit with the mentee's needs. Introverts should not take these decisions personally (Gelberg, 2008). Not every professional approached will be able to step into a mentoring role. Introverts should not allow the fear of rejection to deter them from identifying mentors and building relationships.

Introverts may also find it difficult to form mentoring relationships if they do not enjoy professional socials and experience discomfort in such settings. Managing energy levels, recognizing which activities are most draining, and planning introductory information and questions can help them alleviate anxiety (Gelberg, 2008). Other strategies include bringing a more extroverted colleague to help start conversations or looking for other professionals who seem uncomfortable because they may also be introverted and understand the discomfort. Once introverts are participating in conversations, they can take breaks by excusing themselves to get water or food. These breaks may give them the quiet time they need to prepare for the next conversation.

In order to successfully advise an introverted mentee, mentors can practice several strategies for improving performance and self-confidence. First, mentors can provide reassurance and praise to help a mentee counter any low self-esteem issues (Warner, 2012). Providing positive comments and recognizing strengths will help an introverted mentee feel more confident and dismiss negative feelings. Second, a mentor can coach introverted mentees through problem-solving steps. Introverts may take longer to think through challenging situations, so having a mentor provide guidance for dealing with specific situations can be empowering. Finally, a mentor can initiate conversations about achievements and goals. Introverts generally do not enjoy talking about themselves and their accomplishments, but they will benefit from the practice. Mentors who introduce these topics can help prepare introverted professionals to engage in such conversations with prospective employers (Warner, 2013).

Mentoring Different Races and Genders

A student affairs professional who begins to search for a mentor may start with a prospect's job title, but it is important also to consider a prospective mentor's personal traits. Ragins and Cotton (1999) found that female mentees paired with female mentors were more likely to engage in social activities together, whereas male mentees paired with female mentors reported engaging in fewer social activities together. Male mentees paired with female mentors reported that they did not experience many challenging assignments. Both female and male mentees paired with male mentors indicated that the relationship led to promotions but necessarily to increased compensation (Ragins & Cotton, 1999).

Racial and ethnic background may also make a difference in the mentoring relationship. Mentors of the same race and gender can help mentees navigate racial and gender identity issues, and mentors of a different race and gender can push mentees beyond their comfort zones and challenge them in ways they might not otherwise be challenged (Acomb, 2013). Mentees with mentors from diverse backgrounds can seek out guidance about racial or gender issues but should carefully consider the tone, time, and manner in which they ask questions so that they do not damage the mentoring relationship (Acomb, 2013).

ADVICE FOR SUPERVISORS

Supervisors can play a key role in supporting and developing both networking and mentoring. They can introduce new employees to others, first within the primary work network, and then within the broader institutional network. If supervisors attend professional conferences with employees, they can make introductions through those networks as well. When providing introductions, they afford employees opportunities to build their own networks and find colleagues who share common interests and goals.

Employees may come to view supervisors as potential mentors. If a supervisor desires this role, he or she can formalize the relationship and begin building additional connections with the employee. If becoming a mentor is not desired or possible, the supervisor should be honest with the employee about his or her reasons and should offer to help find another mentor who would better suit the employee's stated needs.

Even if mentoring relationships with direct-report employees do not develop, supervisors, as leaders in the student affairs field, are positioned to share their expertise and experiences through mentoring relationships. Their responsibilities provide broad perspectives on organizational culture and politics, and they have a variety of experiences that younger colleagues can learn from. Supervisors should consider it part of their professional activity to acquire at least one professional to mentor every year. These mentees can be employed in the same institution, be connected through a professional network at another institution, or be assigned through formal mentoring programs available in graduate preparation programs or professional associations. By volunteering to mentor, supervisors can provide invaluable guidance to young professionals as they navigate the higher education field. In the process, they model what their mentees should do when they become supervisors and pass on what they have learned throughout their own careers.

Finally, supervisors should pay attention to each employee's career goals and competency needs in terms of mentoring opportunities. If an employee's goals and competencies can be advanced through a mentoring relationship, the supervisor can make the suggestion and then identify a colleague who can step into the role. Facilitating this process can help advance an employee's development while also building trust within the supervisor-employee relationship.

CONCLUSION

Networking and mentorship are important personal and professional development activities in higher education. At their core, both practices are about connecting with people and developing meaningful relationships, and student affairs professionals must do both with intentionality to maximize outcomes over the short and long term. This involves learning how to make connections and establish relationships; managing the advancement of and conclusion to relationships; and working with special circumstances such as introversion, generational differences, and differences due to racial and gender characteristics. Considerable time and attention is required to create and maintain these connections, but the rewards are increased job performance, additional career opportunities, and lifelong friendships.

QUESTIONS FOR REFLECTION

- How well are you connected in your place of work, and are there any other relationships you need to develop?
- When using social media to maintain network connections, how do you manage professional communication and monitor the use of your accounts?
- What do you need from a mentoring relationship, and what characteristics are you looking for in a mentor?
- What can you do to help colleagues form their networks and develop mentoring relationships?

REFERENCES

Acomb, R. (2013). What makes a successful cross-gender/cross-racial mentor/mentee relationship? *Diversity for Success*, 121–136. Retrieved from http://www.dri.org/DRI/course-materials/2013-Diversity/pdfs/09_Acomb.pdf

Bagunu, G. A., & Quiñones-Ortega, D. N. (2015). Using technology and social media. In M. J. Amey & L. M. Reesor (Eds.), *Beginning your journey: A guide for new professionals in student affairs* (4th ed., pp. 157–175). Washington, DC: NASPA–Student Affairs Administrators in Higher Education.

Brack, J., & Kelly, K. (2012). Maximizing millennials in the workplace. Retrieved from http://www.kenan-flagler.unc.edu/executive-development/custom-programs/~/media/DF1C11C056874DDA8097271A1ED48662.ashx

Cardon, P. W., & Marshall, B. (2015). The hype and reality of social media use for work collaboration and team communication. *Journal of Business Communication, 52*(3), 273–293. doi: 10.1177/2329488414525446

Cennamo, L., & Gardner, D. (2008). Generational differences in work values, outcomes and person-organisation values fit. *Journal of Managerial Psychology, 23*(8), 891–906. doi: 10.1108/02683940810904385

Dulworth, M. (2008). *The connect effect: Building strong personal, professional, and virtual networks*. San Francisco, CA: Berrett-Koehler.

Ensher, E. A., Heun, C., & Blanchard, A. (2003). Online mentoring and computer-mediated communication: New directions in research. *Journal of Vocational Behavior, 63*(2), 264–288. doi: 10.1016/S0001-8791(03)00044-7

Forret, M. L., & Dougherty, T. W. (2001). Correlates of networking behavior for managerial and professional employees. *Group & Organization Management, 26*(3), 283–311. doi: 10.1177/1059601101263004

Gelberg, W. (2008). *The successful introvert: How to enhance your job search and advance your career*. Cupertino, CA: Happy About.

Gladwell, M. (2002). *The tipping point: How little things can make a big difference*. Boston, MA: Little, Brown and Company.

Goleman, D. (2005). *Emotional intelligence*. New York, NY: Bantam Books.

Henderson, D. W. (1985). Enlightened mentoring: A characteristic of public management professionalism. *Public Administration Review, 15*, 857–863. doi: 10.2307/975361

Hahn, J. (2011). Managing multiple generations: Scenarios from the workplace. *Nursing Forum, 46*(3), 119–127. doi: 10.1111/j.1744-6198.2011.00223.x

Kelly, K. E. (1984). Initiating a relationship with a mentor in student affairs. *NASPA Journal, 21*(3), 49–54. Retrieved from http://www.tandfonline.com/uarp

Kram, K. E. (1983). Phases of the mentor relationship. *Academy of Management Journal, 26*(4), 608–625. doi: 10.2307/255910

Langdon, E. A., & Gordon, S. A. (2007). Mentoring for middle management in student affairs. In R. L. Ackerman (Ed.), *The mid-level manager in student affairs: Strategies for success* (pp. 209–234). Washington, DC: NASPA–Student Affairs Administrators in Higher Education.

Meister, J. C., & Willyerd, K. (2010). Mentoring millennials. *Harvard Business Review, 88*(5), 68–72. Retrieved from https://hbr.org/2010/05/mentoring-millennials

Peddy, S. (1998). *The art of mentoring: Lead, follow and get out of the way*. Houston, TX: Bullion Books.

Pentland, L. (2015, October). Mentorship vs. sponsorship, and how to maximize both. *Forbes Magazine*. Retrieved from http://www.forbes.com

Porter, J. (2014, September). Yes, you need a mentor but a sponsor will really boost your career. *Fast Company*. Retrieved from http://www.fastcompany.com/3036037/hit-the-ground-running/yes-you-need-a-mentor-but-a-sponsor-will-really-boost-your-career

Ragins, B. R., & Cotton, J. L. (1999). Mentor functions and outcomes: A comparison of men and women in formal and informal mentoring relationships. *Journal of Applied Psychology, 84*(4),

529–550. doi: 10.1037/0021-9010.84.4.529

Reesor, L., Bagunu, G. A., & Gregory, L. (2015). Making professional connections. In M. J. Amey & L. M. Reesor (Eds.), *Beginning your journey: A guide for new professional in student affairs* (4th ed., pp. 177–202). Washington, DC: NASPA–Student Affairs Administrators in Higher Education.

Salimbene, S. (1981). Non-frontal teaching methodology and the effect of group cooperation and student responsibility in the EFL classroom. *English Language Teaching Journal, 35*(2), 89–94. doi: 10.1093/elt/XXXV.2.89

Scandura, T. A., & Pellegrini, E. K. (2007). Workplace mentoring: Theoretical approaches and methodological issues. In T. D. Allen & L. T. Eby (Eds.), *Handbook of mentoring: A multiple perspective* approach (pp. 71–91). Malden, MA: Blackwell.

Stenken, J. A., & Zajicek, A. M. (2010). The importance of asking, mentoring and building networks for academic career success: A personal and social science perspective. *Analytical and Bioanalytical Chemistry, 396*(2), 541–546. doi: 10.1007/s00216-009-3275-x

Warner, J. (2012, September 21). Coaching and mentoring [Web log post]. Retrieved from http://blog.readytomanage.com/coaching-introverts/

Yukl, G. (2002). *Leadership in organizations* (5th ed.). Upper Saddle River, NJ: Prentice Hall.

Zachary, L. J., & Fischler, L. A. (2009). *The mentee's guide: Making mentoring work for you.* San Francisco, CA: Jossey-Bass.

Zack, D. (2010). *Networking for people who hate networking: A field guide for introverts, the overwhelmed, and the underconnected.* San Francisco, CA: Berrett-Koehler.

5

PRACTICING POLITICS
The Art of the Possible in the Milieu of the Maddening

David W. Parrott

HIGHER EDUCATION INSTITUTIONS are a complex collection of divisions, colleges, departments, units, and centers populated by diverse groups of people with different personalities, work styles, agendas, skill levels, budget numbers, and ethical principles whose interests and goals often compete and conflict. As a result, the academic milieu can be equal parts supportive and hostile, clear and foggy, welcoming and rejecting, predictable and unpredictable, or rewarding and punishing. To attain an objective, meet a goal, obtain resources, and stave off a negative outcome, leaders of divisions, departments, programs, or initiatives must understand this milieu and master its politics. They have to identify and exploit opportunities to engage in the art of politics—including collaboration, cooperation, and compromise—or live with the consequences of failing to do so. If they fail, they may find themselves vulnerable, isolated, and shut out of decision-making processes that are critical to everyday survival and success in higher education.

Depending on the definition of *politics* used, views of politics can be either positive or negative. The positive view sees politics as a natural part of the process of problem solving and resolving conflict as well as a necessary set of skills, tools, and decision points that must be used to resolve group and/or individual conflict to benefit the greater good. The negative view sees politics as a self-serving, if not entirely dishonest and misleading, activity used to promote the interests of one or a select few over those of others. This author has a positive view of politics and acknowledges that those with more negative views represent a small but thriving part of the academic milieu. But this small group does not define the academy or constitute a critical mass within higher education.

This chapter will focus largely on the positive view of politics and emphasize building trust rather than engaging in manipulative behaviors. The end goal is to build long-lasting, robust relationships that can withstand the challenges of the higher education environment. This chapter will examine:

- definitions of politics,
- the maddening academic milieu, and
- how to practice the art of the possible in the milieu of the maddening.

POLITICS DEFINED

Definitions of *politics* commonly refer to the exercise of power; the distribution of beliefs and standards; competition among individuals, collectives, or entities pursuing their interests; and conflict resolution. According to *Dictionary.com* (n.d.), *politics* is:

1. The science or art of political government.
2. The practice or profession of conducting political affairs.
3. Political affairs.
4. Political methods or maneuvers.
5. Political principles or opinions.

6. The use of strategy or intrigue in obtaining power, control, or status.

In the *American Heritage Dictionary* (2011), *politics* is defined as:

1. The art or science of government or governing, especially the governing of a political entity, such as a nation, and the administration and control of its internal and external affairs.
2. Intrigue or maneuvering within a political unit or group in order to gain control or power.
3. Political attitudes and positions.
4. The often internally conflicting interrelationships among people in a society.

It is important to distinguish force and naked power from politics. Although force and naked power rear their ugly heads in the academic arena—for example, to resolve a disagreement, professionals may be threatened with termination—in their unfettered form, force and naked power are unattainable resources for many and are inferior choices for all. Politics is something other than force or naked power. According to Andrew Heywood, (2015), a best-selling international author of texts on politics and former vice chancellor of Croydon College, "Politics is a particular means of resolving conflict . . . by compromise, conciliation, and negotiation, rather than by force and naked power. This is what is implied when politics is portrayed as 'the art of the possible'" (p. 8). For Heywood (2015),

> politics, in its broadest sense, is the activity through which people make, preserve and amend the general rules under which they live. . . . politics is thus inextricably linked to the phenomena of conflict and cooperation. On the one hand, the existence of rival opinions, different wants, competing needs and opposing interests guarantees disagreement about the rules under which people live. On the

other hand, people recognize that, in order to influence these rules or ensure that they are upheld, they must work with others. (p. 2)

The idea of working with rather than against others is addressed in the expression "politics makes strange bedfellows." Today's enemy can become tomorrow's ally, and yesterday's friend can become today's adversary. The astute administrator therefore builds relationships for the long term that can withstand the vagaries of decision making and the inevitable changing of allegiances when issues arise, evolve, and are resolved. It is this yin and yang of conflict and cooperation that fires the engine of politics. In the context of higher education, these two apparently contradictory forces are complementary and interdependent.

UNDERSTANDING THE MILIEU OF THE MADDENING

To navigate the political landscape of a particular institution, student affairs professionals must develop an understanding of, and an appreciation for, the unique milieu in which they work. A *milieu* consists of "the people and the physical and social conditions and events that provide a background in which someone acts or lives" (*Cambridge Dictionaries Online,* n.d.). Each academic milieu is unique because the type, size, history, purpose, and mission of each institution varies. Different institutions also have different demographics and exist in different state and regional political environments.

Student affairs professionals can use theoretical frameworks to understand the complex milieu of their institutions and how to navigate them. One useful framework for understanding various types of higher education institutions and behaviors within them is provided by Robert Birnbaum (1991) in *How Colleges Work*. Birnbaum described four models of organizational functioning: the collegial model, the bureaucratic model, the political model, and the anarchical model.

- In the *collegial* model, group decision making is king. Value is placed on inclusive group processes that build consensus and allow people to share power. Small liberal arts colleges and many academic departments at teaching colleges are examples of this model.
- In the *bureaucratic* model, processes are king. Clearly identified authority and responsibility centers are organized hierarchically with well-delineated boundaries. In this model, multiple systems and processes ensure that the work of units and subunits follows a path to centralized decision makers. Community colleges and offices of financial aid and international student services are examples of this model.
- In the *political* model, relationships are king. Like the bureaucratic model, this model has well-delineated boundaries between units and subunits; however, the units and subunits have competing agendas and rival each other for resources. Personal relationships among the organization's leaders determine resource dissemination and conflict resolution. State institutions are examples of this model.
- In the *anarchical* model, autonomy for individual units is king. Autonomy permits quick decision making, speedy processes, and generally uniform direction. Collaboration, communication, and cooperation are encouraged, not imposed. Large, complex, multimission institutions are examples of this model.

Organizational perspectives can be described in similar terms (Manning, 2013):

- *Collegial*: "We're all equal colleagues here. Let's discuss this over coffee."
- *Bureaucratic*: "A place for everyone, and everyone in their place."

- *Political*: "I'll scratch your back if you scratch mine."
- *Organized anarchy*: "Don't try to make sense of it—just trust that it works."
- *Cultural*: "We have a legacy and tradition to maintain. This is not about us but about the past and the future."
- *New science*: "We're so interconnected with our environment that it's hard to tell where we start and it stops."

Competing values in higher education that often produce tensions or political conflicts can be categorized as follows (Manning, 2013):

- Individualism versus community
- Interdependence versus independence
- Flexibility versus structure
- Public versus private good
- Competitive versus collaborative

Higher education institutions rarely align with only one model or perspective or champion one set of values. Rather, they often blend characteristics of two or more models or perspectives simultaneously, and proportions of these characteristics may fluctuate based on circumstances. But by using these frameworks as lenses, professionals can look for environmental cues that link organizational perspectives to observed behaviors, and they can make better predictions about political interactions.

What Makes the Milieu Maddening?

The seemingly unpredictable nature of change certainly contributes to the perceived madness in higher education, but there are other reasons why the higher education milieu can be maddening. Leaders make decisions that often appear to be counterintuitive. The well-thought-out idea that appears to be a winner is not approved, whereas the idea that only partially solves the problem is approved and funded—how maddening. Elected or appointed officials, board members, and whole boards often make decisions to further their agendas, but these agendas may be different from or contradict existing goals within the institution, its divisions, departments, or other units. How maddening.

The following examples from this author's experience show the maddening qualities of a higher education milieu and highlight Manning's (2013) tensions. Note the recurring themes of tension between interdependence and independence as well as public and private good, particularly in the following example.

A set of department leaders were flabbergasted that a political appointee had the authority (and the audacity) to require that a construction project follow a process that gave the department less control and revenue and would likely produce a poorer quality product than previously utilized processes. Department leaders discerned the reasoning behind the less-than-popular decision only through a deliberate and painfully slow process of discovery. The political appointee had needed to show that construction projects required less outflow of state revenue and a greater inflow of private revenue. Thus, the political appointee made the new process a requirement despite the loss of departmental control, reduced departmental revenue, and the likelihood of a poorer quality product. In fact, the appointee decided to require the department to use the new process and to attend to and manage appropriately the control, revenue, and quality issues associated with this decision.

Astute observers of such decision-making processes and other aspects of university life should find evidence of positive movement and outcomes, learn to find patterns of success, and begin to strategize. By applying lessons learned, professionals can better practice the art of the possible in the milieu of the maddening.

The following example highlights the tension between competition and collaboration and shows how the conflict might be resolved.

One professional colleague noted that at her institution, there seemed to be three meetings for every scheduled meeting: the meeting before the meeting, the scheduled meeting, and the meeting after the meeting. She also noticed that anyone not invited to the before and after meetings (which could range from highly informal hallway conversations to more formal, agenda-driven, structured meetings) was not regarded as a key player and/or could be the "victim" of the decisions at the scheduled meeting. She learned that strategizing (determining some acceptable solutions and how to broach them) and purposing (identifying the actual as opposed to the stated purpose of the meeting) took place at the first meeting, whereas meaning-making (deciding upon the real meaning behind a particular comment or decision point) was at the top of the agenda at the final meeting along with identifying next steps. Once she unlocked this mystery, she could work on getting herself included in the before and after meetings. Her primary tools for this work were the credibility of the insights and information she provided and her ability to listen well and identify (within the confines of the real purpose and identified strategies for the meeting) pathways to successful outcomes.

Those who are higher up in the hierarchy have a greater understanding of the always changing variables that come together to shape outcomes and decisions—if for no other reason than they are at the table, in the discussions, and members of the governance and decision-making teams that are higher up in the organization. Those in advanced positions can offer insight, information, and interpretations that can make it easier for other professionals to navigate the milieu (see Chapter 12 on supervision).

To effectively engage the politics of a milieu, student affairs professionals must understand and pay attention to people, circumstances, and choices, and they must take note of the ongoing effects of circumstances and choices. In so doing, they are better able to predict behavior and be effective in any environment.

People: Power Centers, Power Players, and Connectors

Key landmarks in the environment to identify are the power centers and power players. Power centers are often units or subunits where money flows to and/or from (the chief financial officer, the business staff, auxiliary services in student affairs, etc.) or where decisions are made (department heads, unit heads, committee chairs, meeting conveners, etc.). Titles and formal responsibilities are perhaps the strongest and most important clues as to who the power players are and where the power centers are located. Presidents, vice presidents, assistant and associate vice presidents, deans, and department heads are examples of positions that come with legitimate power (financial and otherwise) (Bess & Dee, 2008). Legitimate and sometimes not so legitimate forces outside the university also have power within the academic milieu, but they are not always considered part of it (think powerful alumni and donors, legislators, and even spouses of those with big titles).

Power can also be invested in those who have political connections, those who have amassed power through other means, and those who have been delegated the authority to obtain an outcome or reach a goal (Bess & Dee, 2008). The last, but perhaps the most important, people to identify are those who connect others to power: administrative assistants, secretaries, trusted allies, and political and personal friends of those in power. Each of these individuals provides others with opportunities to connect with and ultimately influence those with power.

The following narratives depict the power centers, power players, and connectors within an educational milieu and highlight Manning's

(2013) tensions. Note the recurring themes of the tension between individualism and community, interdependence and independence, flexibility and structure, and competitive and collaborative administrative practices. In the first narrative, one professional identifies the power inherent in a seemingly powerless organization.

> *At one large research institution, the new president recognized that a parent organization made up of a collective of statewide, hometown parent groups was politically powerful owing to its long association with elected state officials and Board of Trustees members. This organization, although friendly and supportive of the institution, historically weighed in on significant issues like tuition and fee increases, student safety, and hate/bias-related events to shape decisions as much in its favor as possible. But the organization had no formal role in the governance structure of the institution and did not appear on any organizational chart. In his initial remarks to the organization, the president said that earlier in his career, he had become an expert in identifying, analyzing, and providing recommendations about ways to respond to power centers in foreign countries. He said that he had analyzed the power structures at his new institution, and he was certain that the parent organization was a political power center. Throughout his tenure, the president demonstrated his ability to reach out to the people in this group and influence them to align with his agenda. He understood their power and influence and respected them enough to interact with them and communicate in a productive manner.*

Another example of using a connector sheds light on the roles of administrative assistants, secretaries, and trusted allies. The people in these roles often serve a connecting, or gatekeeping, role (Simmons, 1998). They control calendars, correspondence, meeting locations and length, and general access to their bosses, and they are some of the most quietly influential and effective members of an organization.

> *One administrative assistant said that she always set up meetings between her boss and one of his colleagues in her boss's conference room because her boss had discovered that was the only way he could get the undivided attention of his colleague. Meetings in the colleague's office were subject to constant interruption. He had attempted to resolve the problem through frank discussion, but he had been unsuccessful. She was able to use her relationship with the colleague's administrative assistant to locate the meetings in her boss's office setting. She enhanced the attractiveness of the location by always having his colleague's favorite flavor of hot tea available for him to brew when he arrived. This settled her boss's nerves, which made the meetings more relaxed, and everyone was able to use the meeting time efficiently. When the inevitable request was made to alternate the meetings so that every other meeting was in the colleague's office, she negotiated a neutral site by suggesting to her boss that he buy lunch at his colleague's favorite restaurant and hold the meeting there.*

The subtle power of a savvy connector made it possible for her boss and his colleague to complete a series of meetings successfully. Managing a delicate political situation deftly, she practiced the art of the possible in the milieu of the maddening.

Circumstances: Being a Player Versus Being a Victim

In the complex and maddening milieu of higher education, professionals' flight response often overwhelms their fight response, and otherwise competent administrators withdraw rather than engage in political machinations. This may be a sound short-term strategy, but it is not a winning long-term strategy. Professionals who withdraw cannot take advantage of the very experiences that will build their skills and abilities. Their withdrawal simultaneously allows more astute administrators to take advantage of an environment with a diminished oppositional force that could otherwise shape decision making and outcomes in a more balanced manner. In the words of a retired vice president for student affairs, "You can engage, participate, and navigate, or you can be a victim. It is not a long-term viable choice to stand to the side and only observe." Another, less generous interpretation was offered by a veteran colleague in student affairs who likened politics in higher education to a poker game: "In every poker game there is at least one person who is being preyed upon. If you look around the table and cannot identify that person, then it is most likely the case that you are the prey. There are no neutral parties in a poker game. The same is true about politics in higher education."

The point is that engaging in organizational politics is risky and intimidating, yet not engaging may be even more risky. Student affairs professionals need to recognize that all organizations are political and shed their naiveté by embracing this reality. Developing a set of strategies for analyzing and navigating the political environment is both a requirement for attaining success and an indicator of professional maturity and effectiveness.

Æsop's (n.d.) cautionary fable about a child and a snake illustrates the kinds of things professionals need to remember as they navigate the landmines, personalities, blind curves, surprises, known knowns (things one knows they know), unknown unknowns (things one is not aware they do not know), and other good and bad parts of the political milieu in higher education.

> *As a child was walking on a path to a relative's house in the cool, wet weather of early fall, the child came upon a snake. The snake cried out to the child and asked to be picked up and carried because it*

didn't want to travel over the wet and cold ground. The child said, "But you are a snake, and if I pick you up, you will bite me!" The snake replied, "Please pick me up, and put me in your jacket pocket so that I can be warm and dry. I will not bite you. Please have pity on me, and get me out of this cold, wet weather." The child felt compassion for the snake and picked it up, put it in her jacket pocket, and continued walking. After a while, the child neared her relative's house and said to the snake, "I have kept you warm and dry and protected you from harm during our travels, and now I have to take you out of my jacket pocket and put you on the ground so that I can go into my relative's house and you can go on your way." With that, the child reached into her jacket pocket and then gently put the snake on the ground. As the child withdrew her hand, the snake bit her. The child cried out in pain and said, "Why did you bite me? I was kind and caring and shielded you from the wet and the cold and kept you safe while we journeyed together. I brought you willingly along with me to advance you in your journey. And you promised that you wouldn't bite me." The snake replied, "You knew what I was when you put me in your pocket."

This tale is about naïveté, misplaced trust, and alliances made with those who have a history of not being trustworthy. The important lesson to learn from the story is that a professional should verify information, remember the history and reputation of those in the interaction(s), and keep in mind that more can be learned from observing others' actions than from listening to what they say. The savvy administrator observes, trusts, and builds alliances with an eye on past behavior, current actions, and future consequences while remaining optimistic, demonstrating a positive demeanor, and expecting success. Professionals who remember this simple cautionary tale and the associated advice may be able to participate more effectively in the political milieu and avoid becoming a victim.

Choices: What Hills Are Worth Dying On?

Student affairs professionals should remember that they will have multiple opportunities for conflict and cooperation on a daily basis but that they have finite amounts of energy, time, and political capital. They must analyze opportunities for conflict and collaboration before determining whether they will engage and to what extent, and how much energy and resources they can and will expend when they engage. When opportunities for conflict arise, they must repeatedly ask, "Is this a hill worth dying on?" If the answer is yes, then they should engage. If the answer is no, then they should engage with caution or choose not to engage.

They can also choose to engage and later choose to disengage; choose to not engage and later choose to engage; or choose to engage with varying levels of energy, enthusiasm, and resource allocation—all dependent upon the circumstances of the particular opportunity for conflict and cooperation. The point is to choose wisely which battles to engage and which to avoid; in that way, professionals conserve scarce resources and increase their chances of remaining viable in the long term. The administrator who fights every battle soon becomes a tiresome, distracting, and no longer useful part of an organization.

The following narrative depicts a hill *not* worth dying on within an educational milieu. It also illustrates Manning's (2013) tensions between interdependence and independence and between competition and collaboration.

> *One of the first decisions made by a new vice president for student affairs (VPSA) was to move Greek Life from one reporting associate vice president (AVP) to another. This was a painful decision at multiple levels. It was the first time this particular AVP had had a department removed, and the new reporting AVP and the Greek Life staff were not in favor of the move. The stage was set for a conflict that could only have one outcome—the VPSA was going to win.*

The current AVP had a one-on-one conversation with the VPSA to explore other options. The VPSA was polite but firm. The realignment would proceed immediately. The current AVP then talked with the Greek Life staff and advised them of the move, told them he would appreciate their cooperation in making the new alignment successful, and said that this was not a hill worth dying on. The battle could not be won.

Over the course of the next 5 years, the VPSA pointed to the level of professionalism and cooperation he received in this matter (self-described as his first major decision) and said it had made all the difference. He had made up his mind, and he was not open to alternative alignments for Greek Life at that time. In his opinion, the staff spent their energy wisely on making the realignment work rather than on resisting the change and protecting the status quo. The VPSA repeatedly complimented the AVP and the Greek Life staff publicly for implementing a difficult decision under adverse conditions in a smooth, positive, and productive manner.

The AVP and the VPSA both noted that the decision was final and that fighting and resisting would have been futile and painful. The realization that this was not a hill worth dying on enhanced the professional standing of the AVP and the Greek Life staff and demonstrated support of the VPSA.

Professionals exercise and demonstrate mature professional judgment by distinguishing between organizational objectives and personal preferences when they choose which conflict opportunities to engage. Organizational objectives are easily defensible because they are closely aligned with organizational objectives, whereas personal preferences are less defensible because they are primarily, if not exclusively, the personal preferences of one or more staff members.

The connection between sound judgment, savvy thinking, and mature decision-making skills and success is illustrated by a short narrative about a conversation between a retired senior administrator from one of the largest research institutions in the country and a group of graduate students. This conversation was convened, initiated, moderated, and observed by this author. The author asked the senior administrator what would be the best advice he could give to graduate students who would soon be embarking on, or re-embarking on, an administrative career path. He answered with no hesitation or uncertainty: "Be careful of the toes you step on today, as they may be attached to the person whose butt you have to kiss tomorrow."

The comment underscored the ways in which the hazards and effects of administrative change magnify the maddening characteristics of the higher education milieu. The senior administrator explained that he had become the supervisor of a former supervisor or become the supervisee of one of his former subordinates five times in his career. Because his interaction style was consistently courteous, professional, transparent, and honest, he had survived and even flourished. On the other hand, several colleagues had become casualties in such political fluctuations of power and direction—in large part because of their previously established deficient interaction styles. In contrast, the respect and political capital that this senior administrator amassed over his career coupled with his proclivity for being a complete professional and a consummate team player made the otherwise turbulent waters of change relatively calm for him. Each administration for which he worked found him to be a valuable member of the team, regardless of what role and level of responsibility he was assigned. He noted that he was proud that he was able to retire on his own terms rather than as the result of the winds of administrative change.

A student affairs professional might serve at one particular institution for 15 years, during which time there might be seven presidents or interim presidents, five provosts or interim provosts, and seven vice presidents for student affairs or interim vice presidents for student affairs. The winds of change can affect many colleagues negatively and positively. Learning to navigate these changes is largely about establishing a reputation as a consistent, dependable, trustworthy, and complete professional and consummate team player who can thrive during change. Remember that change is the only constant, or as Heraclitus of Ephesus (c. 500 BCE) stated: "No man ever steps in the same river twice" (as cited in Mark, 2010).

PRACTICING THE ART OF THE POSSIBLE

The pathway to success in the political environment of higher education is often meandering, full of inclines and declines, and fraught with periods of slow responses and unexpected, lightning-quick responses. Success, therefore, is more about understanding the rhythms of the political environment; being prepared for rapid changes in the decision-making process; attending to and being purposeful about the pacing, timing, and sequencing of messages; ensuring that the content and style of message resonates with decision makers and stakeholders; and seasoning those actions with a sprinkling of perseverance. It is also true that attending to all of this may not lead to success. Such is the milieu of the maddening. This section will address these topics and conclude with several practical tips for professionals who wish to master the art of the possible in the milieu of the maddening.

Timing, Messaging, and Engaging Stakeholders

Student affairs professionals set the stage for success when they understand the definition of politics and the nature and characteristics of the milieu, or the people, circumstances, and choices associated with higher education administration. But to be successful, they also need to adopt, apply, and refine certain skill sets. One of the most valuable skill sets is the ability to be sensitive to the pacing, timing, and sequencing of requests, topic introductions, recommendations, and associated interactions while attending to the content of the message. Pacing refers to how soon or how late a subject is addressed, whereas timing refers to the best point at which to bring up a topic or make a recommendation or request. Sequencing involves the order in which a topic is introduced in relation to other topics. Equally critical to those three elements is the content and style of message. To be successful, professionals must choose words that resonate with stakeholders and, equally important, avoid words that will be perceived as unnecessarily negative. It is also important to bring stakeholders to the discussion and use their feedback to shape the outcome—doing so is a time-honored method of strengthening an initiative, request, or recommendation.

The following narrative highlights the importance of timing, pacing, and sequencing.

> *A number of years ago, a high-ranking administrator at a state institution worked for several years to implement a new-student retention program. She was having little success at getting the necessary resources even though her research was sound, her rationale was sound, and the institution was in need of such a program. Her message was that she needed more resources and more staff to accomplish this important work on behalf of the university. She had worked tirelessly by herself to do the research and to write the recommendation. But the state was experiencing a series of budget cuts, and her request was falling on deaf ears. Soon after, she retired, and the university did not fill her position, in large part because of the budget cuts. Nevertheless, administrators still expected that a retention program for new students would be put in place.*

In the 12–18 months after her retirement, a new president, vice president for student affairs, dean of students, and director of residence life were hired in part to attend to the retention of new students and the needs of underrepresented students. The director of residence life believed the time was ripe for a retention program for new students and underrepresented students that could be produced within the existing budget footprint of the university.

The director of residence life approached his supervisor, the dean of students, and asked if he could form a committee to create a new retention program that would be inexpensive, funded by a small fee to participants, and implemented by existing staff. Since this was a campus with a requirement for new students to live on campus, it would be for residential students. The permission was given to proceed with a committee and to explore and make recommendations that would fit the needs and parameters of the current administration.

In a short time, a recommendation was made to create this new retention program. The program was designed to have voluntary attendance, to be funded in large part by a small fee to be paid by participants, to be implemented by existing staff, to be 3 days and 2 nights in length, to take place in the days just before classes started, to allow participants to move into their residence hall room early, and to have a primary outcome of connecting new students to one another and to the campus. The twin focus on new students and underrepresented students was a critical part of the recommendation.

The president and vice president approved the recommendation, and the program was implemented. The key points in the recommendation were as follows: there would be no increased cost to the university, the cost to participants would be low, and there was the strong possibility that the program would have a significant positive effect on new-student and underrepresented-student retention (these effects were later supported by longitudinal research).

In this case, timing, sequencing, and careful attention to the milieu when styling the language in the recommendation were important factors in the process of getting approval for the long-needed retention program. Ideas that had not been viable under one administration came to fruition under another set of leaders, and the professionals who made the second recommendation used lessons learned from the first to design a message that addressed budget and resource limitations as well as the need for a retention program. Their recommendation also included stakeholders. By including stakeholders, they improved their understanding of stakeholder needs, increased their credibility and chances of success, and created buy-in from otherwise disaffected groups.

Reciprocation

Savvy administrators look for opportunities to use their resources to assist another colleague or unit. Their first goal is to be consummate team players, and their second goal is to position themselves to be able to call in favors later. They know that giving something to someone often motivates that person to return the favor.

Professionals who are adept at providing favors (and if really adept, doing so before being asked) and who use the exchange of favors (including both tangibles and intangibles) to facilitate relationship building are better able to find political solutions. For example, student affairs practitioners who are courteous and show respect are often treated with courtesy and respect. Practitioners who demonstrate professionalism and honesty, particularly under adverse conditions, will likely be treated in the same way by colleagues and stakeholders. The following narrative shared by a distinguished colleague illustrates this point.

One veteran colleague makes it a practice to speak to me one-on-one before he disagrees with me publicly. He painstakingly sets out his reasoning and gives me ample time to prepare for his public disagreement, which may occur at a meeting and/or in writing. The fact that he respects me enough to do this motivates me to provide him with the same courtesy. We get along famously. We are known for our collegial relationship—for collaborating with others, for supporting one another, and for disagreeing in a civil manner. He has been a model for me in learning to do this. I have a strong desire, and make it my regular practice, to alert him in the same respectful manner in advance of a public disagreement. Our colleagues, who have witnessed the power of this technique, have initiated this practice also. It takes transparency to a new level and adds to the high level of trust throughout the organization.

Professionals successfully navigate political issues by compromising, negotiating, and reciprocating—giving something to someone in exchange for that person giving something to them. Though unethical people can abuse this exchange process (for example, by bribing someone), it is a normal part of a healthy environment and is critical to practicing the art of the possible in the milieu of the maddening.

Practical Tips

To practice the art of the possible in the milieu of the maddening:

- ◆ **Identify decision-making paths.** Student affairs professionals should observe and analyze how decisions are made in units, subunits, and across the institution. They should learn who serves as blockers, who serves as facilitators, and where funding sources are. They should pay particular attention to the history of decision making on the topic(s) for which they are currently working.

- **Pay attention to messaging.** It is critical that student affairs professionals attend to the pacing, timing, and sequencing of recommendations and decisions. The style and content of messages should be customized and always include stakeholders.
- **Have credibility.** Student affairs professionals bring credibility to the table by providing accurate and valuable information, valued skills, and workable solutions and ideas. Bringing something of value to the table enhances relationships and sets the stage for success.
- **Build coalitions.** Student affairs professionals should understand the value of coalitions and networking. It is easy to build coalitions on matters of common interest. Networking can be used to move beyond existing coalitions (and beyond existing organization's reporting lines and political boundaries) to build new coalitions. Professionals should aspire to be credible and sought-after coalition members because of their transparency, dependability, and value. The quality and diversity of a professional network is much more critical than the size.
- **Use resources.** Once student affairs professionals understand the milieu in which they work, they can use networking, coalition building, and reciprocity to leverage their insight, influence, and credibility in organizations. They should understand the value of the decision-making setting and use the home-court advantage when possible. Neutral sites can also add value. Professionals should never forget that it is important to offer administrative support, technological support, or other incentives to get stakeholders to see the value of a particular decision-making setting.
- **Be persuasive.** Politically savvy student affairs professionals should be charming and persuasive, but not aggressive. The

famous actor Cary Grant suggested that the definition of charm was the ability to elicit the answer "yes" without ever asking the question. Professionals should use persuasion to build trust rather than erode it. One method of doing this is to focus on the pros and the cons of a decision to demonstrate transparency, then explain why the pros (or the cons) matter more in the circumstances under discussion.

- **Find role models.** Student affairs professionals should identify others within their organization who are successful with navigating politics. They should observe these role models, talk to them, and uncover their strategies for success; professionals should then emulate these role models in their own interactions.
- **Listen more than speak.** Much can be learned about power structures and decision-making paths by listening to conversations. Student affairs professionals should avoid the temptation to talk too much. Instead, they should make strategic, concise, and thoughtful comments—less is more in political circumstances. Professionals should focus on responding appropriately given the circumstances and the culture of the organization.
- **Be humble.** Student affairs professionals should respond to victories as if they have experienced them many times and respond to setbacks with the grace of an adult rather than the selfishness of a child. It is important in all interactions to make a positive, long-lasting impression.
- **Maintain perspective.** It is important to remain upbeat in the face of setbacks. Student affairs professionals should remember that particular events are not directed at them. It can be helpful to practice the mantra of those who refuse to

become defensive: "These events are happening, but they are not happening to me. I am present, but I am not the intended target, though I might be affected by the residual turbulence." Professionals who find that they have become the intended target should go back into the conflict and demonstrate what a mature interaction looks like by finding out what to do to move forward. Then learn from the process, and improve it the next time.

CONCLUSION

This chapter provided a positive perspective on the political environment in higher education and discussed ways in which student affairs professionals can navigate the competing demands and values in higher education institutions. Professionals should understand their academic milieus, including the tensions common to them, and know how to engage successfully by building relationships across an institution. Through intentional and careful practice, student affairs professionals can effectively manage the art of the possible in the milieu of the maddening.

QUESTIONS FOR REFLECTION

- After reading the chapter, do you perceive politics to be largely positive or negative? Why?
- Which of Birnbaum's institutional types would you use to classify your institution? How does the institutional type affect the politics of the institution?
- Which of Manning's (2013) tensions have you seen in your institution? In what way?
- Consider a request you may have made of your supervisor or a program or initiative you have proposed that was either not successful or not as well received as you had hoped. Consider the timing, pacing, and sequencing of the request/proposal. How might you have changed the timing, pacing, and sequencing of the request or proposal?

REFERENCES

Æsop. (n.d.). The farmer and the viper. Retrieved from https://aesopsfables.wordpress.com/the-farmer-and-the-viper/

Bess, J. L., & Dee, J. R. (2008). *Understanding college and university organization: Theories for effective policy and practice. Volume II: Dynamics of the system.* Sterling, VA: Stylus.

Birnbaum, R. (1991). *How colleges work: The cybernetics of academic organization and leadership.* Hoboken, NJ: John Wiley & Sons.

Heywood, A. (2015). *Politics.* New York, NY: Palgrave Macmillan.

Manning, K. (2013). *Organization theory in higher education.* New York, NY: Routledge.

Mark, J. J. (2010). Heraclitus of Ephesos. In *Ancient history encyclopedia.* Retrieved from http://www.ancient.eu/Heraclitus_of_Ephesos

Milieu. (n.d.). In *Cambridge dictionaries online.* Retrieved from http://dictionary.cambridge.org/us/dictionary/english/milieu

Politics. (n.d.). In *Dictionary.com.* Retrieved from http://www.dictionary.com/browse/politics

Politics. (2011). In *American heritage dictionary of the English language* (5th ed.). Boston, MA: Houghton Mifflin Harcourt.

Simmons, A. (1998). *Territorial games: Understanding and ending turf wars at work.* New York, NY: American Management Association.

6

CONFLICT AND RESOLUTION IN THE WORKPLACE

Merna Jacobsen

CONFLICT AND THE search for effective ways of resolving conflict most surely began with the first interaction between humans. The search for ways of resolving conflict continues today, and for good reason. As part of the human condition, conflict has both constructive and destructive properties and is able to transform or destroy interpersonal relationships and group dynamics.

Proof of the persistent quest for effective conflict resolution methods can be found by examining current and historical approaches to conflict around the world; the examination reveals myriad methods aimed at resolving conflicts and preserving relationships. For instance, ancient Albanian Law called for community members to "beat a matter," a process of deliberation and resolution based on the word *kuvendim*, which meant to "sit down with a group of people in order to submit, analyze, examine, sift, weigh, and find a solution to a problem or a dilemma that concerns them" (Marin, 2006, p.71). In ancient Russia, if resolution did not emerge after coming together for collective thinking and persuasive speaking by renowned orators, conflicts were settled by a physical fight, referred to as "to go wall against wall" (Marin, 2006, p. 177).

In the modern world, conflict resolution methods span cultures.

The Acholi of Uganda emphasize forgiveness, reconciliation, and the centrality of relationships (VisionThought, 2010). The Babemba tribe of South Africa uses a ritual to reestablish relationships. If a member of the tribe has acted out or caused discord, that individual is placed in the community square where community members recount the positive deeds and actions of others, then welcome the individual back into the community (VisionThought, 2010). The Baka people of Cameroon stress cooperation, sharing, the common good over personal advantage, and the equal distribution of power and leadership. Individuals who generate conflict are subject to avoidance, a withdrawal of attention, and peer pressure (Marin, 2006). The Maori of New Zealand utilize the *hui*, an open-ended meeting with no time constraints or predetermined outcomes; participants move around a circle to share persuasive speeches that subsequently form the basis of their decisions (Marin, 2006). These few examples demonstrate that the search for effective methods of managing conflict spans history and cultures.

There are good reasons to both embrace conflict in the modern workplace and explore methods of resolving conflict. Researchers have long espoused the transformative benefits of productive conflict; it can alter attitudes, behaviors, and relationships and replace negative or destructive patterns of behavior with positive and constructive patterns (Burgess & Burgess, 2003). However, the positive, transformative effects of conflict are elusive—according to De Dreu (2007), they exist in only a very narrow set of circumstances—and the many negative effects of conflict include time off-task, high stress levels, the deterioration of job satisfaction, increased employee turnover, and stifled innovation. Given conflict's high potential for transformation coupled with its equally potent negative effects and elusive positive effects, student affairs professionals must have competency in conflict resolution skills.

This chapter will explore:

- conflict theories and models,
- applications of conflict theories in the workplace,
- organization and employee development in conflict resolution, and
- key competencies in conflict resolution.

DEFINITIONS, THEORIES, AND MODELS

Definitions

Themes related to the ideas of incompatibility and competition and to perceived or actual threats are common in definitions of *conflict*. *Businessdictionary.com* (2016) defined *conflict* as "friction or opposition resulting from actual or perceived differences or incompatibilities." Prevost (as cited in Furlong, 2005) defined conflict as occurring "when a boundary and its norms are challenged, threatened, or circumvented" (p. 91). Boulding (1962) integrated into his definition the ideas of perceived incompatibility and competition over goals or resources. Henderson and Coning (as cited in Azakasi, 2016) defined conflict as "a state of human interaction where there is disharmony or a perceived divergence of interests, needs or goals" (p. 1). *Merriam-Webster's Online Dictionary* (n.d.) included "a difference that prevents agreement" in its definition. Mayer (1990) noted that perceived threats to needs, interests, or concerns were central to the development of conflict.

It is helpful to distinguish between conflict and *conflict management*, which *BusinessDictionary.com* (2016) defined as "the practice of recognizing and dealing with disputes in a rational, balanced and effective way." Managing conflict means knowing when to confront and when to avoid a conflict, and it requires understanding the issues around which the conflict revolves.

Theories and Models

Several theorists have supported the transformational benefits of conflict. Morton (1973) focused not only on the advantages of conflict but also on cooperation as a means of resolving conflict. Morton recognized that conflict stimulates interest, identifies problems, and promotes change, thereby leading to the establishment of new norms and productive solutions. Coupled with cooperative behaviors like mutual problem solving, openness, mutual regard, and persuasion, conflict can transform interpersonal, group, and organizational dynamics. To determine whether a conflict would have constructive or destructive outcomes, Morton (1973) examined the characteristics of the conflict, the prior relationship of those involved in the conflict, the nature of issues, the environment in which the conflict occurred, the influence of interested third parties, the strategies and tactics employed, and the consequences to each of the participants. Morton's (1973) focus on these variables provided an early framework for conflict analysis.

Fisher and Ury (1991) introduced interest-based principled negotiation and advanced knowledge in the field of transformational conflict with their groundbreaking work *Getting to Yes*. Position-based negotiation throws disputants into a competition in which a conflict is seen as a "winner takes all" zero-sum game; the consequence is a tug-of-war in which the achievement of goals for one party means the loss of goals for the other. Conversely, interest-based negotiation focuses on mutual gain and the satisfactory achievement of goals and needs for both parties; disputants are encouraged to focus on the mutual interests of the parties rather than on positions. Fisher and Ury (1991) offered four tenets of interest-based principled negotiation:

- Separate the people from the problem.
- Focus on interests rather than positions.

- Invent options for mutual gain.
- Insist on using objective criteria.

Furlong (2005), in *Conflict Resolution Toolkit*, offered eight models for diagnosing and analyzing conflict. Foremost among these is the circle of conflict diagnostic model described by Christopher Moore (1986). Moore identified five types of conflicts:

- Relationships
- Data
- Values
- Structures
- Interests

According to Moore (1986), relationship conflicts are caused by strong emotions, stereotyping, and repetitive negative patterns of behavior. Data conflicts involve questions of the validity and completeness of information; data can be hard (statistics) or soft (perceptions and assumptions). Conflicts can also emerge when there is a clash of values—either workplace values or the moral, religious, and personal values that guide individuals. Structural conflicts emerge from the organization and involve issues related to time, geography, the exercise of power and authority, approaches to decision making, and other structural elements. Competing interests are another source of conflict. Moore (1986) noted that disputants have three interests: (a) Procedural interests concern how a process is handled or a conflict is resolved—whether the process is timely, safe, fair, and orderly. (b) Psychological interests concern how participants are treated during conflict. Does the process keep participants emotionally safe? Are disputants allowed to save face? (c) Substantive issues refer to the fact that every disputant wants something of substance out of the conflict.

In his diagnostic model, Moore (1986) provided strategies for resolving each of the conflict types. Effective strategies to use in **relationship** conflicts include the following:

- Control participants' emotions by setting up ground rules.
- Promote the expression of emotions by legitimizing feelings.
- Clarify perceptions.
- Improve communications.
- Encourage positive attitudes about problem solving.
- Block repetitive negative behaviors, which may require making changes to the structure.

Effective strategies to use in resolving **data** conflicts include the following:

- Agree on what data are important.
- Agree on a process by which data will be collected.
- Develop common criteria to assess data.
- Engage third-party experts to break data deadlocks.

Effective strategies to use in resolving **values** conflicts include the following:

- Allow parties to agree to disagree.
- Identify a superordinate goal that all parties share.
- Allow one set of values to dominate, or prevent a conflict from being defined in terms of values.

Effective strategies to use in resolving **structural** conflicts include the following:

- Examine and adjust roles, resources, the use of time, the physical environment, and decision-making processes.
- Move from positions to interests.
- Change the type of influence used in the conflict.
- Modify the external pressures on disputants.

Effective strategies to use in resolving **interest-based** conflicts include the following:

- Develop integrative approaches and solutions that allow mutual gain for all parties.
- Promote trade-offs.

Kaufman, Elliott, and Shmueli (2013) used the idea of frames to understand or analyze conflict. They asserted that disputants view a conflict through a particular frame or lens that is largely determined by their experiences, values, and beliefs. This frame acts as a sieve through which disputants gather, filter, and organize information. Frames are powerful in that they are often more influential than data or reason. Frames distinguish disputants from one another and drive behaviors and attitudes during conflict. Thus, analyzing conflict involves understanding these frames. Kaufman et al. (2013) discussed six common frames and argued that understanding or analyzing the frames held by disputing parties is the first step toward managing frames or *reframing*, which is essential to conflict resolution.

- **Identity.** In the context of the conflict, disputants may see themselves as having a particular identity based on their professional roles (e.g., expert) or self-defined gender or ethnic identities. Conflicts escalate when disputants feel that their identity is being threatened.
- **Characterization.** These frames involve stereotypes or strong views and judgments that disputants hold about the other parties, and they govern not only how disputants view one another but also how they interact. Judgments one party holds about the other may be used to justify that party's behavior and undermine the legitimacy and credibility of the other.

- **Power.** Disputants frequently hold differing views about what type of power is legitimate, honorable, or dishonorable.
- **Process.** The same is true of processes. Differences in power and process frames influence not only how disputants behave during conflict but also their willingness to engage and the manner in which they express themselves.
- **Risk and information.** Some disputants view conflict through this frame. Their assessment of the risk posed by the conflict determines their willingness to engage.
- **Loss versus gain.** Participants may frame the conflict in terms of how much they stand to lose or gain. Disputants may reject proposed solutions that represent perceived losses.

Analyzing the frames of a conflict can help in understanding a past conflict or to better manage a current conflict, resulting in *reframing* (Kaufman et al., 2013). Sometimes the use of frames can help those involved in the conflict to better comprehend the root of the conflict and the issues and factors that might lead to change and possibly resolution. Even in seemingly intractable conflicts, where the frames have been entrenched over time, frames might be altered through deliberate intervention to make resolution possible. However, reframing is not an easy process and requires that those involved in the conflict be willing to take risks and be open to new perspectives.

CURRENT APPLICATIONS OF CONFLICT RESOLUTION THEORY IN THE WORKPLACE

Conflict theory is currently applied to understanding and managing teams and work groups, understanding conflict's transformational role, and assessing disputants' preferences for certain styles of conflict resolution. Conflict can be categorized as constructive or destructive, and methods of conflict resolution can be categorized as formal or informal.

In *Overcoming the Five Dysfunctions of a Team*, Lencioni (2005) argued that conflict is central to healthy, high-functioning teams. Describing conflict in terms of a continuum, with constructive conflict on one end and destructive conflict on the other, Lencioni posited that constructive conflict, in which members robustly debate workplace issues, is desirable because it strengthens teams. On the other hand, destructive conflict, which may involve personal attacks, undermines the functioning of a team. Lencioni offered four tools for mastering conflict:

- conflict profiling through the use of conflict styles instruments (see the next section on conflict assessments),
- conflict norming in teams to establish ground rules and agreements about how conflict will be handled,
- intentional mining for conflict to ensure issues surface in a timely manner, and
- real-time permission to hold one another accountable.

Patterson, Grenny, McMillan, and Switzler (2002) focused on the transformational power of conflict and emphasized moving from conflict to action. In their view, conflict is not something that can be handled in a transactional fashion. They argued that in conflict situations, two characteristics are true: the stakes are high, and emotions run high. They advocated elevating and strengthening relationships through dialogue, and they highlighted the far-reaching and long-lasting consequences of mishandled conversations on both individuals and organizations.

The Thomas–Kilmann conflict mode instrument provides a situational approach to conflict resolution and promotes the value of self-awareness (Kilmann, 2015). Since preferences for certain conflict resolution styles play an important role in conflict resolution, it is essential to be aware of these preferences and to assess them. The Thomas–Kilmann conflict mode instrument measures preferences for five styles of conflict resolution—avoid, accommodate, compete, collaborate, compromise—along assertiveness and cooperation axes. Avoidance and accommodation are both unassertive, but avoidance is also uncooperative. Competition and collaboration are both assertive, but competition is uncooperative. Compromise represents a midpoint between assertiveness and cooperation. Each style may be appropriate, depending on the situation (Kilmann, 2015). The skill and will to utilize each style and the wisdom to recognize when a particular style is appropriate are hallmarks of effective conflict resolution.

Organizations should have both formal and informal methods of conflict resolution, and employees should be informed about both. Formal methods include grievance processes and litigation. Informal methods, also referred to as alternative dispute resolution, include:

- Self-negotiation
- Mediation
- Arbitration
- Dialogue

Informal methods honor the notion that it is most desirable that disputants resolve the conflict at the lowest level possible. Using informal resolution methods reduces the number of formal grievances filed, develops the capacity of employees to resolve conflicts, and creates an environment in which employees are willing to come forward with issues and concerns. Informal resolution methods are less costly, more timely (e.g., they reduce the time spent disputing), and less stressful than formal methods of dispute resolution; and because disputing parties are in more control of outcomes, sustainable outcomes are likely (Gunn, 2016).

Not all disputes can be resolved by informal methods. Formal methods are appropriate when disputants are unable to represent or speak for themselves or when conflicts cannot be resolved informally. Robust and well-known procedures for filing complaints and grievances are necessary to ensure that conflicts are resolved in a productive and timely manner.

Not all researchers take a positive view of conflict or the ability of conflict to be managed for transformative results. After performing a comprehensive review of conflict studies, De Dreu (2007) noted that task-related conflicts are more likely than relationship or values conflicts to realize positive effects, and only if the conflict is of moderate intensity. Trust and psychological safety must be high, and if group members experience conflict during the decision-making process, they will opt to delay or procrastinate rather than debate or continue to push for a high-quality decision. Finally, positive effects are more likely to be related to innovation and decision quality (De Dreu, 2007).

EXAMPLES OF COMPLEX WORKPLACE CONFLICTS

The following three scenarios portray complex workplace conflicts involving multiple parties and issues. Moore's (1986) circle of conflict framework is used to identify the types of conflicts inherent in the situation and strategies that might be used to address each. These scenarios illustrate how student affairs professionals can use Moore's (1986) framework to dissect and address even the most complicated and emotion-laden conflicts.

A Clash of Values

A young higher education professional, Tom, was one member of an office of 10 individuals at a large research institution with several million dollars in federal grants. The bulk of its students receive federal financial aid. A year ago, Tom revealed to his colleagues that he was

HIV positive and had AIDS. He also revealed that he had contracted the disease through unprotected homosexual sex. After his revelation, one of his colleagues, Nora, engaged in a number of behaviors that made Tom and several others in the work environment uncomfortable. Nora's behaviors included disinfecting office equipment touched by Tom, commenting to other workers that Tom was being punished by God for being homosexual, and leaving Bible verses on Tom's desk. When Tom decided to leave the institution for a new position elsewhere, Nora staged a celebration at the office on the day after his departure. When confronted about her behavior, Nora recited Bible verses and justified her behavior by stating that her religious faith was more important than others' opinions.

This scenario is a clear example of what Moore (1986) called a *values conflict*—generally considered one of the most challenging types of conflict to resolve. Religious values, workplace values, and values associated with accepting others are inherent in the scenario. In this situation, the nature of the institution and the policies, regulations, and laws governing the organization should be considered. A public institution that receives federal funds has laws prohibiting harassment and the establishment of a hostile environment. Although individuals can hold any values and beliefs they choose, their behaviors must be in compliance with the institution's governing policies and laws. When deciding what to do in a situation like this, it is critical to separate personal beliefs from behaviors. Nora cannot be disciplined for her beliefs, but she can be disciplined for violating the institution's policies and laws.

A Conflict Between a Department and a New Leader

Roland was in his first 6 months as the director of a student affairs department with approximately 30 employees. His short tenure had been rocky. The previous director had been with the department for more than 30 years, starting as an undergraduate student worker and working his way into leadership. The two assistant directors in the department were hired by the previous director (as were most of the staff) and were both loyal to him and philosophically aligned with him. The previous director's approach to student affairs work was to deliver services, act in loco parentis, and to work on behalf of students.

Roland had immediately expressed expectations that the department adopt a facilitator model, adjust the mission of the department to align with the learning mission of the institution, and engage students in leadership roles. Roland also expected that individuals with academic preparation in the higher education field would be hired for particular positions.

Roland had discussed his philosophies and ideas about management during his interview process, and though these were antithetical to the culture and practices of the department for the past 30 years, they resonated with the vice president for student affairs and other executive leaders on campus. Roland's philosophy about how the department should be run represented a fundamental paradigm shift for the department, and department members were shocked that Roland had been hired rather than an internal candidate.

The employees believed that Roland was too much of an outsider and too different to be their leader. They routinely referred to Roland by derogatory names and called the day he was hired "Doomsday Tuesday." After 2 months in the department, Roland eliminated a layer of management positions to streamline the department and reduce administrative costs. This action eliminated promotional opportunities. Roland made the change against the advice of his assistant directors and without consulting or engaging any of the employees in discussion. His decision was met with shouting at subsequent staff meetings. Some employees went to the vice president for student affairs to complain and ask that he be removed. Events that should not have been problematic escalated into major conflicts. A consultant was hired to assist the department and determine whether Roland could continue in his role.

This scenario illustrates multiple categories of conflict described in Moore's (1986) circle of conflict model. The emotional reaction of the employees and their derogatory characterization of Roland are typical of *relationship* conflicts. Different philosophies about how to run the department reflect *values* conflicts. The difference of opinion concerning the elimination of positions and the decision-making process associated with this action are *structural* conflicts.

Several strategies based on Moore's (1986) model might effectively resolve the conflicts. Ground rules about expressing emotions could be established and these rules could include prohibiting the use of derogatory language and stereotypical labels. Department members could also focus on shared goals to resolve the values issues. Establishing transparency around the decision-making process and providing information about the new organizational structure could address structural problems.

A Conflict Based on Assumptions

From the day Sharon assumed her leadership role as department director, it was obvious that the staff was actively trying to force her to resign. She has now decided to quit. The stress of coping with two years of shunning, uncooperativeness, and outright hostility has taken its toll. Her physical and emotional health is suffering, and she has lost confidence in herself as a leader.

To investigate the cause of the problem and determine whether the conflicts in the department could be resolved, Sharon's supervisor—the assistant vice president (AVP) for student affairs—hired a consultant. The consultant's investigation revealed that the conflict started with assumptions made by staff members at the time of Sharon's hire. The search committee involved in the hiring process conducted by the

AVP had included employees from the department. The committee reviewed several applicants and forwarded their top three candidates to the AVP. Sharon was not among the top three. The AVP ignored the recommendations of the search committee and hired Sharon. The employees on the search committee assumed that Sharon and the AVP were friends and that she had been hired for that reason. They accepted this assumption as fact, shared this "fact" throughout the organization, and used it to organize the employees against Sharon. The employees made an intentional plan and committed themselves to driving Sharon out of the organization in retaliation. However, the facts were that Sharon had never met the AVP and had no prior relationship with him. Sharon was not aware that she was not among the top candidates chosen by the search committee and had no idea why the AVP had decided to hire her over other candidates.

This scenario illustrates at least three conflict categories from Moore's (1986) circle of conflict model. The lack of complete and accurate information regarding Sharon's hiring is a *data* problem. The hostile treatment of Sharon is a *relationship* problem. The obvious flaws in the hiring process point to a *structural* problem. To resolve this conflict, accurate information must be disseminated. A meeting in which members of the staff are provided with facts is the starting point. Staff can then begin the process of deconstructing their long-held false assumptions. Although the deconstruction process may be emotional for those involved, it will initiate a new relationship between Sharon and her staff. The hiring process problem is a structural issue not controlled by the group. The group members may want to address this issue, or they may decide that it is more important to repair work relationships within the office.

COMPETENCIES IN CONFLICT RESOLUTION

Key Competencies

Five key competencies can help student affairs professionals master constructive conflict and conflict resolution.

- **The ability to manage resolution processes.** Resolution processes, including informal methods (e.g., mediation, arbitration, negotiation, dialogue) and formal methods (e.g., grievances, litigation) are governed by codes of ethics and professional standards. Familiarity with standard practices, and better yet, training or certification in some methods, is helpful. For example, those who act as mediators must know how to mediate a process that allows parties to vent, after which the mediator and parties set an agenda and then generate and select solutions and make a plan to implement the solutions. Those who understand such resolution processes and the professional standards governing them can address conflict more effectively, are more likely to prevent conflicts from escalating, and are less likely to do unintentional harm.
- **The ability to communicate for resolution.** Effective conflict managers need a variety of communication skills to help disputants stay in dialogue, establish trust, and reduce defensiveness. The ability to frame and reframe issues is essential to effective problem solving.
- **The ability to convene and facilitate groups in conflict.** Those who convene groups in conflict must be proficient in advanced facilitation skills, agenda design, and facilitation processes and techniques.
- **The ability to analyze conflict.** Effective conflict managers carefully analyze situations to select appropriate interventions

and ensure they are not acting from bias or perception. Conflict analysis skills are essential to understanding conflict and exploring options for mutual gain.
- **The ability to implement a course of action for moving forward.** To make progress in conflict situations, conflict managers must do more than express emotions and identify issues. Conflict managers must work with others to determine effective solutions and future steps. A few key behaviors can help in doing this in an intentional and disciplined fashion. First, conflict managers must be able to break down complex conflicts and assist others in making meaning of the components of a conflict. It is also critical to be able to correctly identify the issues and root causes of the conflict. Assisting in identifying high-leverage solutions and engaging in robust reality testing of those solutions ensures better outcomes. Finally, using both short and long-term agreements is more likely to produce sustainable resolutions.

Strategies for Developing Conflict Competencies

Student affairs professionals can develop conflict competencies in the following ways:

- Observe and interview exceptional conflict managers. Professionals can learn strategies and gain wisdom and lessons learned from the field from these managers.
- Debrief significant events and conduct after-action reviews of how conflicts were handled. Doing this work encourages reflective practice and corrective behavior.
- Engage in on-going training in resolution methods and skills to ensure that legitimate processes are used. Such training may include dialogue skills like talking, listening, framing, and being assertive, as well as communication skills to diffuse situations.

- Seek feedback from trusted mentors and engage in self-awareness exercises, such as assessing personal communication style, conflict style preferences, biases, and personal triggers.

Several associations provide professional development in conflict resolution competencies. These include the Association for Conflict Resolution, the International Association for Conflict Management, the American Arbitration Association, and the National Association for Community Mediation. These associations offer publications and professional development events. The International Association of Facilitators offers professional training in a broad range of facilitation skills, as does the Institute of Cultural Affairs. In addition, there are several books on the topic of conflict management, including the ones cited in this chapter.

ADVICE FOR SUPERVISORS

In their work on managerial mediation competency, Poitras, Hill, Hamel, and Pelletier (2015) noted that supervisors are increasingly called upon to intervene in workplace conflicts and that their leadership in conflict situations can affect employee engagement and satisfaction. Poitras et al. (2015) asserted that supervisors must have skills in three domains inherent in conflict resolution:

- **Cognitive.** Supervisors should be able to understand concerns and identify underlying interests. According to Poitras et al. (2015), "Parties should perceive that their manager understands what matters to them" (p. 108). They must be able to formulate questions, facilitate input from the parties involved, and accurately define problems and concerns.
- **Emotional.** Supervisors must be able to find ways in which emotions can be addressed constructively so that they do not

escalate the conflict. They must be able to establish processes that allow for the expression and legitimization of emotions. They must also be able to restate emotions.
- **Behavioral.** Supervisors must be able to use facts to challenge the perspectives held by disputants, encourage the exploration of solutions, and facilitate implementation.

In addition, supervisors enhance conflict management among employees in the following ways:

- **Model behaviors.** When supervisors model essential behaviors, they set the tone for constructive conflict and effective conflict resolution in the workplace. By addressing conflicts openly without defensiveness or judgment and by being committed to making things better, not worse, they give those they supervise permission to engage in conflict. They must treat both controversies and people with respect to reinforce their commitment to constructive conflict. Supervisors can achieve genuineness only if they are comfortable with conflict and not afraid to lean in to their discomfort. They must be aware of their biases and maintain neutrality in conflict situations to model appropriate behaviors.
- **Create a culture that embraces conflict.** Supervisors should shape the organizational culture around conflict by defining patterns of behavior and interactions. For example, they should set expectations regarding conflict (e.g., issues should be addressed in a timely fashion; conversations should include the appropriate parties only). Supervisors can use several methods for establishing patterns:
  - Norm the group around conflict issues during the early stages of team development.

+ Demonstrate effective communication skills in difficult conversations.
+ Incorporate core values and the associated desired behaviors into employee orientation and onboarding programs. Language is one of the most important tools available to supervisors to establish a healthy conflict culture. Respectful but direct language, free from toxicity, sets the tone for interactions.

- **Attend to and trust process.** The most important role of the supervisor is to ensure that conflict resolution processes exist and that these processes are fair, equitable, and accessible. Effective processes must include complete and accurate data, objective criteria, a common understanding of neutrality, an equal voice for all disputants, and ethical standards that are known and adhered to by all. Supervisors should ensure the organization has a robust conflict management system with both formal and informal processes available to employees.
- **Encourage employees to develop their capacity for self-negotiation.** Strengthening the capacity of employees to resolve conflict issues has several benefits. It relieves the pressure on supervisors to act as intermediaries; it prevents conflicts from escalating into more serious and intractable issues; it establishes a culture of resolution for the organization; and it builds both the competence and confidence of employees to resolve issues. Effective ways to build capacity include providing on-going training in conflict resolution, modeling appropriate behaviors, and coaching employees in conflict management and resolution.

CONCLUSION

This chapter discussed the ever-present and honorable search for effective means of resolving workplace conflicts through processes that will transform relationships and groups. Conflict theories emphasized interest-based approaches to foster constructive conflict. By embracing the transformational possibilities inherent in conflict, student affairs professionals can encourage better problem solving and support new norms concerning conflict resolution. To make meaning of complex issues and emotions and make progress toward resolution, disputants and third parties must engage in conflict analysis.

Because managers and supervisors are increasingly being called upon to intervene in workplace conflicts, they must develop competency in cognitive, emotional, and behavioral domains. They must also model behaviors associated with effective conflict resolution. Most importantly, they must understand and trust in the conflict resolution process so that they can resolve conflicts and establish an effective conflict-resolution culture in the workplace.

In conflict resolution, problems can be solved for today, or they can be solved for tomorrow. Investing in effective conflict resolution in the workplace is an investment in the future of the organization. How conflicts are resolved reveals the quality of the organization's thinking and the intensity of the organization's commitment.

QUESTIONS FOR REFLECTION

- Recall a conflict (from either your professional or personal life) and use Moore's (1986) circle of conflict model to analyze the types of conflicts inherent in that situation.

- Reflect on your own conflict resolution style (or complete a self-assessment such as the Thomas–Kilmann instrument). What is your typical response to conflict? Does your style create problems for you or others? Are you aware of your own effectiveness in conflict resolution?

- Create a professional development plan to build your understanding of the process of staying in dialogue and the skills you need to engage in that process.

REFERENCES

Azakasi, S. J. (2016). *Conflict analysis of dinner for two video: Definitional issues and theoretical frameworks.* Retrieved from http://www.primepeace.org/doc/CONFLICT-ANALYSIS-OF-DINNER-FOR-TWO.pdf

Boulding, K. (1962). *Conflict and defense.* New York, NY: Harper and Row.

Burgess, G., & Burgess, H. (2003). What are intractable conflicts? *Beyond Intractability.* Retrieved from http://www.beyondintractability.org/essay/meaning-intractability

Conflict. (n.d.). In *BusinessDictionary.com.* Retrieved from http://www.businessdictionary.com/definition/conflict.html

Conflict. (n.d.). In *Merriam-Webster's online dictionary* (11th ed.). Retrieved from http://www.merriam-webster.com/dictionary/conflict

Conflict management. (n.d.). In *BusinessDictionary.com.* Retrieved from http://www.businessdictionary.com/definition/conflict-management.html

De Dreu, C. (2007). The virtue and vice of workplace conflict: Food for (pessimistic) thought. *Journal of Organizational Behavior, 29*(1), 5–18. doi: 10.1002/job.474

Fisher, R., & Ury, W. (1991). *Getting to yes: Negotiating agreement without giving in* (2nd ed.). New York, NY: Penguin Books.

Furlong, G. T. (2005). *The conflict resolution toolbox: Models and maps for analyzing, diagnosing, and resolving conflict.* Mississauga, Ontario: Wiley Canada.

Gunn, R. (2016). Alternative dispute resolution in a work setting. Retrieved from http://www.mediate.com/articles/gunn.cfm#1

Kaufman, S., Elliott, M., & Shmueli, D. (2013). Frames, framing and reframing. Retrieved from http://www.beyondintractability.org/essay/framing

Kilmann, R. (2015). A brief history of the Thomas–Kilmann conflict mode instrument. Retrieved from http://www.kilmanndiagnostics.com/brief-history-thomas-kilmann-conflict-mode-instrument

Lencioni, P. (2005). *Overcoming the five dysfunctions of a team: A field guide for leaders, managers, and facilitators.* San Francisco, CA: Jossey-Bass.

Marin, I. (2006). *Collective decision making around the world.* Dayton, OH: Kettering Foundation.

Mayer, R. J. (1990). *Conflict management: The courage to confront.* Columbus, OH: Battelle Press.

Moore, C. W. (1986). *The mediation process: Practical strategies for resolving conflict.* San Francisco, CA: Jossey-Bass.

Morton, D. (1973). *The resolution of conflict.* New Haven, CT: Yale University Press.

Patterson, K., Grenny, J., McMillan, R., & Switzler, A. (2002). *Crucial conversations: Tools for talking when the stakes are high.* New York, NY: McGraw-Hill.

Poitras, J., Hill, K., Hamel, V., & Pelletier, F. (2015). Managerial mediation competency: A mixed-method study. *Negotiation Journal, 31*(2), 105–129. doi: 10.1111/nejo.12085

VisionThought. (2010, September 20). Maat, Imhotep & rituals of peace: Authentic models of conflict resolution in African culture [Blog post]. Retrieved from https://visionthought.wordpress.com/2010/09/20/maat-imhotep-rituals-of-peace-authentic-models-of-conflict-resolution-in-african-culture

ETHICS AND ETHICAL DECISION MAKING

Peggy C. Holzweiss

IN AN INCREASINGLY complex higher education environment, with its diverse set of constituents and their competing interests, student affairs practitioners at every level must frequently react to challenging situations and make good decisions with minimal preparation. Practitioners can apply principles in the field, such as the principle of doing no harm, to the decision-making process as a method for identifying and prioritizing options. However, using these principles does not prevent lapses in judgment or making quick decisions that lead to unintended consequences.

This chapter will explore:

- competencies in ethics in higher education,
- professional standards and codes of conduct,
- common ethical dilemmas in student affairs,
- older models of ethical decision making,
- a new model of ethical decision making,
- applications of the model, and
- the supervisor's role in guiding professionals' ethical development.

ETHICS IN HIGHER EDUCATION

Ethics is commonly defined as a set of principles that guide moral behavior and involves personal values, organizational contexts, and community norms (Beu, 2003; Blimling, 1998; Dalton, Crosby, Valente, & Eberhardt, 2009; Lovell & Kosten, 2000; Reybold, Halx, & Jimenez, 2008). In guiding behavior in the workplace, ethical decision making protects others from harm and ensures a higher quality of professional performance (Cimino, Rorke, & Adams, 2013). It is therefore not surprising that ethics is a desired professional competency in the field of higher education and student affairs (Blimling, 1998; Henning, Cilente, Kennedy, & Sloane, 2011; Waple, 2006).

However, there is disagreement about where and when student affairs professionals develop competencies in ethics. According to Kuk, Cobb, and Forrest (2007), higher education and student affairs faculty believe professionals learn these competencies during graduate preparation programs. As these researchers noted, student affairs professionals believe that these competencies are developed through experience. In fact, competencies can be developed in either environment or both, but the two perspectives illustrate why training and development efforts in graduate programs may not fully address the expectations of all constituent groups.

Graduate preparation programs teach student affairs practitioners about ethical foundations by reviewing codes of conduct and basic principles of the field. Yet these programs do not teach what ethics looks like in real world applications, so when student affairs educators enter professional practice and "are literally surrounded by ethics in its most practical form whenever they are doing their business" (Janosik, Creamer, & Humphrey, 2004, p. 357), they do not know how to resolve dilemmas. Introductory knowledge without experience with ethical situations is not sufficient preparation. It is therefore wise for student affairs professionals to adopt personal practices for enhancing these skills.

A list of specific competencies in ethics for student affairs educators to develop at various stages of their careers have been developed by ACPA–College Student Educators International and NASPA–Student Affairs Administrators in Higher Education (2015). The Personal and Ethical Foundations list emphasizes:

- increasing awareness of personal values and beliefs,
- creating a personal code of ethics,
- managing areas of incongruence between personal and institutional values,
- understanding the influence of organizational culture on ethical decisions,
- reflecting on and evaluating ethical decisions,
- identifying other professionals who can provide consultation, and
- modeling good ethical behavior for others.

After becoming familiar with the competencies identified at each career stage, professionals can conduct a self-assessment. They can then confirm or enhance their own assessment by adding in an assessment from a supervisor or work colleague. Once they have identified areas of growth, professionals can create a list of goals. For example, they might plan to read research and best practices on the topic, find a mentor to guide their development, and have regular discussions on the topic with colleagues. Finally, if they revisit personal practices on an annual basis, professionals can become more aware of when and how competencies in ethics are used in the work environment.

PRINCIPLES OF ETHICAL PRACTICE AND CODES OF CONDUCT

After examining professional competencies in ethics, student affairs practitioners should review the foundational values of the higher education field (Cuyjet, Longwell-Grice, & Molina, 2009; Welfel & Lipsitz, 1984). Kitchener (1985) identified six principles of ethical practice in higher education, including the following:

- autonomy (allowing for independent choices),
- nonmalfeasance (doing no harm),
- beneficence (doing good for others),
- justice (acting fairly),
- fidelity (trustworthiness), and
- veracity (honesty).

Dalton et al. (2009) noted that the Council for the Advancement of Standards in Higher Education added one more principle: affiliation (building community).

Career fields focused on human relationships share these ethical principles, and student affairs professionals can refer to them when discussing issues encountered in the higher education field. (For a thorough review of ethical principles and standards for the field, see Ortiz, O'Brien, & Martinez, 2015).

In addition, a variety of established codes of conduct found within professional association guidelines prescribe how student affairs practitioners should act in specific functional areas, such as student orientation, residence life, and academic advising. However, there are a number of reasons why student affairs professionals should not depend on these codes to fully inform their ethical decision making.

1. Representative administrators who have their own beliefs, values, and organizational contexts develop and update the codes (Blimling, 1998; Stark, 2015). These administrators must work cooperatively to adopt a one-size-fits-all set of standards to govern professional behavior (Blimling, 1998; Stark, 2015), which may not work in specific situations.
2. Codes of conduct are often vague, share only general guidance for decision making (Blimling, 1998; Reybold et al., 2008), and are disconnected from what occurs in the daily life of a student affairs professional (Dalton et al., 2009; Janosik et al., 2004; Reybold et al., 2008; Shapiro & Stefkovich, 2005). The codes are designed to be broad enough to apply to various institution types and organizational contexts, but they do not provide the specific direction a professional needs to make good ethical decisions.
3. Student affairs professionals may not be familiar with or remember the codes of conduct; they may neglect to implement them; or they may find them difficult to use (Humphrey, Janosik, & Creamer, 2004; McDonald, Ebelhar, Orehovec, & Sanderson, 2006). Although some professionals may have been exposed to codes of conduct during their academic preparation programs (Kuk et al., 2007), they may not have had practice applying the codes or discussed different behavioral standards in the field. For these reasons, ethics training that focuses on codes of conduct may not have a significant influence on professionals' decision-making capabilities (Artino, 2007).

Student affairs professionals need more than knowledge of ethical principles and codes of conduct in order to meet the challenges they will face in various organizational contexts. But they should know the principles and codes, and they can benefit from considering them in the light of the culture of their specific institutions. Professionals can review each of the seven guiding principles for the field to identify the values they prioritize and then compare those with the values their leaders' prioritize. For example, a professional working in academic advising who prioritizes student autonomy may encourage students to select the courses they will take. But the organization's leaders may want advisors to take a more active role in directing students' selections. By understanding these subtle differences in values, the professional can refine priorities, decide how to put personal beliefs into practice within a specific organizational culture, and forecast leaders' reactions to decisions.

COMMON ETHICAL DILEMMAS IN HIGHER EDUCATION

Once professionals have examined ethical principles and codes of conduct, they should consider the types of dilemmas they will encounter in the higher education environment. Shapiro and Stefkovich (2005) identified four primary types of dilemmas in the field of education.

1. **Justice** concerns issues of fairness, equity, and individual rights together with the ideal of the greater good. Student affairs professionals may need to apply policies consistently to address this type of dilemma.
2. **Critique** concerns inequities in society and involves challenging inconsistencies. For example, a professional who observes discriminatory practices must decide whether to address the situation.
3. **Care** concerns loyalty, trust, cultures, and relationships. Student affairs professionals may focus on advocacy for a student who needs more than the normal amount of assistance.

4. **Profession** concerns community standards and professional codes of conduct. Student affairs professionals might need to decide whether to report policy violations.

Student affairs practitioners should also examine specific situations that occur within these broad dilemma types so that they can determine whether their personal values will influence decision making, whether competing interests exist, and what options they might consider to resolve the dilemma appropriately (Humphrey et al., 2004; Magolda & Baxter Magolda, 2011). In the higher education environment, several ethical challenges or dilemmas are common across functional areas. Janosik (2007) identified the following:

- acting when one has knowledge of a problematic issue,
- treating others fairly,
- respecting private and confidential information, and
- knowing when to set loyalty aside for the benefit of the greater good.

Dalton et al. (2009) added:

- reporting alcohol usage by staff members,
- having personal relationships with students and defining appropriate boundaries, and
- favoring specific individuals or groups.

Young (2011) contributed organizational dilemmas such as:

- making decisions based on immediate resource needs that may not align with institutional values,
- disciplining a student athlete when it could hurt the institution's reputation, and
- focusing on the needs of one student group to the detriment of another.

Student affairs professionals can practice responding to challenging situations by discussing the broad dilemma types and specific situations with supervisors and colleagues. In doing so, they can consider diverse perspectives on a situation, and these perspectives may influence the factors that inform their decision-making process. Seeing a situation from multiple perspectives helps elucidate problems that may arise from various approaches. Taking the time to analyze ethical dilemmas with others helps student affairs professionals improve their critical thinking skills and better prepares them for similar situations they may encounter in their daily practice.

ETHICAL DECISIONS

As representatives of their institutions, student affairs professionals should respect legal boundaries when making decisions, model for students what integrity looks like, and always do what is best for the institutional mission. Understanding ethical principles, conduct codes, and common dilemmas provides a foundation to work from, but student affairs professionals must go beyond foundational knowledge to build skills in ethical decision making. As Blimling (1998) noted, ultimate responsibility "rests with the individual to make a moral judgment" (p. 66).

Dalton et al. (2009) suggested that an individual needs experience, practice, and reflection to make good ethical decisions. In the higher education environment, satisfying these conditions poses a challenge. Even professionals who have been working for a number of years may not have the full range of experience or practice necessary to recognize and/or resolve the ethical situations they encounter. In addition, they may overlook reflection even though it is a necessary component of student affairs practice (ACPA & NASPA, 2015). Professionals generally focus on addressing the task-oriented demands of their positions and do not make time for the philosophical reflections that can lead to improved performance (Sterling, 2015).

Without experience, practice, and reflection to inform their ethical decision making, student affairs professionals may rely solely on their personal judgment to resolve dilemmas, but doing so leaves them vulnerable to their lack of knowledge, and they may make poor choices by failing to completely understand a situation. Poor choices may lead to outcomes that adversely affect other people or the individual's career (McDonald et al., 2006; Reybold et al., 2008). For instance, when a situation occurs that requires a professional to make an ethical judgment, the professional may not recognize the problem or have the critical thinking skills necessary to analyze and resolve it; the professional may not understand available options or know whether to act (Dalton et al., 2009; Sternberg, 2015). Magolda and Baxter Magolda (2011) observed that professionals may not fully understand how their personal values align with the institution's values; therefore, even established professionals entering midlife should continue to increase self-awareness and continually consider how their values affect their professional practice. Magolda and Baxter Magolda (2011) explained that personal values may prompt professionals to choose not to act on an ethical situation—they may fear that their action will reflect badly on their reputation or negatively affect the organization or its leaders.

A variety of cultural characteristics may contribute to poor decision making or may affect student affairs professionals' readiness to make good ethical decisions, but professionals may not be aware that these characteristics affect the manner in which they make decisions. Sometimes cultural norms reinforce conformity or contribute to a lack of clarity regarding ethical principles. Political conflicts between individuals or groups can influence professionals' judgments. These effects are more pronounced when professionals do not receive systemic training or continued education regarding proper decision making in the workplace (Liddell, Cooper, Healy, and Stewart, 2010).

Consider how students from different cultures may view the act of plagiarizing a paper. For example, a student includes direct passages from several journal articles in a research paper and does not properly cite the authors or include quotation marks to signify that those passages are someone else's work. After the student turns in the paper, the instructor discovers the passages, fails the student for that assignment, and sends the student to the conduct office for disciplinary action. If the student comes from a culture emphasizing individualism, such as the United States, the student may explain that there was a need to plagiarize in order to finish the paper on time and get a better grade. Personal gain motivated the plagiarism (Hofstede, Pedersen, & Hofstede, 2002). Now substitute a student from a collectivist culture such as China. This student may explain that the passages improved the quality of the paper and enhanced the reputations of the teacher and university. The student may not see anything wrong with the behavior and may be baffled by the disciplinary action. A desire to benefit the organization as a whole motivated the plagiarism. The act of plagiarism is the same but the underlying values leading to the behavior are very different.

There are other instances when student affairs professionals must take underlying values into account when determining whether behavior is ethical or unethical. For instance, some students may want to include family members in meetings even though the information being shared is of a private or confidential nature. Or a staff member may choose not to share his or her concerns about a new policy because to do so would undermine the leader's authority. It is a mistake for student affairs professionals to assume that students, or even other professionals, share their values and will react as they do in specific situations. If they increase their knowledge of cultural differences, professionals can more easily identify how people from different backgrounds are likely to approach situations and make ethical decisions.

Without a knowledge of different backgrounds and cultures, professionals may rely on authority figures to resolve dilemmas for them (Blimling, 1998). Alternatively, they may use a majority vote to resolve ethical issues; they may work toward consensus; or they may use rules and regulations to guide decision making (Reybold et al., 2008). Reybold et al. (2008) noted that ethical development seemed to occur through a trial-and-error approach but that professionals who obtained leadership positions became more aware of decision-making processes and outcomes. Reybold et al. (2008) speculated that as professionals move into positions of increasing authority and make important decisions with a far-reaching impact, their critical thinking improves.

To improve decision-making capabilities at all levels, it may be critical to teach student affairs professionals how to respond to challenging situations. Many ethical decision-making models (Dalton et al., 2009; Hornak, 2009; Humphrey et al., 2004; Vaccaro, McCoy, Champagne, & Siegel, 2013) suggest that professionals take deliberate steps such as the following:

- recognize the problem,
- classify the type of dilemma,
- identify possible outcomes,
- apply ethical principles,
- decide on a course of action, and
- assess, evaluate, and/or reflect.

However, student affairs professionals usually do not have time to take these steps; they often react but do not analyze the problem, outline options, and weigh different solutions and their impact. They are more likely to do those things after they have made decisions and experienced the consequences. To counteract the tendency to react, it is necessary to apply a new model of ethical decision making that addresses the needs of student affairs professionals.

THE STUDENT AFFAIRS ETHICAL DECISION-MAKING MODEL

The student affairs ethical decision-making model includes five behavioral steps that student affairs professionals can take to make better decisions.

1. **Recognize the emotions that the situation generates.** Magolda and Baxter Magolda (2011) noted that professionals may recognize a general feeling of discomfort. They may not understand why they feel uncomfortable, but they know that something is not quite right and feel uneasy about it. When professionals recognize their feeling of discomfort, they move to the next step—even if they do not know why the situation bothers them.
2. **Make time to analyze the situation.** Professionals should postpone any action until later so that they have time to analyze why the situation feels uncomfortable. For example, a student may share with a student affairs professional that she overheard another student discussing details of what sounded like a sexual assault on that student's significant other. It is not clear from what was overheard whether the student perpetrated the assault or had knowledge of it occurring. The student affairs professional is unsure if this should be reported and feels uneasy about addressing sexual assault issues. The professional can ask to get back to the student the next day in order to review campus processes; this lets the student know that her concerns have been heard, and it gives the professional time to analyze personal

feelings of discomfort. Stepping away for even a few minutes to make a phone call or a restroom break can provide professionals with an opportunity to view a situation more clearly and react in a calm manner. Professionals who take this extra time to analyze their reactions are better able to think critically and make good decisions (Frisby & Traffanstedt, 2003; Gunia, Wang, Huang, Wang, & Murnighan, 2012).

3. **Consult with others, especially trusted others, before making decisions.** It is helpful for student affairs professionals to describe their feelings of discomfort to someone before identifying the ethical problem, acknowledging personal values, and reviewing possible options and outcomes. Even if a decision has already been made, there may still be time to change direction or modify the decision. It can be helpful to gather input from others in order to understand the actions to take to rectify a problematic decision (Cimino et al., 2013). When possible, professionals should seek multiple consultants to assist in analyzing a situation and determine what outcomes can be achieved through various actions. Outside perspectives can help professionals identify any unintended consequences that may result from the decision and recognize any precedents that may guide the decision.

Student affairs professionals should carefully consider which trusted sources they will confide in. Confidants may include a supervisor, colleague, or even a neutral third party such as a member of a professional network or a significant other. A primary consideration should be maintaining confidentiality and privacy for the parties involved. For instance, when a discussion needs to include specific details about another person's situation such as that person's disciplinary background, academic performance, or sexual assault status, a significant other may not be the best confidant. Alternatively, when a situation involves a colleague, a neutral third party who does not know anyone in the immediate work environment may be a good choice. Even if identifying information such as names is not disclosed, an insider confidant who recognizes the characteristics of the situation may be able to determine who is being discussed. Professionals should remain vigilant about protecting the privacy and confidentiality of the individuals involved in a situation, regardless of whom they select as a confidant.

4. **Choose a course of action after acknowledging the dilemma and consulting with others.** A student affairs professional should first determine whether a situation is within the scope of his or her authority to resolve. The best course of action might be to report the situation to someone who does have the authority to address it; such a person might be a supervisor, a human resources professional, or a member of the campus police. Choosing not to act is also an option, but it may not be the best course of action because often situations become more difficult if nothing is done (Sternberg, 2015). Writing down details about the situation serves as a record of what happened that the professional can consult in case the situation arises again or becomes worse. If the professional chooses to confront the person(s) involved in the situation, he or she should discuss with a trusted confidant how the conversation will be approached, what might go wrong, how to prepare for it, and what the desired outcome will be.

5. **After the action has been implemented, discuss the situation with someone to reflect on and evaluate what happened.** A student affairs professional can have this discussion with a

confidant, the person serving in the consultant role, or someone new to the situation. Someone who hears the entire story from start to finish can provide a different perspective and make suggestions about how to be more effective if the situation arises again in the future. Privacy and confidentiality must be maintained in this final step.

APPLICATION OF THE MODEL

One of the more challenging ethical dilemmas student affairs professionals face is deciding what to do when they observe a supervisor making poor choices. The supervisor's poor choices might manifest as bullying behavior toward others, inappropriate relationships with staff or students that cross established boundaries, mismanagement of resources, unfair treatment of others, or failure to meet expectations or align behavior with institutional guidelines (Cimino et al., 2013). Any one of these behaviors may generate discomfort.

These are the steps student affairs professionals can take when they observe such behaviors:

1. **Acknowledge discomfort.** It is the first sign that the situation is significant enough to warrant evaluation.
2. **Make time to think through the situation.** The unethical act observed may not require immediate attention, and in many cases, it may be best for a professional to put some distance between the observation and the action they are considering so that they can think more rationally and less emotionally about what was observed. If a supervisor has exhibited unethical behavior, it is important to take time to reflect because any action a professional takes could have personal and professional repercussions.

3. **Consult a trusted confidant to discuss the supervisor's troublesome behavior and analyze actions to take to resolve the situation.** A discussion can help a student affairs professional identify the consequences of taking an action, such as losing his or her job, having unsupportive colleagues who make work difficult or unpleasant, or being compelled to look for another job (Cimino et al., 2013; Young, 2011). Carefully selecting a confidant and sharing only the necessary details can help a professional protect everyone involved from unintended consequences.
4. **Take action of some kind.** In situations involving supervisors, an institution may have an anonymous reporting mechanism. Another option may be for a professional to document what happened without reporting it. If the problem has occurred only once, it may be an aberration rather than a pattern of behavior. Writing down the details of what happened in a private journal kept at home provides a record of the details to consult in case of future problems. If a second incident occurs, the original documentation can provide the facts necessary to establish a pattern of behavior. Depending on a professional's relationship with a supervisor, direct confrontation may be an option, but it might be more effective to have a relevant third party intervene. That approach reduces possible negative consequences for the reporting professional.
5. **Discuss the situation from start to finish with a trusted confidant.** Only necessary details should be shared, and anything that would constitute a breach of confidentiality or privacy should not be disclosed. If the situation involves a supervisor, a professional may find the work environment less comfortable. The professional may need to mend his or her relationship with the supervisor or feel compelled to look for a new job. A trusted friend or colleague who acts as a

sounding board can help the professional evaluate the situation and address the new challenges.

ADVICE FOR SUPERVISORS

Student affairs professionals benefit from working in an environment that promotes good ethical behavior. They also benefit when they follow a model for good decision making when ethical challenges arise. Supervisors have a critical role in shaping the work environment and promoting good ethical behavior since they lead others toward common goals and influence how work is conducted. They can help create an environment of ethical openness by engaging employees in regular discussion and encouraging employees to analyze challenging situations (Reybold et al., 2008). For example, by taking time during a staff meeting to discuss an ethical situation that is making national headlines, supervisors signal that employees can address such problems collaboratively in the organizational environment. Questions to address might include how the situation affects the institution and what actions would be appropriate in the context of the institution. In this way, supervisors establish norms to guide staff members with dilemmas they may encounter and reinforce acceptable standards of behavior.

In discussions about ethics, supervisors could ask staff members about the ethical issues they have observed or experienced in the course of their daily work. The conversation could include identifying barriers to good decision making, such as not understanding how or when to report a situation or whether the situation warrants a report. During a periodic review of the code of conduct for the unit, all staff members could be asked to contribute ideas about what might arise and how they might approach the situations. By inviting employees to discuss dilemmas, supervisors promote their active engagement in ethical practices and improve the overall performance of everyone in the organization. During discussions, supervisors may be able to identify organizational culture issues that pose barriers to good decision making.

Supervisors should set aside any expectations they may have about what employees should know. Even student affairs professionals with many years of experience struggle with ethical issues. Although having regular conversations about ethics can encourage professionals to share their concerns, they are likely to keep this information to themselves if they perceive a lack of support. When professionals acknowledge that they do not know the answer to a question, they are leaving themselves open to criticism. If they know that their supervisor is available to them if they wish to consult about an ethical situation and that sharing that information will not adversely affect how the supervisor perceives their work, they will be more likely to address ethical issues regularly.

Supervisors are uniquely positioned to connect organizational values and expectations to the daily practice of student affairs professionals because of the many meetings they attend and the information they have access to. When introducing a new policy, supervisors can explain why the policy exists, what the institutional leaders hope to accomplish with the policy, and how employees will contribute to the overall mission by following the policy. Supervisors may also find it helpful to explain the history and political climate behind the new policy. Employees may have only a superficial understanding of why the policy is important and may choose to ignore or work around requirements because they find that complying with those requirements is burdensome or unnecessary. When the supervisor explains the impact of the policy on organizational resources and constituents, employees are more likely to support it and make good decisions.

Supervisors also need to guide employees in developing ethical competencies. This effort begins when a new staff member joins the team. Supervisors help new staff members define what it means to be an ethical professional within the organizational context by discussing the guiding principles and codes of conduct that define work within the office, the values the supervisor prioritizes, why those values contribute to the success of the office, and professional behaviors that are desirable in challenging situations. Once supervisors establish a good foundation for ethical performance for the professionals they supervise, they should include the topic of decision making in employees' annual performance reviews. A discussion of this topic might involve assessing an employee's competencies and identifying skills he or she should work on over the course of the next year. By supporting skill building in various ways (e.g., funding a workshop, purchasing a book), supervisors signal that the office is invested in ethical practices.

Supervisors should also reinforce good ethical decision making throughout the year. They can take note of employees who react emotionally to a situation before they have had an opportunity to assess the situation rationally. When they observe emotionally driven decision making, supervisors can meet with those employees to review the situation. Supervisors who ask employees to discuss a situation and consider better ways to handle similar situations in the future help those professionals develop personal strategies that will enhance their skills and improve their performance.

CONCLUSION

In the final analysis, the individual is responsible for developing professional ethical competencies, including understanding personal values, seeking perspectives from other professionals, balancing individual and community needs, and knowing the institutional context (Liddell et al., 2010). Attending conferences and engaging in consultations with others can help student affairs practitioners develop these competences. While participating in professional association conferences, whether local, regional, or national, practitioners have the opportunity to consider current events and emerging topics and contemplate their personal values. They can ask other conference participants how they view the events and topics, discuss concerns about community needs, and analyze institutional contexts.

When they have ethical questions of any kind, student affairs practitioners should seek advice and feedback. Ethical behavior is not an isolated activity; rather, it is shaped by the organizational culture and the behavior of others. Practitioners should seek other perspectives to help them develop a personal code of ethics and establish professional boundaries. By discussing their beliefs with colleagues, they can determine what they will or will not tolerate within the organization's environment.

It can be difficult to determine the ethical context of an institution when job searching. Student affairs practitioners should understand their personal and professional values before they embark on a job search because they will need to look for signs that their values and the institution's values match. To determine whether these values match, practitioners can take the following steps:

1. Assess the language of the job posting and the way in which the job is advertised to determine what the organization values in its employees and where they search for possible applicants.
2. Review both the organization's and the institution's websites. In a typical job search, a student affairs practitioner becomes acquainted with the mission and goals of both, but practitioners should also examine the way in which information is communicated and to whom. Are representatives accessible? Is the language inviting? What do these things say, if anything, about standards and professional conduct?

3. Peruse institutional media releases and local or campus newspaper stories from the last year. What success stories does the institution promote? What articles have been written about the institution, and do the articles raise organizational culture issues that cause concern?
4. Generate questions from research to ask during a job interview. Observe reactions to the questions. Do the representatives address the questions directly, or do they avoid answering? Ask about the organizational culture and the institutional culture and how they compare.
5. If possible, find students or staff members not on the official interview agenda to talk to about these issues. Walk around campus before or after the interview and find someone to talk to about the values the institution espouses. After gaining a better understanding of institutional and organizational values, a practitioner can determine whether the environment is a good fit. A mismatch of values or an uneasy feeling might indicate that the professional would be faced with challenging ethical dilemmas.

It is essential that student affairs practitioners develop competencies in ethical decision making. To do this, they must set aside time for reflection and consult with others who can help them analyze situations and decide upon appropriate courses of action (Shapiro & Stefkovich, 2005). When they act to resolve an ethical dilemma, practitioners experience personal satisfaction, prevent others from experiencing harm, and increase their understanding of what ethical decision making looks like in their work environment (Sternberg, 2015; Young, 2011). As Sternberg (2015) observed, even if a practitioner's ethical action is unsuccessful, taking action at least symbolizes a willingness to act, and "a series of those symbolic statements, as made by courageous people around the world, have brought down unethical individuals and governments alike" (p. 184).

QUESTIONS FOR REFLECTION

- Which of Kitchener's (1985) values do you prioritize? Why?

- What ethical dilemmas have you encountered while working in higher education? How did your personal values influence how you viewed the situation?

- How can you help other student affairs professionals make better decisions when they are confronted with an ethical dilemma?

- What consequences are you prepared to accept if your ethical decisions do not go as planned?

- Under what circumstances would you leave an institution for ethical reasons?

- What role does the difference between "intent" and "impact" play in ethics?

- How can you differentiate between an honest mistake and a breach of ethics?

REFERENCES

ACPA–College Student Educators International & NASPA–Student Affairs Administrators in Higher Education. (2015). *Professional competency areas for student affairs educators.* Retrieved from https://www.naspa.org/images/uploads/main/Professional_Competencies.pdf

Artino, A. R. (2007). Assessing ethical dilemmas in educational research: Does formal ethics training make a difference? *Journal of College and Character, 8*(5), 1–18. doi: 10.2202/1940-1639.1616

Beu, D. (2003). Ethical behavior: Does being accountable matter? *Journal of College and Character, 4*(4). doi: 10.2202/1940-1639.1353

Blimling, G. S. (1998). Navigating the changing climate of moral and ethical issues in student affairs. In D. L Cooper & J. M. Lancaster (Eds.), *Beyond law and policy: Reaffirming the role of student affairs* (New Directions for Student Services, No. 82, pp. 65–75). San Francisco, CA: Jossey-Bass.

Cimino, A. N., Rorke, J., & Adams, H. L. (2013). Supervisors behaving badly: Witnessing ethical dilemmas and what to do about it. *Journal of Social Work Values and Ethics, 10*(2), 48–57. Retrieved from http://jswve.org

Cuyjet, M. J., Longwell-Grice, R., & Molina, E. (2009). Perceptions of new student affairs professionals and their supervisors regarding the application of competencies learned in preparation programs. *Journal of College Student Development, 50*(1), 104–119. doi: 10.1353/csd.0.0054

Dalton, J. C., Crosby, P. C., Valente, A., & Eberhardt, D. (2009). Maintaining and modeling everyday ethics in student affairs. In G. S. McClellan & J. Stringer (Eds.), *The handbook of student affairs administration* (3rd ed., pp. 166–186). San Francisco, CA: Jossey-Bass.

Frisby, C. L., & Traffanstedt, B. K. (2003). Time and performance on the California Critical Thinking Skills test. *Journal of College Reading and Learning, 34*(1), 26–43. doi: 10.1080/10790195.2003.10850154

Gunia, B. C., Wang, L., Huang, L., Wang, J., & Murnighan, J. K. (2012). Contemplation and conversation: Subtle influences on moral decision making. *Academy of Management Journal, 55*(1), 13–33. doi: 10.5465/amj.2009.0872

Henning, G. W., Cilente, K. M., Kennedy, D. F., & Sloane, T. M. (2011). Professional development needs for new residential life professionals. *The Journal of College and University Student Housing, 37*(2), 26–37. Retrieved from http://www.acuho-i.org/journal

Hofstede, G. J., Pedersen, P., & Hofstede, G. H. (2002). *Exploring cultures: Exercises, stories, and synthethic cultures.* Yarmouth, ME: Nicholas Brealey.

Hornak, A. M. (2009). Ethical issues for community college student affairs professionals. In C. P. Harbour & P. L. Farrell (Eds.), *Special issue: Contemporary issues in institutional ethics* (New Directions for Community Colleges, No. 148, pp. 53–62). San Francisco, CA: Jossey-Bass.

Humphrey, E., Janosik, S. M., & Creamer, D. G. (2004). The role of principles, character, and professional values in ethical decision-making. *NASPA Journal, 41*(3), 675–692. doi: 10.2202/0027-6014.1393

Janosik, S. M. (2007). Common issues in professional behavior. *NASPA Journal, 44*(2), 285–306. doi: 10.2202/1949-6605.1796

Janosik, S. M., Creamer, D. G., & Humphrey, E. (2004). An analysis of ethical problems facing student affairs administration. *NASPA Journal, 41*(2), 356–374. doi: 10.2202/0027-6014.1796

Kitchener, K. S. (1985). Ethical principles and ethical decisions in student affairs. In H. J. Canon & R. D. Brown (Eds.), *Applied ethics in student services* (New Directions for Student Services, No. 30, pp. 17–29). San Francisco, CA: Jossey-Bass.

Kuk, L., Cobb, B., & Forrest, C. (2007). Perceptions of competencies of entry-level practitioners in student affairs. *NASPA Journal, 44*(4), 664–691. doi: 10.2202/0027-6014.1863

Liddell, D. L., Cooper, D. L., Healy, M. A., & Stewart, D. L. (2010). Ethical elders: Campus role models for moral development. *About Campus, 15*(1), 11–17. doi: 10.1002/abc.20010

Lovell, C., & Kosten, L. (2000). Skills, knowledge, and personal traits necessary for success as student affairs administrator: A meta-analysis of thirty years of research. *NASPA Journal, 37*, 553–572. doi: 10.2202/0027-6014.1118

Magolda, P. M., & Baxter Magolda, M. B. (2011). How do professionals navigate situations when their professional beliefs clash with their supervisors' or organizations' beliefs? In P. M. Magolda & M. B. Baxter Magolda (Eds.), *Contested issues in student affairs: Diverse perspectives and respectful dialogue* (pp. 453–465). Sterling, VA: Stylus.

McDonald, W. M., Ebelhar, M. W., Orehovec, E. R., & Sanderson, R. H. (2006). Ethical decision making: A teaching and learning model for graduate students and new professionals. *The College Student Affairs Journal, 25*(2), 152–163.

Ortiz, A. M., O'Brien, J., & Martinez, C. R. (2015). Developing a professional ethic. In M. J. Amey & L. M. Reesor (Eds.), *Beginning your journey: A guide for new professionals in student affairs* (4th ed., pp. 43–66). Washington, DC: NASPA–Student Affairs Administrators in Higher Education.

Reybold, L. E., Halx, M. D., & Jimenez, A. L. (2008). Professional integrity in higher education: A study of administrative staff ethics in student affairs. *Journal of College Student Development, 49*(2), 110–124. doi: 10.1353/csd.2008.0013.

Shapiro, J. P., & Stefkovich, J. A. (2005). *Ethical leadership and decision making in education*. Mahwah, NJ: Erlbaum.

Stark, L. (2015). Why ethics codes fail. *Inside Higher Ed*. Retrieved from https://www.insidehighered.com/views/2015/07/21/essay-why-scholarly-ethics-codes-may-be-likely-fail

Sterling, L. (2015). Students' and tutors' perceptions of the use of reflection in post-registration nurse education. *Community Practitioner, 88*(4), 38–41.

Sternberg, R. J. (2015). Ethical impotence. *Journal of College and Character, 16*(3), 180–185. doi: 10.1080/2194587X.2015.1057154

Vaccaro, A., McCoy, B., Champagne, D., & Siegel, M. (2013). *Decisions matter: Using a decision-making framework with contemporary student affairs case studies*. Washington, DC: NASPA–Student Affairs Administrators in Higher Education.

Waple, J. N. (2006). An assessment of skills and competencies necessary for entry-level student affairs work. *NASPA Journal, 43*(1), 1–18. doi: 10.2202/0027-6014.1568

Welfel, E. R., & Lipsitz, N. E. (1984). The ethical behavior of professional psychologists: A critical analysis of the research. *The Counseling Psychologist, 12*(3), 31–42. doi: 10.1177/0011000084123004

Young, R. B. (2011). Give in or get out? Responding to professional challenges. In R. B. Young (Ed.), *Special issue: Advancing the integrity of professional practice* (New Directions for Student Services, No. 135), pp. 79–87). San Francisco, CA: Jossey-Bass.

PART II

PROFESSIONAL DEVELOPMENT

8

AUTHORING PERSONAL AND PROFESSIONAL SUCCESS

Peggy C. Holzweiss

ACPA–COLLEGE STUDENT EDUCATORS International and NASPA–Student Affairs Administrators in Higher Education (2015) jointly developed a comprehensive list of competencies needed for practice in student affairs. One specific competency in the Personal and Ethical Foundations area suggested that student affairs professionals should "seek environments and collaborations that provide adequate challenge such that personal development is promoted" (p. 17). This statement implies that practitioners should approach their own development with intentionality and plan for the types of experiences they need to be successful in student affairs.

This chapter will address how student affairs professionals can:

- be intentional about their professional development,
- assess their development needs,
- prepare for emerging opportunities,
- recognize natural transitions in career progression, and
- determine what factors are involved in obtaining advanced degrees, finding work–life balance, and supporting employees in their development from a supervisory role.

BEING INTENTIONAL ABOUT PROFESSIONAL DEVELOPMENT

As student affairs practitioners begin their careers, their professional development may be influenced by a number of factors such as the positions they hold, the institutions they work for, the expectations of colleagues and mentors, and their personal needs, professional goals, and career interests. As they acquire more experience, their development may be influenced by additional factors such as the skills and abilities they need for advancement, their family obligations, and the career outcomes they desire. If they do not plan intentionally, they leave their development to happenstance and are likely to find later that they have become dissatisfied with their work environments and job roles and that their personal needs are not fulfilled.

This section will discuss the theory of self-authorship (Baxter Magolda & King, 2012) and review ways in which professionals can use the theory to purposefully identify and work toward desired benchmarks. The section will conclude with an explanation of the imposter syndrome and the ways in which it stalls the healthy development of professional identity.

Self-Authorship

The theory of self-authorship describes the process by which individuals learn to rely on personal values and beliefs to make life decisions (Baxter Magolda & King, 2012). Although the theory applies to adult development well beyond the college years, it is an especially relevant lens through which to look at the college student population, consisting as it does of students who are beginning to discover their personal values and beliefs and who often need guidance as they form and reform their identities. The theory also sheds light on the development process professionals experience as they embark on or advance through their careers.

Baxter Magolda and King (2012) described self-authorship as a continuum of how individuals define meaning in their lives through their worldview, relationships, and identity. On one end of the continuum, individuals define meaning through external influences such as family beliefs or social expectations. They do not yet view these influences through a critical lens; instead, they accept these beliefs and expectations as norms dictating the way that life ought to be experienced. On the other end of the continuum, also known as self-authorship, individuals define meaning through internal influences such as beliefs, values, and experiences, and they make decisions in accordance with these internal influences.

At some point in their development, individuals reach a "crossroads" where there is a mix of both internal and external influences (Baxter Magolda & King, 2012). During this phase, individuals begin to question the ways in which external influences dictate their decisions, start developing personal opinions about the meaning of their lives, and initiate a shift from relying on external influences to looking for internal congruence between values and behaviors. Individuals are able to identify when external influences are affecting personal decisions and begin to choose to be guided by internal influences instead.

Individuals can be described as self-authors of their lives when they regularly trust their internal voice, develop a personal philosophy of life, and make decisions that are aligned with their personal philosophy even if external influences are unsupportive or provide a contrary view (Baxter Magolda & King, 2012). The process of achieving self-authorship involves continuous self-evaluation and adjustment if an individual is to lead an authentic life, and the process can span many years of an individual's development. Baxter Magolda (1998) found that only a few elements of self-authorship emerged during graduate school, which means that most of the crossroad experiences and the development of self-authorship occur during the postgraduate phase of life when many adults are engaged in the full-time working environment. It also means that individuals must navigate their sense of self as they establish a professional identity.

Self-authorship is further developed in professional practice when individuals can focus on:

- working with multiple perspectives,
- identifying similarities and differences,
- collaborating effectively with others,
- anticipating possible future trends and challenges,
- managing the competing demands of multiple stakeholders,
- building intercultural maturity, and
- coping with ambiguity. (Baxter Magolda, 2014)

Baxter Magolda and King (2012) described a three-step assessment process for helping college students apply self-authorship concepts that student affairs professionals can adapt to their own process of evaluating professional identity development. The first step is for professionals to recognize important personal characteristics. A professional taking this step might acknowledge his or her academic history, known strengths, areas of challenge, and career goals and expectations. The second step is to identify important experiences in previous work situations and explain their effect on the professional's identity (Baxter Magolda & King, 2012). These experiences could involve part-time positions, internships, or full-time employment and include any significant experience with either a positive or a negative outcome. Examples include starting a job at a new institution, being in a leadership position for the first time, or experiencing disciplinary action for a mistake. Once a professional identifies the experiences, he or she should reflect on the impact of those experiences and assess the ways in which they challenged or changed the professional's personal beliefs, values, or behavior. The final step is to examine each of the experiences and assess how meaning was developed. This involves evaluating each situation and determining how external influences and internal values affected outcomes (Baxter Magolda & King, 2012).

An example can illustrate the assessment process described by Baxter Magolda and King (2012). After being disciplined for ignoring an established process in order to help a student with a unique set of circumstances, a professional evaluates the experience by acknowledging:

- why she exhibited the original behavior;
- what the external influences were on the original behavior;
- what internal values were involved in the original behavior; and
- how (or if) internal values and behavior have changed as a result of the disciplinary action.

In this situation, the professional's internal value of helping others may have been competing with the external influence of a student asking to be exempt from a process. A professional who is still developing self-authorship may have made the decision to ignore the process because she found it difficult to decline the student's request. The disciplinary action might prompt her to evaluate her decision and adjust her behavior so that it is more in line with organizational demands. A professional who has achieved self-authorship may have made the decision to ignore the process because she believes that helping others is more important than any organizational rule, especially if there are special circumstances. In this case, the disciplinary action may not change her values or behavior. Instead, she may accept it as a price to pay for making decisions aligned with her philosophy of life.

Student affairs professionals can use the theory of self-authorship to frame their professional identities and help them make conscious decisions regarding their development. Using the assessment process, individuals can evaluate previous professional experiences and assess the impact those experiences have had on their development. The assessment process measures an individual's progress toward self-authorship because each experience represents additional learning and development. When professionals have reached self-authorship or crossroad benchmarks and can recognize when external influences are impacting decisions but use an internally developed philosophy to guide their decisions, they can continue to refine their self-authorship identity.

The Imposter Syndrome

Although intentional self-authorship can guide the development of professional identity, the imposter syndrome can interfere with it. This syndrome is defined as feeling inadequate or unworthy and being consumed by self-doubt (Clance, 1985), and it is often experienced by those viewed as successful high achievers (Parkman & Beard, 2008). These individuals attribute their success mainly to external factors such as working long hours, knowing the right people, or being held to lower standards than others; they do not attribute their success to their personal skills and competencies. Although it is sometimes attributed to females, the imposter syndrome is likely to be experienced by both sexes (Parkman & Beard, 2008), but being the first one in a family to achieve professional success may increase the chances that a professional will feel like an imposter (Harvey & Katz, 1985).

Individuals experiencing the imposter syndrome often work hard to achieve success and perceive that if they were more competent in the position, they would not have to work so hard (Parkman & Beard, 2008). This perception is linked to having perfectionist tendencies, having high expectations of colleagues and subordinates, and exhibiting workaholic behaviors such as staying late at the office and conducting business over the weekend. Individuals experiencing the imposter syndrome can experience burnout (Hutchins, 2015; Parkman & Beard, 2008), and they affect the organization as a whole through "ineffective workplace performance patterns, negatively influencing peers and subordinates, and derailing the institution's succession plan" (Parkman & Beard, 2008, p. 30).

Combating imposter syndrome means first identifying it. For example, a supervisor or colleague may notice that a practitioner's behavior pattern includes regularly responding to e-mails regardless of when they are sent, taking a dominant role in every project, and being the last person to leave the office every day. When this pattern is detected, the supervisor or colleague could share these observations with the practitioner and express concern for what kind of stress the individual may be under. This conversation can initiate a discussion about the professional's feelings of being overwhelmed or of not wanting to fail (Hutchins, 2015; Parkman & Beard, 2008). Professionals who are experiencing the syndrome can have discussions with supervisors about workload issues, and these discussions can help them set realistic goals and identify causes of the feelings of inadequacy. Finally, turning to mentors or personal support systems for affirmation can remind professionals about the skills and abilities they have developed and can help them connect those competencies to workplace successes.

ASSESSING PROFESSIONAL NEEDS

The self-authorship theory defines specific competencies that self-authored professionals exhibit in the workplace, such as collaborating effectively with others, managing diverse perspectives, and working effectively in ambiguous situations (Baxter Magolda, 2014). These skills are a set of outcomes student affairs practitioners can work toward when building and refining identity. To become authors of their own development, practitioners must start by identifying areas in which they need to grow.

Professional standards and competencies for the field are another source of guidance concerning development (Knight, 2014). The Council for the Advancement of Standards in Higher Education (CAS; 2015) has provided detailed descriptions of what professionals should know or be able to do when performing work in one of the many functional areas in higher education. Although these standards are often used to assess program effectiveness and student learning, student affairs practitioners can use the standards to evaluate their own abilities as they align themselves and their abilities with job responsibilities. Knight (2014) explained that practitioners should be able to apply these standards consistently because they are the "best or promising practices" (p. 6) in the field. As they review job responsibilities against the standards for the functional area, practitioners can determine which responsibilities they have the most experience with and which they may still need to develop. They can then create a list of outcomes and a plan for obtaining additional training or practice.

Student affairs educators can also use the professional competencies developed by ACPA and NASPA (2015) as a self-evaluation tool. The long list of competencies covers broad areas such as personal and ethical foundations; law, policy, and governance; social justice and inclusion; and advising and supporting. Each of the competency areas outlines development at the basic or foundational level, the intermediate level, and the advanced level. Practitioners can assess their competencies by reviewing each competency area and writing down experiences that demonstrate mastery of the listed skills and knowledge. Such experiences might include activities occurring in graduate preparation programs, internships, and full-time jobs; individually selected development activities such as participation in training sessions, conferences, and webinars; and additional development activities such as reading scholarly literature and discussing ideas with colleagues. Practitioners who review and align each listed competency with examples from their professional background can more easily determine which skills, abilities, and knowledge they need to develop.

Professionals can also look to current trends in higher education to determine what to prioritize for development. For instance, Knight (2014) suggested that because of the increasing demand for higher education to be accountable for outcomes and rising tuition, "evidence-based practices are the gold standard" (p. 6). This means that professionals should prioritize assessment processes, research skills, and the ability to use data to perform analyses. Other researchers have emphasized the need for skills in supervision, planning, development, conflict management, team building, collaboration, and resource management (Roberts, 2007; Saunders & Cooper, 1999). Professionals can sort these skills and prioritize them according to personal preference.

Biddix (2011) recommended studying the career paths and skills developed by senior-level leaders in higher education. By reviewing hundreds of résumés, Biddix (2011) identified director-level positions as the most common route to senior-level leadership; dean positions were a secondary route. Student affairs practitioners who aspire to senior-level positions may therefore need to prioritize preparation for director and dean positions and gain experiences in the associated competencies to advance successfully. In addition, Biddix (2011) recommended that practitioners use skills and abilities performed at the senior level as competency goals for development. These competencies include budgeting, personnel management, compliance procedures and reporting, and community outreach, which involves working with constituents.

Biddix (2011) found additional professional development priorities in the functional areas associated with senior leaders, and thus recommended that practitioners obtain experience in and knowledge of areas such as enrollment management, financial aid, development and fundraising, and registration. Practitioners do not need full-time experience in these areas to learn more. By simply taking advantage of opportunities to develop partnerships or by requesting membership on committees, practitioners can better understand the competencies they need for these functional areas as well as the challenges these areas present. In addition, leadership roles in national organizations can sometimes provide professionals with skills in budgeting, development, and fundraising, which are required of senior leadership.

Student affairs practitioners should also stay current with what is happening in higher education to assist their development plans. Signing up for the free daily e-mails provided by *The Chronicle of Higher Education* or *Inside Higher Ed* can help practitioners stay abreast of challenges and trends from across the country and around the world. Even scanning just the headlines every day can provide practitioners with a general sense of the issues institutions are struggling with and what might affect the student affairs profession in the near future. Regularly reviewing scholarly literature in the field can also help practitioners stay current with research findings and apply those findings to the work environment (Chernow, Cooper, & Winston, 2003).

When attending conferences, student affairs professionals should move beyond their comfort zone. For example, when a list of available sessions is posted, professionals may naturally gravitate to those sessions that are closely aligned with their job responsibilities. However, selecting sessions that target a wider variety of functional areas helps expand learning opportunities and offers different perspectives of current trends. Professionals who increase awareness in this way can discover new methods to order developmental goals.

Finally, professionals can identify priorities for development by regularly scanning job postings, finding postings that match their career goals, and evaluating requested qualifications against personal competencies. When they do not meet the qualifications, professionals can create a list of skills and experiences to obtain. They can also share with supervisors what they have discovered and request assistance in developing these qualifications. In this way, they can be proactive and seek support for their development.

PREPARING FOR EMERGING OPPORTUNITIES

Once priorities for development have been established, student affairs professionals should be intentional about how experiences are obtained. Self-advocacy is an important skill. Professionals should share development priorities with their supervisors, and then ask for assistance in identifying opportunities and experiences that can build competencies. As a second step, professionals should ask to participate in specific experiences that will provide a broader view of organizational functions and leadership. These experiences may include participating in governance activities (Rosser & Javinar, 2003) or serving on institutional committees (Chernow et al., 2003). Even requesting regular conversations with a division leader on challenging topics such as the political environment can help improve understanding of the systemic perspective of higher education organizations. All of these activities enhance knowledge and provide different lenses by which to view current trends and future challenges.

Another strategy student affairs professionals should consider to prepare for emerging opportunities is to be open to other functional areas for either career options or professional development experiences. It may be possible to cross-train or cultivate a long-term project with another unit. This type of challenging experience can benefit professionals by introducing them to a different functional area while they remain in their full-time position. It can also benefit organizations by strengthening relationships across the campus, and these stronger relationships may in turn make operating processes and procedures more efficient. Professionals may decide that since they are open to other functional areas, they should apply for full-time positions in those areas. Taking this step has the benefit of offering entirely different environments and can prepare professionals for future leadership roles.

Chernow et al. (2003) recommended that student affairs practitioners get involved in professional association activities and leadership to prepare for emerging opportunities. Finding experiences within these associations can help practitioners build a network, which can in turn help them discover new opportunities. Members of the network become acquainted with each other's work through association activities and may actively recruit for new positions, publication or presentation opportunities, or collaborative projects. Practitioners who are involved in association activities also gain from experiences that are not available at the institutional level; these experiences can include working on a task force that will affect a large sector of the profession or hosting a conference that a majority of professionals will attend. These opportunities have the potential to have long-lasting effects on professional identity and should be included in a practitioner's development plans.

IDENTIFYING NATURAL TRANSITIONS

Determining when a job no longer meets one's development needs can be challenging. Student affairs professionals may find themselves wanting to be loyal to their employer or unprepared for the next step. Both scenarios can result in remaining in a position when there are no more opportunities for growth. The self-authorship framework can help professionals determine when a natural transition point has been reached. For instance, according to the self-authorship theory, when a professional reaches the crossroads on the self-authorship continuum, he or she may begin challenging or questioning external influences and make decisions that align with personal preferences rather than the expectations of others (Baxter Magolda, 1998). A professional who begins to have these kinds of experiences in the workplace has reached a benchmark or point of transition; the environment may no longer align with the professional's stage of self-authorship development. The need to make different decisions may very well signal that it is time to change jobs.

Student affairs practitioners may wish to plan their transition by identifying next steps in a career path. Biddix (2011) determined that reaching the senior leadership level would take between 17 and 23 years of service, depending on institutional type. Progressing through various positions to that level would involve an average of six job changes, or a new position every 3 or 4 years. Practitioners who aspire to the senior leadership level can use this timeline to plan transitions.

Other professionals may not have a clear career path and would not want to plan regular job changes. For professionals in this category, determining when it is time to move on can be a little more challenging. These professionals are often less concerned about moving up to the next level and more focused on satisfaction within the work environment and within their professional roles. Their satisfaction may be affected by longevity at an institution, challenges with leadership or role definition, issues with work–life balance, or concerns about workplace relationships.

Rosser and Javinar (2003) found that the longer professionals worked at an institution, the more they encountered issues that influenced their desire to leave. Those with more years of service had concerns about unfair treatment, not being valued, problems with ambiguity, challenges to their authority, and the ethics of leaders. The researchers also identified quality-of-life issues: minimal investment in professional development, challenging relationships with colleagues, and a lack of feedback and guidance from leaders. Silver and Jakeman (2014) suggested that stress and burnout, financial concerns, lack of institutional support, feeling emotionally burdened from working with students, and a lack of time to make social connections outside of the work environment all contributed to the desire for professionals to leave the field entirely.

It is important for student affairs professionals to identify feelings of unhappiness and resentment as soon as they emerge, as these feelings can signal that a point of transition has been reached. When a professional no longer looks forward to going to work or persistently experiences negative feelings about the organizational culture, it may mean the professional and the position are no longer a good match. Evaluating what is occurring can help professionals take control of the situation and determine what personal decisions must be made. Waiting until emotions rise and stress is constant does not help to approach the situation with a critical eye. Having self-awareness and recognizing when problematic feelings emerge can help professionals find a resolution before the situation becomes worse.

Student affairs practitioners who have not created a clear career path or who are not experiencing dissatisfaction in their current positions may be able to identify natural transition points in two additional ways. One indication is when all the responsibilities of a job have been fulfilled successfully and are in the refinement stage. A second sign that a natural transition point has been reached is when boredom sets in. Boredom signals that the position lacks challenge and that new opportunities for growth and development are needed. However, all professionals should adopt a general philosophy of learning to do their current job well before moving to another one.

CONSIDERING ADVANCED DEGREES

Student affairs professionals whose plans include pursuing senior-level positions or possible teaching opportunities need to consider obtaining a doctoral degree (also referred to as a terminal degree). These degrees are often required for faculty positions, especially at the graduate level (see Chapter 11 for an in-depth discussion of transitioning to faculty roles), and they are often required for senior-level administrative positions (Howard-Hamilton & Hyman, 2009; Saunders & Cooper, 1999). Biddix (2013) found that almost three-quarters of student affairs practitioners holding senior positions had completed doctoral degrees. However, practitioners should obtain professional experience before seeking an advanced degree since positions can still be difficult to obtain if a practitioner does not also have the work experience to complement what he or she has learned in the doctoral program (Daddona, Cooper, & Dunn, 2006).

Types of Degrees

One type of degree that may be of interest is the doctor of jurisprudence (JD) degree. Professionals must attend a law school in order to earn a JD and can pursue faculty appointments as well as senior-level positions such as a vice president for student affairs or jobs working in compliance, contracts and licensing, student conduct, and risk management. More common in higher education is the doctor of education (EdD) or doctor of philosophy (PhD) degree earned in an educational leadership or higher education program. Although the JD is a terminal and valuable degree, faculty and administrators in the field of higher education do not always esteem it as highly as they do the more traditional EdD or PhD degree.

Historically, the EdD degree has been marketed to professionals who wish to retain careers as administrators and possibly teach on a part-time basis, whereas the PhD has been represented as the degree to obtain if a full-time faculty position is the goal. Leist and Scott (2011) reported that while PhD degrees still represent the majority of terminal degree programs offered in the higher education field, the EdD degree is becoming more common. After comparing doctoral degrees offered at various institutions, Leist and Scott concluded that although the different degrees targeted different audiences, the actual program requirements were quite similar. The primary differences concerned credit hours and entrance criteria: earning a PhD required a few more credit hours in the area of research, and PhD applicants were sometimes measured against slightly higher standards to determine whether they were qualified to enter the doctoral program. However, the authors determined that the differences between the different types of doctoral degrees were largely philosophical.

The Timing of Graduate Program Enrollment

In addition to considering the type of degree desired, professionals should think about when to pursue the degree. In fields largely based on practitioners like student affairs, it is wise to consider doctoral programs only after completing a few years of full-time employment. Professionals who complete a master's program and then move straight into a doctoral program may find employment after graduation difficult to obtain. Holding a doctoral degree places professionals in the mid- to senior-level leadership range in terms of educational qualifications, but the lack of full-time experience aligns them with entry-level positions. If a professional's background does not match both educational and experiential qualifications for a position, an employer may look to other candidates to fill positions.

After a few years of full-time employment, professionals may base their decision about when to enroll in a graduate program on several factors. For professionals planning to join full-time graduate programs, timing may be dependent on the amount of personal savings they have acquired and the level of debt they carry. Although the academic department may offer assistantships and fellowships, leaving salaried positions and moving to a graduate student stipend can become a significant financial burden, especially if car loans, mortgages, or previous student loans are part of the situation. Benefits that a full-time employer may have provided such as health insurance or professional development expenses may now become the student's responsibility. However, students who enroll full-time complete the doctoral degree in a shorter time and can completely immerse themselves in the experience of learning without having to try to balance both student and work roles.

For professionals hoping to pursue part-time programs, a supportive supervisor may be a primary factor in the decision to enroll. If the institution offers courses only during day or late afternoon hours, a supportive supervisor will be flexible and allow the professional to be out of the office during the workday to meet academic requirements. Without this flexibility, completing the program may be more challenging. Once the supervisor's support has been obtained, the professional should review institutional policies about missing work. Policies may require professionals to take personal time when courses are held during the workday, or professionals could be asked to stay longer on certain days to make up for the lost time. Some institutions offer fee waivers or other financial incentives for staff members who pursue degrees. These benefits are not always widely advertised, so professionals should inquire about any financial support the institution provides.

The Doctoral Degree Process

Most graduate programs follow a similar format covering two phases. The first phase of the program focuses on courses in both content and research methods. Content courses could include topics such as law and policy, leadership, and organizational development. Research methods courses will address a mixture of quantitative and qualitative techniques such as statistical measures and content analysis. There could also be courses offered in literature review and research design. This phase is often challenging but enjoyable because there are students in the courses to interact with and learn from.

At the end of the first phase, students are often asked to participate in a qualifying exam to verify learning and readiness to move to the second phase. The exam could take different forms, including oral, written, or a combination of both; the exam is typically comprehensive and requires students to synthesize information from all aspects of the curriculum. When a student passes the exam, the student earns all-but-dissertation (ABD) status. ABD represents a significant achievement in a student's progress toward the degree, but in itself, ABD is neither a degree nor a professional qualification.

At some point during the first phase, students are asked to identify a dissertation chair or will be assigned one. These faculty members guide students throughout the dissertation process and will facilitate required steps such as the qualifying exam, proposal defense, and dissertation defense. There will also be a need for a few more faculty members to serve on the dissertation committee. The number of committee members and where they come from are dependent on program requirements. Programs may assign committee members or allow students to select them. Committee members may come from the same academic department or could be from departments across campus. Professionals are encouraged to inquire about the process and policies prior to enrolling so that they understand expectations and timelines.

After the qualifying exam is completed, the second phase begins and focuses on writing a dissertation. A dissertation is an independent research study that can take different forms. The most widely used format consists of five chapters or parts—a statement of the problem, a literature review, the method section, the data analysis and findings section, and a discussion of the findings. The process begins with the student identifying a research topic and working with the dissertation chair to refine the topic until it is in a meaningful and realistic form. Students need to have a good foundation in the scholarly literature and be able to identify gaps in that literature, or areas of research that researchers have not yet explored but should explore to improve understanding or practice.

Once the dissertation topic has been approved, the student can begin working on the proposal, which addresses the statement of the problem, specific research questions, a review of the literature, and anticipated research methods. The proposal format is largely dependent on what the dissertation chair prefers or what the program policies require. A student may be asked to write the first three chapters of the dissertation as the proposal or may only need to write a few pages for each section. The proposal writing process will consist of many interactions with and reviews from the dissertation chair. When the proposal meets the expectations of the dissertation chair, the student can schedule the proposal defense. At this time, all committee members convene to hear the student orally present the proposal. A discussion will occur, and modifications may be made to the study during that process. Once committee members are satisfied with the proposal, they will formally approve it, and the student can begin the actual research.

Completing the dissertation is similar to the proposal process. Once the data have been collected and analyzed, the student can write the final two chapters. The dissertation chair will work with the student to refine the full dissertation and have a final draft ready for the defense process, when the full committee convenes again to hear the student present the results of the study. If committee members believe the research meets expectations, the student will pass the dissertation defense and earn the doctoral degree. Other processes are often involved, such as formatting the dissertation according to institutional requirements. These processes are usually administered through other departments on campus and must be fulfilled before an actual diploma can be awarded. By incorporating these steps into the individual completion plan, the student ensures that he or she addresses all procedures in a timely manner.

Challenges to Anticipate

Many students find the second phase of a doctoral program the most difficult to manage. Research demonstrates that anywhere from 40% to 60% of doctoral students do not complete their degrees (Bair & Haworth, 1999), and many doctoral students cite a lack of structure and time management issues during the dissertation phase as primary causes (Pifer & Baker, 2016). Once exams have been completed, there are no more class meetings to attend, and progress is completely up to the individual student to initiate and sustain. Planning for this stage can be a significant factor in whether or not a student completes the dissertation.

Researchers have demonstrated that when doctoral students participate in support activities such as writing groups, have an accountability partner, or design a formal structure for progression, they are more likely to complete the degree (Bair & Haworth, 1999). One way for doctoral students to build a support system is to recruit a fellow student to serve as an accountability partner. Partners who are at similar stages in the dissertation process can share advice and experiences and support each other at every step. Establishing a partnership may involve scheduling weekly meetings to discuss what each partner has done the previous week and what will be completed during the current week. A simple meeting may be all that is needed to keep moving forward. Another good practice is for doctoral students to follow the regular course schedule even after the first phase ends. For example, if a student typically had Tuesday evening courses for 3 hours, he or she should set aside that same 3-hour period every week for dissertation work. It is also wise for students to follow the academic calendar to maintain a reasonable work–life balance. Students should set aside dissertation tasks when the institution is on a holiday break and resume work when the next academic period begins. Following this plan provides doctoral students with both the structure needed to make progress as well as time for well-earned breaks.

WORK–LIFE INTEGRATION

Full-time professionals also need breaks in their schedule so that they can establish a good work–life integration. The ability to establish a work–life integration can be defined as the ability to make a clear distinction between work time and personal time and to ensure that the two do not cross over on a regular basis. Beer et al. (2015) explained that when professionals fail to pay attention to the balance needed in their lives, both their work satisfaction and personal well-being may suffer. Balancing work time and personal time is especially important for student affairs professionals because the field can be demanding in terms of time commitments. Collins and Hirt (2006) found that professionals employed in functional areas such as residence life or campus activities generally worked significantly more hours per week than other professionals did. These functional areas are often filled with new professionals who are asked to work evening and weekend hours in addition to maintaining a regular workweek (Nobbe & Manning, 1997). Mid-level professionals may not put in the same number of weekend and evening hours, but they have other demands from the work environment that may require them to be in frequent contact with their offices and leaders. Both situations lead to problems with work–life balance.

In an examination of institutional support for finding balance, Jones and Taylor (2013) found that only half of higher education institutions had policies or services addressing issues of balance, with most focusing on family leave policies and flexible scheduling for the workday. The researchers determined that the lack of personal support can lead to dissatisfaction with the workplace. Females and older workers were especially affected by the lack of formal support because they were often the primary caregivers for children or elderly parents and needed more flexibility than policies provided for.

With minimal formal support, student affairs professionals must find informal methods of creating a work–life integration. A good starting point is for professionals to discuss options with their supervisors. Institutional flexibility policies often allow supervisors to use their judgment regarding minor scheduling issues. For example, if a professional has dependents who require him to be away from the office for an hour or two during the regular workday, his supervisor may be willing to let him make up those hours by working through lunch or coming in early. Or his supervisor may allow periodic telework opportunities. Professionals and supervisors should discuss needs and available options to help achieve a good balance.

It is especially helpful to turn off e-mail when not at work (Silver & Jakeman, 2014). Modern technology allows e-mail messages to be sent and received at all hours of the day and from any geographic location.

Yet it is not usually necessary to stay in constant contact with the office. Professionals should consider allowing time off from work issues by avoiding work e-mail entirely when not in the office (colleagues can keep an alternate communication method, such as a phone number, on file in case a true emergency arises). Smartphones can even be set to deliver e-mail messages only during work hours, so the messages will remain invisible during personal time.

Some professionals may find it difficult to let go of work concerns after they leave the office. To combat this challenge, it is helpful to develop friendships with people who do not share the same profession. These relationships can be cultivated through a variety of activities such as volunteering in the community, attending a place of worship, or participating in informal social groups like book or dinner clubs. Beer et al. (2015) also recommended engaging in contemplative practices such as exercise, meditation, or other forms of relaxation and stress reduction. They found that connecting with people who used the same contemplative practices helped people generate feelings of stability and self-awareness.

When work commitments require significant hours in the office, it is still important to find a little personal time to deal with stress or clear the mind. Taking a 10-minute break to walk around the building could be all that is needed to refocus. It is also important to recapture those lost hours at another time. Professionals should consider negotiating time off with their supervisors after significant events or projects have been completed. The downtime may allow professionals to tend to personal tasks that were neglected or provide an opportunity for a short vacation from work responsibilities.

ADVICE FOR SUPERVISORS

Supervisors can help employees be more intentional about their development in several ways. Knight (2014) recommended that supervisors first model the desired behavior. This means acknowledging personal competency gaps, letting employees know what you are doing to advance your development, and being actively engaged in best practices such as reading higher education news or becoming involved in professional associations. When employees observe supervisors being intentional about their own development, they are more likely to emulate the same behavior.

As employees work on their own professional development plans, supervisors can assist by discussing those plans and identifying ways for employees to meet development goals (Knight, 2014). Supervisors may include employees in budget decisions, allow them to supervise paraprofessional or support staff, or invite them to attend leadership meetings. These are all effective ways for supervisors to help employees reach their goals and advance their experience and understanding of the field.

It is also important for supervisors to help employees manage imposter syndrome by fostering awareness of problematic behaviors and working with individuals who may be experiencing feelings of inadequacy (Parkman & Beard, 2008). Combating imposter syndrome may involve defining in explicit language what excellence and success mean as well as discussing clear expectations for projects and work responsibilities. Supervisors can also address imposter syndrome through timely and consistent feedback regarding employees' skills and competencies, paying careful attention to what employees do well and what they still need to work on. If supervisors manage performance by focusing on employees' skills and competencies, they can help employees define their own development in those terms, and they can fix employees' attention on forward progression rather than perfection.

Finally, supervisors can address both work–life balance issues and the imposter syndrome by observing who is working long hours and by asking questions about workload and schedule. If employees cannot finish their work during normal business hours, they may have taken on more than they can handle. On the other hand, long work hours can signal perfectionist tendencies, which may be associated with the imposter syndrome. Once they recognize these signs, supervisors can start a conversation with employees about work–life balance and what strategies they can adopt to alleviate stress. Supervisors who encourage employees to leave work early or come in late or who offer to shift project responsibilities to someone else demonstrate to their employees that finding balance and tending to personal needs are important.

CONCLUSION

This chapter discussed intentional professional development, the theory of self-authorship, the imposter syndrome, and ways that student affairs practitioners can assess their competencies, plan their professional development, prepare for emerging opportunities, create a career path, and recognize natural transition points. By acquiring valuable skills and experiences, practitioners will be better able to prepare for career advancement or other work opportunities that emerge as higher education responds to changing social and economic conditions. Being intentional about professional development involves making decisions about career paths and advanced degrees, but it also involves establishing and maintaining a work–life integration. Practitioners who adopt a purposeful approach to professional development can take advantage of opportunities as they appear.

> **QUESTIONS FOR REFLECTION**
>
> ❓ What external and internal influences affect your decisions regarding your development?
>
> ❓ Do you feel like an imposter in your professional life? How can you correct this feeling with conscious development?
>
> ❓ What methods do you use to assess the competencies and skills you need to develop?
>
> ❓ What strategies have you developed to maintain a healthy work–life balance?

REFERENCES

ACPA–College Student Educators International & NASPA–Student Affairs Administrators in Higher Education. (2015). *Professional competency areas for student affairs educators.* Retrieved from https://www.naspa.org/images/uploads/main/Professional_Competencies.pdf

Bair, C., & Haworth, J. (1999, November). *Doctoral student attrition and persistence: A meta-synthesis of research.* Paper presented at the annual meeting of the Association for the Study of Higher Education, San Antonio, TX.

Baxter Magolda, M. B. (1998). Developing self-authorship in graduate school. In M. S. Anderson (Ed.), *The experience of being in graduate school: An exploration* (New Directions for Higher Education, No. 101, pp. 41–54). San Francisco, CA: Jossey-Bass.

Baxter Magolda, M. B. (2014). Enriching educators' learning experiences. *About Campus, 19*(2), 2–10. doi: 10.1002/abc.21150

Baxter Magola, M. B., & King, P. M. (2012). Nudging minds to life: Self-authorship as a foundation for learning. *ASHE Higher Education Report, 38*(3), 1–138. doi: 10.1002/aehe.20003

Beer, L. E., Rodriguez, K., Taylor, C., Martinez-Jones, N., Griffin, J., Smith, T. R., Lamar, M., & Anaya, R. (2015). Awareness, integration and interconnectedness: Contemplative practices of higher education professionals. *Journal of Transformative Education, 13*(2), 161–185. doi: 10.1177/1541344615572850

Biddix, J. P. (2011). "Stepping stones": Career paths to the SSAO for men and women at four-year institutions. *Journal of Student Affairs Research and Practice, 48*(4), 443–461. doi: 10.2202/1949-6605.6244

Biddix, J. P. (2013). Directors, deans, doctors, divergers: The four career paths of SSAOs. *Journal of College Student Development, 54*(3), 315–321. doi: 10.1353/csd.2013.0056

Chernow, E., Cooper, D. L., & Winston, R. B. (2003). Professional association involvement of student affairs professionals. *NASPA Journal, 40*(2), 43–58. doi: 10.2202/0027-6014.1220

Clance, P. R. (1985). *The imposter phenomenon: When success makes you feel like a fake.* Toronto, Canada: Bantam.

Collins, D., & Hirt, J. B. (2006). The nature of professional life for residence hall administrators. *Journal of College and University Student Housing, 34*(1), 14–24. Retrieved from http://www.acuho-i.org/journal

Council for the Advancement of Standards in Higher Education. (2015). *CAS professional standards for higher education* (9th ed.). Fort Collins, CO: Author.

Daddonna, M. F., Cooper, D. L., & Dunn, M. S. (2006). Career paths and expectations of recent doctoral graduates in student affairs. *NASPA Journal, 43*(2), 203–215. doi: 10.2202/0027-6014.1636

Harvey, J., & Katz, C. (1985). *If I'm so successful, why do I feel like a fake? The imposter phenomenon.* New York, NY: St. Martin's Press.

Howard-Hamilton, M. F., & Hyman, R. E. (2009). Advancing professionally through doctoral education. In G. S. McClellan, J. Stringer, & M. J. Barr (Eds.), *The handbook of student affairs administration* (3rd ed., pp. 388–402). San Francisco, CA: Jossey-Bass.

Hutchins, H. (2015). Outing the imposter: A study exploring imposter phenomenon among higher education faculty. *New Horizons in Adult Education & Human Resource Development, 27*(2), 3–12. doi: 10.1002/nha3.20098

Jones, S. J., & Taylor, C. M. (2013). Work and life balance support of female midlevel noninstructional staff at community colleges. *Community College Journal of Research and Practice, 37*(12), 936–953. doi: 10.1080/10668926.2010.484999

Knight, A. (2014). Excellence in community college student affairs. In C. C. Ozaki, A. M. Hornak, & C. J. Lunceford (Eds.), *Supporting student affairs professionals* (New Directions for Community Colleges, No. 166, pp. 5–12). San Francisco, CA: Jossey-Bass.

Leist, J., & Scott, J. A. (2011). Differentiation...but to what degree? The Ed.D. and Ph.D. in higher education programs. *Academic Leadership, 9*(3), 1–15. Retrieved from http://contentcat.fhsu.edu/cdm/landingpage/collection/p15732coll4

Nobbe, J., & Manning, S. (1997). Issues for women in student affairs with children. *NASPA Journal, 34*(2), 101–111. doi: 10.2202/1949-6605.1014

Parkman, A., & Beard, R. (2008). Succession planning and the imposter phenomenon in higher education. *CUPA-HR Journal, 59*(2), 29–36. Retrieved from http://www.cupahr.org/hew/files/CUPA-HR-Journal-Vol59No2.pdf

Pifer, M. J., & Baker, V. L. (2016). Stage-based challenges and strategies for support in doctoral education: A practical guide for students, faculty members, and program administrators. *International Journal of Doctoral Studies, 11,* 15–34. Retrieved from http://ijds.org/Volume11/IJDSv11p015-034Pifer2155.pdf

Roberts, D. M. (2007). Preferred methods of professional development in student affairs. *NASPA Journal, 44*(3), 561–577. doi: 10.2202/0027-6014.1836

Rosser, V. J., & Javinar, J. M. (2003). Midlevel student affairs leaders' intentions to leave: Examining the quality of their professional and institutional work life. *Journal of College Student Development, 44*(6), 813–830. doi: 10.1353/csd.2003.0076

Saunders, S. A., & Cooper, D. L. (1999). The doctorate in student affairs: Essential skills and competencies for mid-management. *Journal of College Student Development, 40*(2), 185–191. Retrieved from http://www.myacpa.org/journal-college-student-development

Silver, B. R., & Jakeman, R. C. (2014). Understanding intent to leave the field: A study of student affairs master's students' career plans. *Journal of Student Affairs Research and Practice, 51*(2), 170–182. doi: 10.1515/jsarp-2014-0017

9

TAKING THE JOB SEARCH TO THE NEXT LEVEL

Lesley-Ann Brown-Henderson
and Shelia Higgs Burkhalter

THERE ARE VARIOUS reasons for transitioning to a new job. Graduating from college, outgrowing a position, getting married or divorced, deciding to move abroad, or being denied an expected promotion. Schlossberg (1984) described three different types of transitions: anticipated, unanticipated, and nonevents. Anticipated transitions, such as graduating from college and outgrowing a position, are expected. Unanticipated transitions, such as separating from a partner, happen unexpectedly. Nonevent transitions, such as the promotion that never came, are transitions that an individual expected but that did not happen.

Whatever the reason for making the transition to a new position, a student affairs professional's job search priorities are likely to evolve over time. With increased professional experience comes a greater certainty about priorities—needs, wants, values, competencies, negotiables, and non-negotiables. However, the job search process can also become more complex when factoring in relationships, support systems, familial needs, the timing of a transition, and the desired career trajectory.

This chapter will discuss taking the job search to the next level, including:

- making sense of the transition process;
- working with limitations while searching;
- navigating ethical challenges while searching; and
- engaging in mid-level placement conference experiences.

It will also offer advice for:

- working with a search firm;
- searching with a partner;
- using professional connections to learn more about the campus culture and the working environment of the position sought;
- organizing an international job search;
- conducting a mid-level search via placement opportunities; and
- being nominated for positions.

MAKING SENSE OF THE TRANSITION PROCESS

Goodman, Schlossberg, and Anderson (2006) identified four factors that explain a professional's ability to successfully navigate a path in, through, and out of a career transition:

- Self
- Situation
- Social support
- Strategies

These factors, referred to as the "four S's," can be used to understand how an individual makes sense of transitions (Evans, Forney, Guido, Patton, & Renn, 2010; Goodman et al., 2006).

The first factor, *self,* is divided into two categories: (a) personal demographic characteristics and (b) psychological resources. Personal demographic characteristics include characteristics such as race, gender, socioeconomic status, and age. Psychological resources include resources such as attitudes toward change and ability to adapt, which can affect how professionals experience a transition.

Most student affairs professionals face some challenges when securing a new position, but those with marginalized identities are apt to encounter greater challenges. This is because the dynamics of power and privilege related to various social identities (e.g., race, gender, socioeconomic status, age) are pervasive, and these dynamics are encountered at every juncture of a job search process. Professionals with marginalized identities are often made to feel inferior, which negatively affects the psychological resources they use to cope with the transition process. Steele (2010) aptly described a stereotype threat as a "socially premised psychological threat that arises when one is in a situation or doing something for which a negative stereotype about one's group applies" (p. 614). Such psychological threats can have a detrimental effect on self-efficacy and performance.

To counteract these psychological threats, professionals with marginalized identities need to become aware of their social identities and view them as assets rather than liabilities. Yosso's (2005) cultural wealth model describes six types of capital (aspirational, linguistic, familial, social, navigational, and resistant) that individuals of marginalized identity bring with them to any environment. Using this model and its six types of capital, professionals can create a counternarrative to challenge and resist employers' stereotypes and prejudices. In turn, employers can provide support by considering multiple methods of interacting and interviewing job candidates. They can discuss social identities as strengths to give professionals the opportunity to participate in the interview process authentically. They can use the following prompts: "Discuss how your social identities inform your work with students" or "How does your personal narrative inform your professional values and manifest itself in your work?"

To help determine whether a position aligns with personal values, beliefs, and goals, student affairs professionals should investigate the institution's culture, values, mission, and opportunities for growth and development. The investigation can begin with the institution's electronic and print materials, but should not end there. Colleagues and networks can be useful to obtain the personal experiences of professionals who work at the institution. Further, student affairs professionals should be prepared to ask interviewers and employers directly about the culture, values, mission, and growth opportunities they might experience as employees.

The second factor in the model, *situation*, is defined by eight elements that influence the professional's appraisal of the transition:

- *Trigger* refers to the reason for the job search. A trigger could be a change in leadership at the current institution, a family situation, a desire for increased responsibility and advancement, or the loss of employment.
- The *timing* of a job search affects the professional's perception of the process. For instance, if a professional's position is eliminated when the professional is making a decision about being a stay-at-home parent, the timing may be perceived as good even though the trigger for the job search process is negative.
- A professional's appraisal of the transition is influenced by whether the professional believes that the transition is within his or her *control*. As an example, a professional may experience the loss of a job because of budget cuts. The transition itself may be out of her control, yet she may choose to believe that everything happens for a reason, thereby exercising control over her reactions.
- At times, a transition will involve a *role change*. The role change can be related to a promotion or to moving from a

smaller institution where staff members have multiple responsibilities to a large institution where the responsibilities are more specialized.
- The *duration* of a job search can be perceived as "permanent, temporary, or uncertain" (Evans et al., 2010, p. 217). If a professional submits application materials for a few positions and receives positive responses, the transitional period may appear to be temporary. The opposite is true for professionals who submit multiple applications without much response; in this case, the duration of the transition can seem more uncertain.
- Professionals who are job searching may have *previous experience* with a similar transition. They may have experience with the process (e.g., phone interviews, on-campus interviews, negotiations); they may understand available resources (e.g., job search websites, video conferencing technology, cost of living calculators); and they may be familiar with established stress management techniques (e.g., exercising regularly, practicing gratitude, consulting with people in a supportive network). These reference points can help them navigate the job search process successfully.
- While job searching, a professional may be trying to sell a home, support a partner's job search, handle a change in the family structure, or complete a graduate degree. How a professional manages *concurrent stress* affects how cumbersome the search process feels to the professional and is linked to physical health (Holmes & Rahe, 1967).
- The final element of the situation factor is the professional's *assessment* of what initiated the job search (Evans et al., 2010). For example, a professional who is forced to leave an

enjoyable position because his partner has secured employment in another state may not be eager to start the job search process. On the other hand, a professional who has aging parents and is seeking employment closer to them will likely approach the job search with urgency.

The third factor in the model, *support*, describes the systems a professional may have in place for every phase of the job search process (Evans et al., 2010; Schlossberg, 1984). Personal and professional networks can provide decision-making assistance, feedback on career materials and presentations, observations about institutional culture, or advice about negotiating benefits.

The fourth factor in the model is *strategies*, which enable professionals to manage the transition effectively. Student affairs professionals might use strategies such as researching institutions, staying physically active, meditating, journaling, spending time with family and friends, playing music, connecting with nature, praying, talking to colleagues, drawing, or seeing a therapist.

WORKING WITH LIMITATIONS WHILE SEARCHING

When searching for a job, student affairs professionals may be subject to various limitations. They may need to stay in a specific geographic region; they may need to make a lateral career move or a functional area change; or they may be unemployed during the search process. This section will review each limitation and discuss relevant aspects of Schlossberg's (1984) transition model addressing the limitations.

Geographic-Specific Searches

Geographic limitations can be related to family structure, a partner's transition to a new job, an individual's desire to move closer to family, or personal preferences in climate, culture, or lifestyle. Job-posting websites, such as HigherEdJobs.com, Indeed.com, and *The Chronicle of Higher Education,* offer search options for jobs by region and state. Search engines can be customized to send alerts about positions in preferred locations.

Outreach and networking can be used when attempting to secure employment in a specific location. In higher education, it is common for new positions to be created and for individuals to privately announce their departure from the institution before a public announcement is made. Professionals who have a strong, broad, and connected network may find out about these opportunities before the formal process begins. (See Chapter 4 for an in-depth discussion of professional connections.)

Lateral Career Moves

A lateral career move involves accepting a position that is similar to the one the professional already holds and may involve comparable responsibilities or an equivalent salary. Lateral moves can be ideal if there is a need to relocate suddenly, if the current institution is not a good fit, or if family circumstances require a change. A lateral move can also be an opportunity to learn a new skill, transition into a new functional area, work with trusted colleagues, or secure a position at a desired institution. However, professionals should consider the affect a lateral move might have on their career. Opportunities exist, but some factors can undermine a successful transition. For instance, a lateral move may limit future advancement or require a pay cut. Professionals should think about whether a lateral move will help achieve both short- and long-term career goals. To determine whether to make the move, consider all the consequences of the move.

When making a lateral move, it is important to be mindful of what the move may look like to other people. Employers often expect professionals to pursue an upward career trajectory; this paradigm often defines how career success is measured. If a professional applies for a position that does not represent forward progression or if the applicant seems overqualified for the position, questions will likely be asked. The reasons for a lateral move should be discussed in a cover letter to ensure that the candidate is given the strongest consideration. In the cover letter, professionals should share their motivation for applying and discuss the ways such a move can benefit the employer. If professionals are upfront about the situation, they can correct any wrong assumptions prospective employers may have made, and they are more likely to secure a spot in the candidate pool.

Professionals should also be prepared to address their motives throughout the interview process. By communicating a consistent, enthusiastic, and positive message, they can help employers see them as an asset to the organization, especially if they focus on the ways they will enhance the team, office, or institution.

Functional Area Changes

The Council for the Advancement of Standards in Higher Education (2015) identified 45 different functional areas for higher education programs and services, each with its own standards and required skills. Student affairs professionals who are considering a functional area change should become familiar with the requirements of that area, and they should be ready to articulate how their skills and experiences contribute to the stated outcomes. Their first step should be to provide a cover letter and functional (or skills) résumé that focuses on professional competencies for higher education (ACPA–College Student Educators International & NASPA–Student Affairs Administrators in Higher Education, 2015). Employers use these competencies to match a candidate's professional background to the relevant context.

Professionals with experience working in the selected functional area may have a better chance of being hired. Within their current position, professionals can generate opportunities in the desired functional area by volunteering for a new assignment, asking to join a committee or work group, or pursuing additional training or certification.

In the absence of direct experience, professionals can highlight experiences such as cross-institutional partnerships, collaborative relationships with major institutional stakeholders, and contributions to institutional strategic directions. Experiences such as these show that they are able to focus on outcomes outside their current job responsibilities and that they desire to develop connections to other areas of the institution.

Searching While Unemployed

There are a number of reasons why professionals may engage in a job search while they are unemployed. They may have recently completed a graduate degree, been terminated from a position, had their position eliminated, or made a personal decision to resign because of organizational fit, workplace toxicity, family situation, or health. Securing a position when unemployed can be challenging because unemployment may raise questions or doubts in the minds of potential employers. Professionals should decide how they want to share their story, keep it concise, stay positive, and be authentic. Some prospective employers will want to probe beyond prepared statements. Professionals should be prepared to share a bit more, but they should be mindful of what they tell prospective employers. They may find it helpful to practice answering questions about their unemployment status with a trusted colleague or mentor to ensure they are striking the right tone.

In addition to planning and rehearsing their story, professionals can do several things to increase their employment opportunities.

1. Apply for part-time positions. These positions can provide additional experience and increased income while searching for a full-time opportunity.

2. Evaluate different functional areas within higher education and different types of educational institutions. They may provide additional employment prospects.
3. Work or volunteer for an organization outside of higher education.
4. Develop a robust list of references who can offer a positive perspective. Although a supervisor's reference is best, a reference from a strong collaborative partner or subordinate may work as well.
5. Stay current in the field by reading professional literature, maintaining association memberships, and renewing any licensing or certification credentials.

Professionals who have an employment plan and stay active and engaged in the profession are more likely to maintain self-confidence and a positive perspective for moving forward.

Being unemployed is mentally, financially, emotionally, and spiritually challenging. Some unemployed professionals may even experience the five stages of grief and loss: denial and isolation, anger, bargaining, depression, and acceptance (Axelrod, 2014; Kubler-Ross, 1969). While unemployed, professionals may need to manage concurrent stressors concerning their financial situation, a toxic work situation, a loss of confidence, doubts about their career choice, family and personal responsibilities, and the need to secure employment on an escalated timeline. When professionals have unresolved personal issues and additional stressors to overcome, they may have difficulty showing their best selves. To deal with the inner turmoil, professionals should use all available support networks. Family and friends can offer needed emotional support and encouragement. Unemployed professionals can also contact mentors, sponsors, and people in professional networks who can remind them of their skills and abilities. If they use their political and social capital, they can increase their employment opportunities (Pouchot, 2013).

NAVIGATING ETHICAL CHALLENGES

Many professionals search for positions while they are employed. Doing so is advantageous because they feel less pressure to secure a position. In addition, potential employers prefer candidates who are employed because their employment provides evidence of job skills and an organization's willingness to hire (Smith, 2012).

Despite the benefits, professionals who conduct a job search while employed must carefully navigate several ethical challenges. The first challenge is to maintain a clear distinction between work time and personal time. Professionals who blur those lines might conduct a job search using their institution's resources instead of their own. Instead, they should use time away from the office to prepare credentials, draft résumés, write cover letters, practice interview skills, reach out to references, complete applications, and contact potential employers to arrange and conduct interviews. To ensure that their current employer is not negatively affected by their search, they need to establish clear boundaries, and they may need to take vacation time to attend to job search activities.

The second ethical challenge professionals must navigate concerns honesty. As they complete employment applications, professionals should remember to accurately list their education, employment experience, and supervisors (even if their supervisors are not their references), and truthfully respond to short questions. Dishonesty is easily discovered, and it can damage careers and professional reputations.

Interviews present a third ethical challenge professionals must navigate. Many employers ask candidates to explain why they want the position and why they are leaving their current institution. Professionals who have had mixed or negative experiences at their current institution may be tempted to share the details of the situation to explain their motivation for job searching. Even if they are invited to tell their story, they should maintain a positive tone and not engage in negative rhetoric about their current situation. Higher education is a highly networked profession, and what a candidate says during an interview may be repeated to colleagues across the field and ultimately hurt the candidate's reputation. In addition, prospective employers might believe that a candidate has a negative attitude toward coworkers and might think twice about whether the candidate would be a good fit for the position. Professionals should stay positive and direct the conversation to their abilities, goals, and aspirations for the position, department, and institution.

The fourth ethical challenge professionals must navigate concerns confidentiality. Professionals should keep their search confidential until they have notified their current supervisor. To do this, they should ask a prospective employer to maintain confidentiality, and they should refrain from discussing their search with colleagues or subordinates or mentioning their search on social media. If a supervisor finds out about a job search from someone else before they have chosen to notify the supervisor, professionals may face negative consequences such as having to work in a tense work environment; they also risk being fired before they have secured other employment. Their best strategy is to identify an appropriate time to notify their supervisor that they are conducting a search, such as when they request a reference, when the process advances to the finalist stage, or when the institution with which they are interviewing has made the names of its top candidates public.

The final ethical challenge student affairs professionals must navigate concerns integrity. Professionals must stay focused in their current position and honor their work commitments. They are still being paid by their current institution until they have officially separated, and a subpar performance can become a widely shared story and negatively affect their reputation. Professionals should ensure that others recognize their integrity. They should leave electronic and paper files that clearly document their work and that provide direction to others who may need to finish the work they could not complete. Transition reports and notebooks can greatly enhance the experience of whomever occupies the position next, and such reports will be a lasting reminder of the departing employee's professionalism.

ENGAGING IN MID-LEVEL PLACEMENT

Student affairs professionals who are beyond entry level positions may doubt the utility of the placement conference experience, which tends to focus heavily on residence life jobs for entry-level professionals. However, professionals at various levels can find opportunities at placement conferences if they set realistic expectations and are strategic about how they use resources and manage their time. Mid-level professionals can engage in placement conference experiences in the following strategic ways.

- ♦ They should expect to have fewer interviews than less experienced colleagues, and they should expect to dedicate an extensive amount of time to researching the institution, crafting a cover letter and résumé for the specific role, and preparing for the interview. As they prepare, mid-level professionals should take advantage of the resources provided through the placement conferences. For instance, The Placement Exchange provides mid-level professionals with their own space and recruits volunteer coaches to assist with onsite mock interviews, discussions about the job search, and résumé reviews.

- They should focus on résumé development. The résumé of the mid-level professional should focus on positional responsibilities and address major accomplishments and quantify the value the professional added to the institution (e.g., "increased the retention of resident assistants by 30%"). Embedded in these accomplishments are stories of challenge, triumph, strategy, and failure. Professionals should be prepared to share these stories in their interviews.
- They should plan for the interview. It is common for mid-level interviews at placement conferences to last longer and focus on behavioral questions. Employers are looking for depth and complexity in responses. Professionals should highlight lived experiences, core values, and leadership styles and philosophies. For example, mid-level professionals should answer an interview question asking them to describe the role they play on a team with a description of the role they most often adopt and what the role means to them, and they should give specific examples that demonstrate their enactment of the role. The interview also gives mid-level professionals an opportunity to share aspects of their candidacy that may be of interest, such as how they resolve conflict, build relationships, or manage high-pressure situations.
- They should use downtime to contribute to the placement experience of others. For instance, by serving as a coach, they can be a sounding board, provide constructive feedback, or offer advice. They can also take advantage of opportunities to participate in educational sessions or roundtables regarding the job search process. Professionals who give back in this manner have an opportunity to polish their skills, demonstrate their commitment to the profession, and add some activities to

their résumés. Being active in this way also provides a distraction and can help with stress management.

PRACTICAL ADVICE ON SEARCHING

Working With Search Firms

Student affairs professionals may encounter opportunities to be managed by search firms. The goal of a search firm is to develop a robust pool of highly qualified candidates for institutions and ultimately to secure the employment of the most qualified person for the position and institution. The pool of candidates may include professionals who have sought these opportunities but will also include professionals who might not have expressed an interest in or been aware of the opportunities available.

A number of search firms manage higher education job searches while providing a plethora of other types of services. Academic360.com (2016) provides a comprehensive listing of these organizations. Before contacting search firm representatives, student affairs professionals should carefully consider the types of opportunities they are seeking and the firms that have the best reputation for managing those types of searches.

Search firm professionals attend a variety of professional association conferences throughout the year. They can often be found staffing booths in the exhibit hall, connecting with job seekers about the positions their firms represent. Search firm professionals also often present and/or host conference sessions. Attending these sessions can be quite useful, as they frequently share valuable information about everything from refining credentials to preparing for the search. Search firms may also offer valuable individual coaching sessions to increase the pool of qualified candidates, as well as the opportunity to opt into notification lists that send e-mails to candidates based on their backgrounds and experiences.

Colleagues may have opportunities to nominate professionals for search firm positions. Professionals can discuss career aspirations with mentors and sponsors so that they may voluntarily offer nominations. But professionals should not hesitate to solicit nominations directly. Professionals should be sure to give mentors and sponsors all the information they need to make a compelling case for the nomination.

Search firm lists are sometimes populated via specific membership queries secured from national associations. These lists can be used to contact individuals who may be a good fit for an opportunity, or they may be used to reach out to individuals already occupying similar roles to solicit network connections. Professionals should keep their association membership and profile updated to increase the likelihood that they will become part of a search firm list.

Once a connection has been established, a professional should focus on building a relationship with the search firm representative. Professionals should keep in mind that search firm representatives work for the institutions that have hired them. Representatives may become quite personable and provide coaching along with valuable tips and pointers. However, no matter how engaging representatives may be, job seekers must be mindful of their words and actions, as every interaction is likely to be considered part of the review process.

The search process itself can have extended timelines. Building a robust pool of qualified, diverse candidates can be a time-consuming process. Search firm representatives must have a deep understanding of the professionals in the pool via informational conversations, credential reviews, interviews, and reference checks. It is also common to be asked for additional documents such as institutional applications; questionnaires further detailing the professional's credentials and behavioral styles and preferences; a variety of waivers or consent forms for background, credit, social media, and driver's license checks;

diversity statements; leadership statements; and extensive reference lists. One of this chapter's authors was even asked to consent to an "off-list" reference check and to complete a document detailing current salary, preferred salary, and other desired compensatory items (e.g., funds for professional development, housing, technology, moving expenses, etc.). As part of the search firm process, job seekers should be prepared to actively engage in all activities and provide all requested documentation.

Interview types can vary widely—and interviews can be more intensive—when working with search firms, and success is directly correlated with preparation. To prepare for the interviews, professionals should conduct an environmental scan of the institutions, divisions, and departments for which they hope to work. They should review websites, strategic plans, and annual reports. They should understand the environmental factors—national, local, and political—that will affect the work in the roles they are pursuing. They can engage professional colleagues to gain in-depth information about open positions or institutional culture, politics, and climate. (For a more in-depth discussion of environmental scans, see Chapter 2.)

Preparation should also include practice in answering standard, behavioral, and situational questions. Standard interview questions offer the candidate an opportunity to provide information about background and experiences. Behavioral interview questions focus on past behaviors—these answers reveal how the candidate might perform in the future. Situational interviews give the candidate an opportunity to assess problem-solving abilities and expertise. Depending upon the type of position and institutional preferences, the candidate may also be asked to consider a case study relevant to the types of issues he or she might encounter in the position. Finally, the candidate may be asked to deliver a presentation. Delivering a presentation is often an opportunity for the candidate to share his or her vision, demonstrate leadership, tackle an issue, or demonstrate depth and breadth of knowledge.

Candidates should also consider the technological tools and environment they may need for various types of interviews, including phone, video, placement conference, airport, individual, group/panel, and multiday campus interviews. For phone and video interviews, candidates should find an environment that is free from distraction where they will not be disturbed, and they should be sure to have adequate technology. For phone interviews, landlines are preferable to cell phones because landline calls are less likely to be dropped. If using a cell phone, candidates should be sure that the signal is strong and that the cell phone is charged. For video interviews, candidates should ensure that their Internet bandwidth is adequate so that they do not experience interruptions or delays. It is recommended that candidates test their technology (e.g., webcam function and position, microphone quality) with a friend prior to the interview. Candidates should also be attentive to what is visible in the background behind them, and they should ensure that everything that appears on camera looks professional and is not distracting.

In placement interviews, the environment can feel chaotic because of the activity and noise in the background from simultaneous interviews, people passing the table, and so on. Group or panel interviews can feel chaotic as well because a larger number of individuals are asking questions. To succeed in both types of interviews, candidates should concentrate on the person asking the questions and block out distractions.

Airport interviews have historically been reserved for senior-level administrative roles; however, candidates for mid-level roles may also encounter them. These interviews are usually conducted at an airport hotel near the campus to help the search firm confidentially screen a large number of candidates in a relatively short period. Afterward, a smaller group of candidates is invited to come to the campus for interviews.

Multiday campus interviews are usually reserved for the final candidates in the search and are designed to maximize opportunities for campus constituents to become acquainted with each candidate's leadership and experience. These interviews often involve individual meetings with various campus leaders; group interviews with committees, staff, and students; meals with individuals and groups; and presentations on various topics. The schedule does not usually provide significant breaks and can be exhausting, so it is important to prepare mentally and physically for the interview. Before traveling to the interview, candidates should be sure to have extra copies of their résumé, two flash drives with presentations and documents, notes about what they want to say, and a list of questions to ask. It is wise to dress professionally while traveling in case luggage is lost. It is also a good idea for candidates to prepare items such as small snacks or medication they may need to bring along. Candidates should get plenty of sleep prior to and during the interview process so that they are well rested and alert. Once the schedule begins, candidates should request breaks prior to each activity so that they have some time to eat, relieve a headache, or collect their thoughts. Remember that scheduled meals are still part of the interview process. Candidates should be mindful about the meal they select, such as choosing something that is easy to consume and that will not cause a mess. They should refrain from consuming alcohol, even if others are doing so.

Searching With a Partner

As student affairs professionals progress in their careers and lives, the likelihood of conducting a job search with a partner increases significantly. Dual job searches are inherently more complex because they involve all of the individual challenges and concerns multiplied by two. If the partnership also includes family and dependents, the process can be daunting.

The good news is that the landscape has improved for dual-career couples because institutions and companies across the country have begun to devote attention to these issues. In recent years, a number of conferences and collaborative research efforts have been launched, including the ADVANCE Working Group Dual-Career Studies at Columbia University and the Dual-Career Academic Couples Study at Stanford University's Clayman Institute for Gender Research—both studies have contributed to knowledge about the needs of couples conducting a dual-career search (Schiebinger, Davies Henderson, & Gilmartin, 2008). In addition, hiring practices are evolving. Some job search sites and institutions offer dual-career programs, networks, and resources to assist partners with job searches (Schiebinger et al., 2008).

However, dual-career resources do not address all the issues that student affairs professionals need to consider. Professionals should talk with their partners about their individual and collective needs and frequently revisit the discussion throughout the job search process. They should discuss issues related to their values (e.g., career trajectory, salary, location, prestige, family), proposed timelines for conducting each search (simultaneously versus separately), and issues related to quality of life (e.g., salary, childcare arrangements, cost of living, familial or professional support, housing).

Once job search expectations have been identified, professionals can increase the likelihood that both they and their partner will secure employment by thinking strategically about geographic areas, types of institutions, and types of programs at institutions. Professionals may want to consider areas with multiple institutions and companies where jobs are more numerous. For example, the city of Baltimore, Maryland, and the surrounding counties have 18 institutions of higher education and countless companies. By focusing on a geographic area like this, professionals can significantly increase the chance that both they and their partner will secure employment.

Another possibility when both partners work in higher education is to pursue opportunities at large institutions with a variety of divisions and departments. One of the chapter authors and her partner were able to secure positions at the same three large public institutions over a period of 6 years. In all three instances, the couple made use of their professional networks to identify available and anticipated opportunities, which made the search process less awkward and stressful. In two of the three instances, one partner's search lagged behind the other's by only a few months.

It can also be helpful for job-seeking professionals to identify at what point in the job interview process they will share with a potential employer that they have a partner who may need employment as well. The decision of when or if to share about a partner's employment needs with a potential employer might be based on the types of programs an institution offers. If an institution offers dual-search resources, it is probably safe to engage in a dialogue about this need with the potential employer early in the process. If the institution does not have such resources, it may be best for the candidate to wait until the search process progresses before introducing this variable.

Conducting International Searches

International opportunities in higher education include positions at U.S. and international institutions located around the world. Although there is no standard way to secure an international position, using Internet-based resources and networks can be helpful. Online websites such as HigherEdJobs.com, *The Chronicle of Higher Education,* and The Placement Exchange offer international postings from reputable institutions and include application instructions. Other international opportunities can be discovered via Internet searches or private firms, although these resources may not provide the same protections that working with an institution of strong repute does. For instance, when working with known entities, candidates will often encounter an individual who can address their concerns during the application process as well as after placement. Many private firms do not provide this high level of service.

Colleagues have cited learning about international opportunities most often via networking. They networked with colleagues at conferences, chatted with colleagues who were already living and working abroad, conducted informational interviews, and/or attended internationally focused meetings such as NASPA's International Symposium. These kinds of gatherings gave them exposure to professionals who were living abroad.

Applicants for international opportunities typically submit standard credentials, such as a résumé, cover letter, job application, and references. Interviews commonly occur via a telephone and/or video call rather than via campus visits. In these ways, they are not very different from searches for domestic opportunities. However, international job searches have a different rhythm. Domestic positions post sometime between January and March, interviews occur through June, and positions start in July and August. International searches proceed at a different pace, and timelines can be inherently ambiguous. For instance, after a professional receives a verbal offer, 6 months may pass before a formal contract arrives. Weathering the process requires an adventurous spirit, flexibility, adaptability, and patience.

Most international hires arrive at their respective sites without ever having visited in person. However, it is important to research the institution and area thoroughly. In addition, professionals should consider participating in a cultural immersion experience before applying. Study abroad or mission/service experiences are the deepest immersive experiences; traveling abroad is a slightly less immersive experience; and learning a foreign language is the least immersive experience. To prepare for international employment, professionals should consider taking one or two trips abroad so that they can understand what it might be like to live in a culture that is completely different from their own. Such trips provide a frame of reference concerning the norms, customs, language, and cultural idiosyncrasies of an area. An internship experience abroad is an excellent opportunity. One colleague indicated that meaningful internship experiences are fairly easy to arrange and fund; however, many international institutions do not necessarily create an internship of their own volition, so make inquiries about the possibility.

Professionals are likely to find international opportunities within an academic affairs unit. One colleague living and working abroad remarked that "student affairs as a profession is still emerging in international destinations, so there is an inherent seamlessness between academic affairs and student affairs that does not always exist in American institutions." However, the knowledge, skills, and abilities used in student affairs positions are transferrable even if the practices and settings are different. And since professionals with expertise in higher education administration are rare in many international settings, there will be an opportunity to engage in high-level conversations to create new initiatives, programs, and services.

Although living abroad can bring great rewards and adventures, it can also be stressful if professionals fail to consider some key quality-of-life issues, such as cost of living, taxes, housing, support system, family needs (e.g., daycare and school options for children), cultural differences, healthcare, safety and security, transportation, and VISA/paperwork requirements (Benson, 2012). For instance, one colleague was able to negotiate a housing allowance, a driver, local interpreter support, and a robust salary. However, he had to pay health insurance costs out of pocket. Another colleague was offered an amazing health care plan, a robust salary, and a housing allowance; however, negotiations for her children's school tuition did not work out, so she had concerns about finding a good school in the area. Overall, professionals can live quite comfortably in many international destinations if they negotiate for what they need.

Student affairs professionals should be flexible and open-minded when working abroad because international ways of being can be more fluid, less policy and process driven, and less defined than in the United States. For example, when one author of this chapter visited China during a study abroad experience, the driver transporting her to an appointment was involved in a car accident. Instead of exchanging car insurance cards or notifying the police, as drivers would have done in the United States, money was collected from all the individuals in the vehicle to pay off the driver of the other vehicle, and everyone went on their way. Personal and professional values may also be challenged by differing religious beliefs and cultural norms. For instance, lesbian, gay, bisexual, transgender, and queer populations are frowned upon and considered an abomination in Muslim countries, and these populations are often victimized and shunned. Professionals may need to dramatically adjust their expectations about what support looks like and how it is offered.

Although learning the language and engaging with the local community can help professionals create some great adventures, living abroad can be a lonely existence. Professionals should expect that work colleagues who are also "friends" may not be as plentiful as in the United States and that international colleagues may maintain some distance because of cultural boundaries and limitations. Professionals with families may make easier transitions to a new culture because they can engage with a partner about the cultural dissonance. Living in a community with expatriates can provide some support but may give very little exposure to local culture.

Depending upon location, a professional's home may not be equipped with the kinds of amenities found in the United States. For example, appliances such as full refrigerators, ovens, and clothes dryers are not necessarily standard in international homes. In fact, professionals may have to pay a premium fee to have these kinds of amenities.

In a similar vein, adjusting to international cuisine can be challenging. The international cuisine found in the United States does not taste the same abroad; and since the supply chain does not include the same technologies as the supply chain in the United States, food standards are not as robust. This means that it can be challenging to eat locally without becoming ill.

ADVICE FOR SUPERVISORS

The experiences, support, and development that professionals receive from their supervisors will undoubtedly assist them in transitioning to their next roles. Fundamentally, it is important for a supervisor to cultivate employee relationships using open communication. With open communication, supervisors can help professionals identify performance issues, strengths, and opportunities and help prepare them for the next career move. Open communication also allows employees to be honest about their career goals and encourages them to share news of a job search or intent to transition out of the organization.

When a professional first discusses a desire to transition out of the current role, the supervisor can provide opportunities including a stretch assignment, new committee role, or other experience to increase the professional's skills and knowledge. If the search is not time sensitive, the supervisor can offer support for a certification or degree attainment and keep the professional in the organization for a little longer while enhancing the professional's readiness for future positions. If the professional has already begun a job search, a supervisor can support the professional by checking in periodically about the process and sharing expectations about the professional's transition out of the position. Expected work might include updates on ongoing projects or documents explaining how to perform specific tasks. However, a supervisor could also use the job search announcement to discuss counteroffers or additional opportunities that might persuade the professional to remain at the institution.

Finally, supervisors should encourage employees to think about their next career move even if they make no mention of making a transition. Supervisors who understand career goals can help direct the growth and development of employees, offer resources to advance employees' skill development and experience, find relevant mentors for employees, and match employees to potential positions as they become available.

CONCLUSION

It is often said that experience is the best teacher and that with an initial job search under their belt, professionals can apply lessons learned from previous searches to their current process. There are a multitude of factors for professionals to consider when making the decision to move from one role to another, and they can use Schlossberg's (1984) four S's (self, situation, support, and strategies) to help them prepare for the job search process.

QUESTIONS FOR REFLECTION

Self

- How does your personal narrative inform your work with students?
- How can you talk about your identities in a way that strengthens your candidacy for any chosen position?
- What integral aspects of your identities are central to this job search?

Situation

- What precipitating factors are influencing your current job search?
- What aspects of this job search are within your control?
- How can your previous experience with job searches and role changes help you to manage your current transition?

Support

- Who is a part of your professional network, and how can they support you in your search process?
- What role can your support system have as you undergo this transition?
- How can the involvement of a search firm help support you as you search?

Strategies

- What keeps you grounded and focused and will help you manage the stress of a job search?
- How can you find purpose in your current role while you are engaged in a job search?
- What do you need to effectively transition physically, mentally, and emotionally out of your current role into your new position?

REFERENCES

Academic360.com. (2016). Search firms. Retrieved from http://www.academic360.com/resources/listings.cfm?DiscID=125.

ACPA–College Student Educators International & NASPA–Student Affairs Administrators in Higher Education. (2015). *Professional competency areas for student affairs educators.* Retrieved from https://www.naspa.org/images/uploads/main/Professional_Competencies.pdf

Axelrod, J. (2014). The 5 stages of loss and grief. *Psych Central.* Retrieved from http://psychcentral.com/lib/the-5-stages-of-loss-and-grief

Benson, M. (2012). Challenges faced by expats living abroad. *ExpatForum.com.* Retrieved from http://www.expatforum.com/generalconsiderations/challenges-faced-by-expats-living-abroad.html

Council for the Advancement of Standards in Higher Education. (2015). *Standards and guidelines for student services development programs.* Washington, DC: Author.

Evans, N., Forney, D., Guido, F., Patton, L., & Renn, K. (2010). *Student development in college: Theory, research, and practice* (2nd ed.). San Francisco, CA: Jossey-Bass.

Goodman, J., Schlossberg, N. K., & Anderson, M. L. (2006). *Counseling adults in transition: Linking practice with theory* (3rd ed.). New York, NY: Springer.

Holmes, T. H., & Rahe, R. H. (1967). The social readjustment rating scale. *Journal of Psychometrical Research, 11*(2), 213–218. doi: 10.1016/0022-3999(67)90010-4

Kubler-Ross, E. (1969). *On death and dying.* New York, NY: Macmillan.

Pouchot, A. (2013). *Enter the world of mentors and sponsors.* Retrieved from http://www.levo.com/articles/career-advice/how-to-find-mentors-and-sponors

Schiebinger, L., Davies Henderson, A., & Gilmartin, S. K. (2008). *Dual career academic couples: What universities need to know.* Retrieved from http://gender.stanford.edu/sites/default/files/DualCareerFinal_0.pdf

Schlossberg, N. K. (1984). *Counseling adults in transition.* New York, NY: Springer.

Smith, J. (2012, October). The dos and don'ts of job searching while you are employed. *Forbes.* Retrieved from http://www.forbes.com/sites/jacquelynsmith/2012/10/26/the-dos-and-donts-of-job-searching-while-youre-still-employed/#6a59a70e1493

Steele, C. (2010). *Whistling Vivaldi: And other clues to how stereotypes affect us.* New York, NY: W. W. Norton.

Yosso, T. (2005). Whose culture has capital? A critical race theory discussion of community cultural wealth. *Race, Ethnicity, and Education, 8*(1), 69–91. doi: 10.1080/1361332052000341006

10

ACCEPTING AND STARTING A NEW POSITION

Peggy A. Crowe

WHEN A JOB search results in an offer of employment, a new set of processes unfold that can determine the kind of reputation a student affairs professional starts with at the new institution. To negotiate the details of an offer, a nuanced approach must be taken because the professional must advocate for personal and professional needs while also attending to unspoken expectations from the employer (for example, what the employer considers reasonable in terms of negotiation length, start date, compensation, etc.). Similarly, the professional must carefully plan the transition into the new institution and role. Rushing into the new environment without first understanding the organizational culture can result in strained office relationships that can take time to repair.

How student affairs professionals approach job offers, subsequent negotiations, transitions into new environments, and their workplace identity during their first few months can affect their success in the new position. This chapter will focus on what professionals should do after a job offer has been extended, including how they should:

- set the proper tone in negotiations;
- decline a position in a professional manner;
- plan for the first few days and months on the job;

- adapt to the new organizational culture;
- prioritize responsibilities; and
- supervise staff members.

CONSIDERING AND NEGOTIATING AN OFFER

To determine whether a job offer should be contemplated, student affairs professionals should consider the context and environment of the position. Higher education institutions are very complex environments with unique missions and leadership structures, and these complex environments shape daily roles and responsibilities (Amey, Jessup-Anger, & Tingson-Gatuz, 2015). Professionals must consider these multifaceted environments carefully when accepting an offer or considering different offers. Insights into the different campus environments can be gained through the job search process, campus visits (both formal and informal), university websites, and conversations with colleagues who work or who have worked at the institution. Professionals can also talk with students on campus about their experiences and perspectives.

Job offers often come with a short response time, from a few days to a week or two. Candidates should think through some of the organizational culture issues and other important matters and discuss personal and professional needs with the offering institution before proceeding to the job offer stage. When a job offer is made, professionals should ask about the deadline for providing a response and use as much of that time as needed to clarify any questions.

While considering the environment, professionals should think about the job itself. Through the job search process, professionals will have opportunities to learn more about the roles and responsibilities of the position and to become acquainted with the variety of projects that might be part of the daily routine. Professionals should consider whether the position will be professionally challenging. Questions to ask include the following: Does this position/role afford opportunities to move to the next professional role? What skills, competencies, and knowledge will be needed to help move the team forward? If the position requires the acquisition of a new set of skills or the development of additional competencies, then the job may meet the professional's needs. If the role is similar to previous roles the professional has held, additional thought may need to be given to the offer before accepting it.

Professionals should also assess how personal and professional needs align with organizational leadership and membership. It is important for professionals to evaluate how their interactions with senior leaders (e.g., directors, deans, vice presidents), administrative support staff, paraprofessionals, and other higher education professionals during the interview process contributed to their overall sense of belonging in the environment. Professionals should ask questions such as, Do these individuals seem to share my professional values? Would they help me be satisfied in the role? Feeling comfortable and natural during the job search process may be an indication that the environment and position is a good fit. Interactions that are more forced and uncomfortable or that generate an uneasy feeling may be a sign that the offer should be declined.

Next, professionals should carefully consider the institutional context before accepting a job offer. A trend toward decreasing enrollment or the elimination of staff positions at the institution may signal funding challenges. Conversely, a newly renovated student center may indicate institutional support for the cocurricular environment. By examining the institution's mission and how that mission is translated through various parts of the campus, professionals can gain insight into opportunities for growth or unique experiences.

Finally, professionals should research the geographic location of the institution. Begin with the local community and examine news stories, notices for things to do around town, crime reports, real estate costs, and dining and shopping options. Professionals should ask questions such as, Do the community activities or resources match my personal interests? Is the surrounding area affordable and safe? If the local community cannot meet all personal needs, professionals should consider where else those needs could be met. For example, a larger town an hour away or a metropolitan area within a 3-hour driving distance may be a better fit. Determining whether the local and surrounding communities address most personal needs is an important factor in deciding whether or not to accept a job offer.

If the environment matches personal and professional needs, student affairs practitioners may need to consider another set of variables, including how they will socialize or adjust to the organization, how the institution circulates information, and how decisions are made and who makes them (the institution's organizational strategy). Tierney (1991) described socialization as a process of becoming aware of and indoctrinated to the values, beliefs, and norms of an organization. Determining how the socialization process will occur may necessitate a conversation with the hiring manager. For instance, a professional could ask about whether she will receive support as she transitions to both the local area and to the job itself; whether she will receive assistance with finding housing or schools or possible jobs for a partner; whether she will be given help in identifying professional development opportunities, understanding what orientation activities she will be asked to attend, or clarifying how she will be supported through the first few weeks in terms of workload and resources.

It is also important to gain a better understanding of how the organization may be viewed or supported throughout the broader institution.

To gain a better understanding of what the first few months may require, professionals should ask questions about relationships between departments, any challenges or issues that may be of concern, or the reputation of the office. Although these issues can be discerned through the interview process, professionals will have additional information needs once a job offer is extended. Obtaining answers to lingering questions can impact the decision to accept or reject a position.

Once a professional believes a job is worth accepting, the negotiation process can begin. It is crucial to address any needs before accepting the offer, because after accepting an offer, negotiations are no longer possible.

Although the negotiation process can be challenging, it is a normal part of the hiring procedure, and it is imperative for professionals to understand it and develop good negotiating skills. A balance must be achieved between advocating for personal and professional needs and understanding what the institution can or should provide. For instance, if a professional does not pay enough attention to his needs, he may face unforeseen lifestyle or development problems. On the other hand, if he asks that the employer meet all his needs and desires, he will seem unreasonable and appear unprofessional or create hard feelings. Professionals can conduct research and consult with mentors to find a good balance for each item that they wish to negotiate.

When starting the negotiation process, many professionals think of salary first. The job description can provide a frame of reference for what flexibility may exist in the salary. If a salary range is not included in the posting, then a figure will be shared with the job offer. In either case, professionals should always ask if the salary is negotiable. If the salary is not negotiable, the person extending the offer will say so. If the salary is negotiable, professionals should be honest about their needs. Professionals should enter the negotiation process with a good understanding of what it will cost to live in the new geographic location in their preferred lifestyle. They should research what housing options exist in that area and what it will cost to obtain desired amenities. It is important to factor in commuting costs, such as mass transportation or fuel, maintenance, and parking for a personal vehicle. Any costs associated with personal hobbies and interests should also be considered.

Based on this information, a professional can create a monthly budget that includes all housing, utility, entertainment, and obligatory payments, such as utilities, car payments, student loans, and so on. Once a monthly total is calculated, a professional can multiply that figure by 12 to determine the approximate annual take-home pay. To calculate gross pay, a professional should determine the tax rate (local, state, federal) and add it to the total. Gross pay should be used to negotiate salary. If a salary that meets or exceeds personal needs can be negotiated, then this item can be set aside and other factors can be considered. If the salary does not meet the established figure, then a professional may need to consider declining the job offer or adjusting his or her lifestyle preferences.

Student affairs professionals need to consider other items during the negotiation process in addition to salary. In the current resource climate of higher education, institutions sometimes have limitations regarding both salary ranges and standard benefits. Recent annual reports can be researched to determine whether funding has been on the decline. In addition, media sources can be reviewed for local or state trends to determine whether funding or other resources are being cut. If funding seems to be an issue or policies limit salary flexibility, professionals may benefit from being creative in terms of the items or options they negotiate. Options to consider when negotiating include travel funds, moving or relocation expenses, professional development funds, advanced training opportunities, health and wellness memberships, parking, membership in professional organizations, time off for involvement in professional development opportunities, future opportunities for advancement, opportunities to supervise others, international trips with student groups, and tuition reimbursement for pursuing an advanced degree. Professionals should determine what items they consider nonnegotiable; that is, what items if not granted as part of the job offer would cause them to decline the offer. Nonnegotiable items might include a lower limit on the salary or professional items such as travel funds and opportunities for development. Professionals will find that it is easier to make a decision if they distinguish what they must have from what they would like to have.

If nonnegotiables are not met, if a better opportunity is identified, or if the job environment does not match personal and professional needs, then a job offer must be declined. Steinfeld (2013) offered a few tips for declining gracefully. First, to protect their professional reputation, student affairs practitioners should keep any information about job offers private until they have accepted an offer and formally declined any others. They should wait to share news about an accepted position until they have signed a contract with the institution. This process can take some time, and there are always opportunities for problems to arise until the paperwork is complete.

To respond to an offer that must be declined, a professional should make a telephone call to the person who extended the offer and discuss the decision directly. Although it may be easier and more comfortable to respond by e-mail, a phone call indicates a greater degree of respect. Given the amount of time invested in the job search process, professional courtesy should be exercised. During the conversation, the professional should express gratitude for the job offer and the consideration paid to him or her during the process. Then the professional should relay his or her decision to decline the offer and provide a reason for declining to accept it. For example, if a professional declines an offer because the salary was too low and she would be unable to pay all her bills, she should share that reason. If she would have accepted the offer if the salary had been higher and she says so, the employer may decide to increase the salary. On the other hand, if a professional declines a position because he feels the organization is not a good fit, he should be cautious in his language and discuss his needs and not the problems he observed at the institution when explaining his decision. In addition, once a professional accepts an offer, he or she should contact any other institutions to terminate candidacy. This simple professional courtesy allows those institutions to save time and move forward with viable candidates.

UNDERSTANDING AN INSTITUTION'S CULTURE

Although most higher education professionals support a common mission to serve students (and help, guide, educate, and challenge them), this work is realized in very different ways at different colleges and universities depending on multiple factors such as institution size, student/faculty/staff demographics, location, pedagogy, history, leadership, management, and external relations. During the job transition process, student affairs professionals should set out to understand the context, history, and culture (both organizational and campus) of their new institution.

Institutional Culture Classifications

Cultures at colleges and universities can be classified in terms of governance (Chaffee & Tierney, 1988); planning styles (Hearn, Clugston, & Heydinger, 1993); and leadership (Birnbaum, 1988). Birnbaum (1988) combined these categories in the following four-model typology:

- The *collegial* institution, a community of equals, shares power and decision-making functions.
- The *bureaucratic* institution uses a hierarchical structure to concentrate power and decision-making functions at the top or in various centers of the institution.
- The *political* institution consists of various interest groups competing for power and resources.
- The *anarchical* institution, a loosely organized community, gives autonomy to individual units.

As Birnbaum (1988) noted, "When we study [colleges and universities] as organizations, we see groups of people filling roles and working together toward the achievement of common objectives within a formal social structure" (p. 1). Professionals can better understand the social structure of an institution if they determine which model describes it. They can then get a better sense of what to expect in terms of governance, leadership, and styles of decision making. (See Chapter 2 for an in-depth discussion of organizational culture.)

Campus Climate Framework

After the institution's type has been determined, professionals should delve into specific aspects of campus culture that they are likely to encounter. (Some of the relevant information will be obtained during the job search process, but more information will have to be gathered during the transition process.) An analysis of campus culture might include a review of classifications of campus culture, such as the three models identified by Dougharty and VanHecke (2014).

The first model, created by Rankin and Reason (2008), uses a six-phase process to examine campus climate in terms of:

- access and retention,
- research and scholarship,

- inter- and intragroup relations,
- curriculum and pedagogy,
- university policy and service, and
- external relations.

By focusing on these areas and how they manifest throughout an institution, professionals can ascertain expectations for work performance and products. This model can help a new employee understand the institutional climate more in-depth, including enrollment demographics, retention rates, support within units, curricular and policy support of campus values, and the roles external constituencies play in shaping campus culture.

The second model, proposed by Cameron and Quinn (2011), uses an assessment instrument to understand campus climate via six dimensions:

- dominant characteristics,
- organizational leadership,
- management of employees,
- organizational glue,
- strategic emphases, and
- criteria for success.

This assessment instrument can help professionals identify competing values across an organization and the type of leadership they are likely to encounter. Professionals can also use this assessment to predict what their experience will be in the work environment. (A free version of the instrument can be found at http://www.ocai-online.com/products/ocai-one).

The third model, created by Hurtado, Milem, Clayton-Pederson, and Allen (1999), uses a four-dimensional framework to understand campus climate. This model evaluates:

- the historical context of exclusion and inclusion of diverse groups at the institution,
- the structural or compositional foundations regarding the representation of diverse groups,
- the psychological environment consisting of beliefs about and attitudes toward diverse groups, and
- the behavioral climate affecting the interaction of diverse groups.

All the assessment models can be used to understand what professionals might encounter at a new institution, what roles they may be expected to fill, and where opportunities for change may exist. Dougharty and VanHecke (2014) emphasized that by using such tools and reflecting on the environment in which they are about to enter, professionals are better able to adapt successfully to the new organization.

The next section discusses what professionals can expect from a transition and how they can plan for inevitable changes. It reviews how to prioritize tasks on the first day and beyond, manage expectations, start the supervisory relationship, and reflect on lessons learned throughout the process.

PLANNING FOR THE TRANSITION

With a better understanding of an institution's campus and organizational culture, student affairs professionals can begin planning for the transition period, a time of tremendous learning, growth, and development. Magolda and Carnaghi (2004) described this period in terms of professionals' "joys and anxieties as they formulated their professional identities, managed stress, satisfied supervisors' expectations, mediated cultural conflicts, and remained true to their own values" (p. xiv). By defining the transitional period in this way, professionals may be better able to resist the pressure to act as if they have all the required skills, confidence, and competence on day one.

Professionals should consider the following steps in planning a transition.

1. **Think about what needs to be learned in the first few days and/or weeks in the new role.** Professionals should ask questions such as, What more do I need or want to know about my institution, division, and department? They should consider what others expect the position to contribute to the immediate working environment and how those expectations align with the mission of the division and the institution. What responsibilities are repeatedly mentioned? Is anything in the organizational culture emphasized? What are the needs of the students? Thinking about these issues will help professionals decide what to prioritize in the first few months and help them identify things they may need to learn more about within the first few days.

   In addition, professionals should create a list of questions for their supervisor to help determine the supervisor's style, needs, and expectations. Professionals supervising others in the office should develop a similar list of questions for them; their answers provide insight into how they view their roles, what challenges or issues they are facing, what support they need from their supervisor, and what they expect from the supervisory relationship. It is important to not neglect professionals on the front line, such as administrative support staff and paraprofessionals. To better align their behavior with expectations, professionals should find some time to become acquainted with each person in the office and learn about their responsibilities and needs.

2. **Develop a specific plan for accomplishing goals.** Professionals should ask themselves, What do I hope to achieve in my first days, weeks, and months? They should consider creating an itemized agenda with calendar milestones. To begin building relationships, within the first few days on the job professionals should schedule individual meetings with everyone in the office. Within the first two weeks, professionals should meet with their supervisor, colleagues, and frontline staff to identify their needs, goals, and expectations. To become acquainted with job responsibilities, professionals should focus on completing all relevant paperwork and attending training and orientation sessions within the first week; or read all the existing files and develop questions about ongoing projects to discuss with their supervisor within the first two weeks. Professionals should consider adding some unique activities to their plan, such as spending time on campus each week randomly chatting with students to learn more about their experiences.

Professionals should also review the competencies and rubrics for student affairs educators published by ACPA–College Student Educators International and NASPA–Student Affairs Administrators in Higher Education (2015; 2016) and determine which skills they need to develop. Higher education professionals tend to focus on the development of the students with whom they work; however, they should also attend to their own development, particularly as they become socialized in a new role. Professionals can use the three domains of development identified by Baxter Magolda (2001)—cognitive–epistemological, interpersonal, and intrapersonal—to conduct self-assessments of competencies, identify areas for growth, create development plans, build effective working relationships, and accept all imperfections as part of a personal identity.

If attending to these developmental issues while adapting to a new job, professionals may need to remain in close contact with mentors and support systems, journal about experiences, or ask for help from a supervisor or new colleagues. These activities can help professionals cope with the stress of adapting to a new organizational culture as they move through the first days and months on a job, when things are likely to feel chaotic (Tull, Hirt, & Saunders, 2009).

3. **Share transition plans.** Professionals should share their transition plans with their supervisor and mentors. These individuals can help professionals prioritize responsibilities and provide direction if goals do not match expectations. Professionals should identify a mentor or trusted colleague outside the institution who can serve as an accountability partner during the early phases of a transition process. Having a willing listener to discuss issues with every few days can help professionals cope with stress, as well as provide alternative perspectives about what is occurring.

4. **Track, reflect upon, and acknowledge accomplishments.** Professionals should take time to think about the first day, week, month, and college term of their journey. The transition to a new role takes time, and it is important for professionals to remember how far they have come, what they have learned, and where they are going. Professionals can share their experiences, successes, and challenges with their mentors, support system, or supervisor. It is important for professionals to never forget that this position is more than likely not their *last* job; rather, it is preparation for their *next* job. Professionals should assess

the competencies they are building and the reputation they are creating, and let others (e.g., family, friends, colleagues) join in the celebration.

ADVICE FOR SUPERVISORS

A supervisor is (or should be) the person who is best poised to assist a newly hired student affairs professional during the job interview process and with socialization to the new role. A supervisor can lend experience, expertise, and wisdom to career socialization, adapting to a new organizational culture, and transitioning through the first several months on the job.

Using the synergistic supervision model, Tull (2006) outlined several ways that supervisors can support professionals during the transition period. Tull (2006) recommended the following advice for supervisors:

- **Establish open lines of communication and build trust.** A supervisor should spend time with the new employee while the employee becomes oriented to the new position. After providing guidance on specific job responsibilities, the supervisor should offer observations about the context in which the professional is now working. One good way to begin this conversation is to discuss the overall budget of the department and the way in which the department fits within the larger division or institution. The way in which funds are spent often reflects priorities, important initiatives, and institutional values. Discussing the budget can also help the new employee understand limits placed on funding. For instance, an institution that has recently experienced decreasing enrollment numbers may focus on monitoring spending and making decisions that are aligned with realistic budget parameters.

- **Support the new employee's career socialization process.** When an employee first joins the team, the supervisor should explain the history of the department and division and should share his or her observations of the current culture. These observations can provide the new employee with a valuable perspective on the origins of the unit and various roles within the university. Whenever possible, the supervisor should discuss the political environment and identify best practices for navigating relationships across the institution. As the new employee works through the first days and weeks in the job, the supervisor should check in regularly and ask about the transition process and its challenges or solicit observations the employee has made about the institution's culture. A new team member may be reluctant to approach his or her supervisor for guidance for fear that doing so will convey incompetence. Supervisors should support and encourage new employees by approaching them first and being open and honest when providing information or feedback. This will help supervisors build the trusting relationships necessary to maintain a successful work environment.
- **Assist the new employee with professional development.** This may involve challenging the employee in appropriate ways. As a starting point, a supervisor should review the competencies for the position in order to have a candid conversation with the new employee about the competencies the employee may still need to develop. The supervisor should assist in developing a plan for building those competencies. This may include asking the new employee to work with different groups across campus, attend training sessions, or read books and articles. The supervisor should encourage the employee to discuss the

development opportunity, including what was learned or what may still be unclear.

- **Consider the employee's career goals, and regularly highlight opportunities that align with those goals.** If conferences or special certifications or training can be financed, a supervisor should share that information and challenge the employee to try new activities. For instance, an employee who attends the same conference every year may not gain the experiences needed to grow and develop. Instead, asking an employee to represent the office at a different conference can stretch the professional and encourage learning. This development will help the employee grow within a current position and prepare the professional to advance in his or her career.

CONCLUSION

This chapter discussed the process of considering, negotiating, and accepting a job offer and making the transition to a new role. To ensure the best possible outcomes, professionals should carefully consider and plan each step of the negotiation, acceptance, and transition process. For instance, they should engage in a deliberate assessment of the institution's culture to prepare for the new environment and the various responsibilities and roles within the new position. Similarly, professionals should focus on building relationships with all members of the work environment within the first days and weeks on the job; in this way, they promote the effective functioning of the entire team. By regularly reflecting on and celebrating accomplishments during the transition period, professionals can develop confidence in their abilities and their professional development prospects.

QUESTIONS FOR REFLECTION

- What personal and professional needs should you consider? Which ones are nonnegotiable?

- What professional competencies do you bring to a new position, and which ones do you hope to develop?

- How will the new institutional culture challenge you to learn, develop, and grow?

- What are your plans for the first days, weeks, and months in your new job?

- Who serves as your support system to help you deal with stress and celebrate your accomplishments during the transition process?

REFERENCES

ACPA–College Student Educators International & NASPA–Student Affairs Administrators in Higher Education. (2015). *Professional competency areas for student affairs practitioners.* Retrieved from https://www.naspa.org/images/uploads/main/Professional_Competencies.pdf

ACPA–College Student Educators International & NASPA–Student Affairs Administrators in Higher Education. (2016). *ACPA/NASPA professional competencies rubrics.* Retrieved from https://www.naspa.org/images/uploads/main/ACPA_NASPA_Professional_Competency_Rubrics_Full.pdf

Amey, M. J., Jessup-Anger, E., & Tingson-Gatuz, C. R. (2015). Unwritten rules: Organizational and political realities of the job. In M. J. Amey & L. Reesor (Eds.), *Beginning your journey: A guide for new professionals in student affairs* (4th ed., pp. 17–41). Washington, DC: NASPA–Student Affairs Administrators in Higher Education.

Baxter Magolda, M. B. (2001). *Making their own way: Narratives for transforming higher education to promote self-development.* Sterling, VA: Stylus.

Birnbaum, R. (1988). *How colleges work. The cybernetics of academic organization and leadership.* San Francisco, CA: Jossey-Bass.

Cameron, K. S., & Quinn, R. E. (2011). *Diagnosing and changing organizational culture: Based on Competing Values Framework* (3rd ed.). San Francisco, CA: Jossey-Bass.

Chaffee, E., & Tierney, W. (1988). *Collegiate culture and leadership strategies.* New York, NY: Macmillian.

Dougharty, W. H., & VanHecke, J. R. (2014). Assessing campus and divisional cultures. In A. Carry (Ed.), *Executive transitions in student affairs: A guide to getting started as the vice president.* Washington, DC: NASPA–Student Affairs Administrators in Higher Education.

Hearn, J. C., Clugston, R., & Heydinger, R. (1993). Five years of strategic environmental assessment efforts at a research university: A case study of an organizational innovation. *Innovative Higher Education, 18*(1), 7–36. doi: 10.1007/BF01742195

Hurtado, S., Milem, J., Clayton-Pederson, A., & Allen, W. (1999). *Enacting diverse learning environments: Improving the climate for racial/ethnic diversity in higher education* (ASHE-ERIC Higher Education Report Vol. 26, No. 8). Washington, DC: The George Washington University.

Magolda, P. M., & Carnaghi, J. E. (2004). *Job one: Experiences of new professionals in student affairs.* Lanham, MD: University Press of America.

Rankin, S. R., & Reason, R. D. (2008). Transformational tapestry model: A comprehensive approach to transforming campus climate. *Journal of Diversity in Higher Education, 1*(4), 262–274. doi: 10.1037/a0014018

Steinfeld, T. (2013, April). Declining a job offer—the right way! *Forbes.* Retrieved from http://www.forbes.com/sites/trudysteinfeld/2013/04/01/decline-a-job-offer-the-right-way/#672560f86e29

Tierney, W. G. (1991). Organizational culture in higher education: Defining the essentials. In M. Peterson (Ed.), *ASHE reader in organization and governance in higher education* (pp. 126–139). Lexington, MA: Ginn Press.

Tull, A. (2006). Synergistic supervision, job satisfaction, and intention to turnover of new professionals in student affairs. *Journal of College Student Development, 47,* 465–480. doi: 10.1353/csd.2006.0053

Tull, A., Hirt, J. B., & Saunders, S. A. (2009). *Becoming socialized in student affairs administration: A guide for new professionals and their supervisors.* Sterling, VA: Stylus.

11

BECOMING A FACULTY MEMBER

Mimi Benjamin and John Wesley Lowery

THOSE WHO HAVE worked as administrators in higher education sometimes express an interest in transitioning into teaching at the graduate level; however, they may not understand the work of higher education graduate faculty, and they may not recognize that making this transition is the equivalent of starting a new career. This chapter provides those interested in full-time faculty and adjunct teaching positions, including transitioning administrators and doctoral students with no prior experience in administration, with the information they need to make informed decisions.

This chapter will discuss:

- the history of higher education preparation programs;
- graduate program characteristics, including program focus and degree type;
- faculty responsibilities and work;
- faculty roles; and
- steps to take to make a successful transition from an administrative position.

A BRIEF HISTORY OF PREPARATION PROGRAMS

Graduate programs for higher education professionals began in the early 1900s when Teacher's College at Columbia University developed a graduate certificate for deans of women at the request of graduates who were then working in that role. Deans of women at the time embraced professional training more quickly than deans of men, many of whom questioned the value of graduate training (Schwartz, 2010). Initially, the certificate program for deans of women consisted of existing courses offered at Teacher's College, but it quickly grew into a distinct master's program and, within a decade or so, a doctoral program was offered as well (Koch, 1966; Lloyd-Jones, 1949). Students in these programs were provided with both "theoretical knowledge... [and] also a practice period or internship" (Sturtevant, 1928, p. 261). At the same time, Lois Kimball Mathews (1915), author of *The Dean of Women*, developed a summer program to prepare deans of women.

Higher education administration had already emerged as a field of study in the 1890s at Clark University (Goodchild, 2013), and in 1931, a graduate program focused on student affairs that also prepared deans of women was established at Syracuse University (Leonard, 1934). Several additional graduate programs in student affairs were established in the years following World War II (Anderson, 1948; Jones, 1948; LaBarre, 1948), and many more were established in the 1960s and 1970s (Coomes, 2013). Also in the 1960s and 1970s, statements intended to guide the education of student affairs professionals (Robinson, 1966) were issued by multiple professional organizations, including the Commission on Professional Development (1964) of the Council of Student Personnel Associations in Higher Education (COSPA); the American College Personnel Association (ACPA; Saddlemire & Knock, 1979), and the American Personnel and

Guidance Association (APGA; 1967). Organizations and the guidelines they issued include the following:

- COSPA and APGA (1969) jointly published "Guidelines for Graduate Programs in the Preparation of Student Personnel Workers in Higher Education."
- The Association for Counselor Education and Accreditation (ACES; 1977) published the "Standards for the Preparation of Counselors and Other Personnel Services Specialists" and shortly after established the Council for Accreditation of Counseling and Related Educational Programs (CACREP) with APGA. CACREP identified counseling as the central focus of graduate preparation programs, whereas ACPA (Saddlemire & Knock, 1979) had a broader focus that included student personnel education (with either counseling, developmental, or administrative emphases).

In the years since, guidelines concerning the education of student affairs professionals have been issued by the following organizations:

- The Council for the Advancement of Standards for Student Services/Development Programs (CAS; 1986), founded in 1979, published "Preparation Standards and Guidelines at the Master's Degree Level for Student Services/Development Professionals in Postsecondary Education." Like the earlier ACPA document (Saddlemire & Knock, 1979), which had served as a starting point, the CAS (1986) guidelines identified multiple program emphases, including student development, administration, and counseling. However, in subsequent revisions of its graduate preparation standards, CAS (2012) endorsed a single model for the curriculum.
- The newly named Council for the Advancement of Standards in

Higher Education (CAS; 2012) developed its "Master's-Level Student Affairs Professional Preparation Programs Standards and Guidelines" and identified three key curriculum areas:

+ foundational studies;
+ professional studies, including student learning and development theories, student characteristics and the effects of college on students, individual and group strategies, student affairs organization and administration, assessment, evaluation, and research; and
+ supervised practice.

- The Council for the Advancement of Higher Education Programs' (CAHEP, 2010), which is affiliated with the Association for the Study of Higher Education (ASHE), published "Guidelines for Higher Education Administration and Leadership Preparation Programs at the Master's Degree Level."
- CACREP (2009), which once accredited student affairs programs because student affairs was considered a subspecialty of the counseling profession, merged college counseling and student affairs into a single specialty area: student affairs and college counseling; however, in its 2016 standards, CACREP (2015) moved even further away from accrediting student affairs programs and renamed the specialty area "college counseling and student affairs" as part of a larger effort to unify the counseling profession. Although CACREP no longer accredits student affairs programs, some programs accredited under its standards are still operating, and CACREP's past and current standards continue to influence student affairs programs' curriculums, especially those of programs grouped with counseling departments.

GRADUATE PREPARATION PROGRAM CHARACTERISTICS

Graduate preparation programs can be differentiated by program focus or emphasis (see Figure 11.1) and types of degrees offered. The three areas of program emphasis are:

- student affairs,
- higher education, and
- counseling.

These areas are not mutually exclusive; a curriculum can reflect all three areas and emphasize topics within these areas (e.g., social justice or intercollegiate athletics). To assess which areas a program emphasizes, the curriculum, courses, course descriptions, and program admissions materials should be reviewed, not only program titles or names.

Figure 11.1. **Graduate Program Emphases and the Program Standards Influencing their Curriculum**

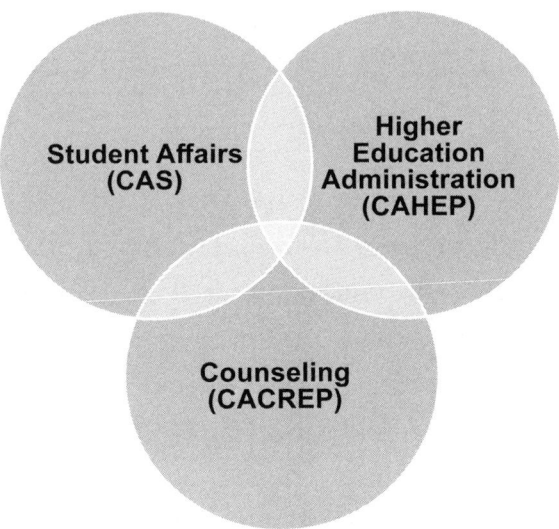

Different programs may offer the following degrees or combinations of degrees:

- master's degrees
- master's and doctoral degrees
- doctoral degrees

Master's-degree-only programs are the most common, followed by programs offering both master's and doctoral degrees; far less common are programs that offer only doctoral degrees (NASPA–Student Affairs Administrators in Higher Education, n.d.). Teaching opportunities in each type of degree program differ: Compared to doctoral degree programs, master's degree programs are more likely to provide students with adjunct teaching opportunities. Doctoral program faculty are often hesitant to relinquish their positions to students, preferring to teach doctoral courses themselves.

FACULTY RESPONSIBILITIES AND WORK

Teaching, research, and service are the primary functions in faculty positions. Institutional type will dictate, to some degree, the emphasis placed on each, particularly with regard to promotion and tenure.

Teaching

Faculty in higher education programs teach in classrooms or online or both. Teaching is the primary responsibility of adjunct faculty members, whereas those in visiting, clinical, or tenure-track faculty positions may be expected to give as much or more time to research. Components of the teaching function include course preparation, grading, and instruction. Some departments also consider academic advising to be a part of teaching.

Expectations regarding teaching can vary greatly depending on the institution and institutional type. "Teaching load" refers to the number of courses per term that a faculty member will teach. At institutions classified as "Doctoral Universities: Highest Research Activity" (colloquially referred to as "Research I Universities") (Carnegie Classification of Institutions of Higher Education, n.d.), full-time tenure-track graduate faculty regularly teach two courses each semester, often called a "2–2 load." At master's and baccalaureate colleges, teaching loads of three to four courses per semester are common. Informal surveys indicate that higher education faculty at the graduate level commonly teach between two and three courses per semester, although course releases can be granted for a variety of reasons, including grant buyouts, significant administrative responsibilities, and special accommodations for new faculty. In some programs, summer teaching will be an option. In other programs, summer teaching may be a departmental requirement. In either case, summer teaching includes additional compensation.

Tenure-track faculty members are evaluated on the quality of their teaching, but the weight this factor is given in the tenure and promotion process(es) depends on the institution. Some institutions, particularly master's and baccalaureate colleges, give greater weight to teaching in the promotion process(es), but research institutions give greater weight to scholarship.

Research

Faculty members are responsible for contributing to scholarship in their field, and this responsibility is emphasized to greater or lesser degrees depending on the faculty role held and the institutional type. Tenure-track faculty members are expected to conduct original research and disseminate that research through presentations and publications. New tenure-track faculty especially should understand the department and institutional expectations regarding research, as some institutions may place greater weight on peer-reviewed articles, single-author publications, books, and external funding for research, whereas other institutions may value a broader range of research activities. Although nontenure-track faculty may not have the same scholarship requirements as tenure-track faculty, individuals in nontenure-track positions who hope to secure a tenure-track position would be wise to put effort into this area to improve their marketability.

Service

Faculty members' additional contributions to their institution are categorized as service and can include serving on departmental, college, and university committees; assuming leadership roles in institutional governance; and working with colleagues in student affairs in a formal capacity as a member of an advisory or search committee. Faculty tenure and promotion guidelines do not limit service to the department and university; they recognize and value service to the higher education profession (e.g., service to professional organizations; leadership on NASPA's Faculty Council or ACPA's Commission for Professional Preparation Directorate qualifies as organizational service). Service on institutional committees such as the promotion committee allows faculty to assist their institution and learn more about the promotion process prior to engaging in it themselves. Although service is expected of those in the tenure and promotion process(es), it may not be required of nontenure-track faculty members.

FACULTY ROLES

Those who wish to pursue a teaching career in higher education preparation programs need to consider a variety of possible roles: adjunct faculty; visiting faculty; and full-time, tenure-track faculty. Administrators who have already completed their doctoral studies and who are considering a faculty career might consider adjunct teaching and visiting professor opportunities. Full-time, tenure-track faculty options are limited, and applicants for those positions are often quite strong. Candidates for tenure-track teaching positions will often need multiple publications and a clearly articulated research agenda to be competitive. Current or future doctoral students should consider which opportunities are of greatest interest, and during their graduate study, they should make decisions about their teaching and research experiences that will serve their goals.

Adjunct Faculty

Two common models describe how programs employ adjunct faculty. Some programs use adjuncts only when they have unanticipated or short term needs for instructors owing to full-time faculty sabbaticals, departures, or reduced teaching loads. Alternatively, some programs use adjuncts on an ongoing basis, and adjuncts regularly teach a particular course or set of courses.

Adjunct opportunities might be available on the individual administrator's home campus if the institution has a student affairs/higher education program, or opportunities might exist at nearby campuses that are within commuting distance. For those who cannot commute to a program, or for whom an adjunct role at their employing institution or a nearby institution is not possible, teaching online may be an option if the online program does not use a hybrid model that requires teachers and students to travel to campus for some classes or activities.

The practical and political challenges of these options may differ significantly. In some situations, adjunct faculty members may need to be appointed by the provost's office; in other situations, the department is free to hire individuals without a specific provost appointment. Some campuses may require that adjuncts gain approval to teach at the graduate level. At unionized institutions, filling adjunct faculty positions from within the ranks of the professional staff may not be an option.

Teaching load and service responsibilities may vary depending on the institution. Adjunct faculty members in student affairs and higher education programs typically teach one class a semester, or perhaps only one course a year. Adjuncts typically are not expected to take on additional departmental service responsibilities or advising duties, although they may be asked to if the adjunct position is in a very small department. For example, a one-person department may need adjuncts' assistance with recruitment and admissions processes.

Adjuncts who are full-time administrators and who add on the teaching role can gain experience as they "test out" an interest in full-time faculty work (and because they embody both practitioner and faculty identities, students often consider their instruction to be current and credible). However, adjunct faculty often have limited involvement with the academic department because of their other job responsibilities. They may not be able to attend faculty meetings or participate in departmental committees that make decisions about the curriculum. As a result, adjunct faculty members may be less informed about or feel less connected to the academic department.

Adjuncts may find themselves in the challenging position of holding dual roles with students, and they should consider this in advance of taking the adjunct position. For example, professionals who employ graduate assistants and teach them in the classroom may find it difficult to separate the individual's performance in one setting from the individual's performance in the other. Administrators involved in student conduct or campus grievance procedures may face similar challenges. Administrators may also find it difficult to balance the responsibilities of the full-time job and the responsibilities of the adjunct role, which include teaching time, preparation, grading, and meeting or advising students outside the classroom.

Visiting Faculty

Unlike adjunct faculty, visiting professors or those taking postdoc positions have a unique opportunity to try out the teaching role on a full-time basis for a year or perhaps two—individuals who accept these roles know that they are temporary. As visiting professors, they can amass significant experience in the areas of teaching, research, and service while being a full participant in the life of the academic department. However, visiting professors will likely have to search for a job while they are working, and after moving to a location for a year, they will have to move again at the conclusion of that year (either because they are not hired for a longer-term position or because no longer-term position is available). Sometimes, but not always, announcements for visiting positions will indicate whether opportunities exist for tenure-track employment at the institution. To individuals interested in a full-time position in the department (if one is available), a visiting position may feel like a yearlong interview.

Tenure-Track Faculty

Given the limited number of tenure-track faculty positions, finding one, particularly in a program that is a good fit, can seem an impossible task; but to many, the full-time, tenure-track position is the ultimate goal. Ideally, the assistant professor on the tenure-track has support for the transition: course releases, research and start-up funding, a graduate assistant, and helpful colleagues who can shepherd the individual through the promotion and tenure processes. Depending on the timing of the transition and the role from which the individual is transitioning (administrator to tenure-track faculty or full-time student to tenure-track faculty), the identity shift can be more or less challenging.

Some professionals who transition to tenure-track positions hold onto their practitioner identities and ideologies and successfully bridge their administrator and teacher identities (Reybold, 2008). In a study of faculty members, Kniess, Benjamin, and Boettcher (in press) found that teacher participants viewed their connections with the work of higher education and professionals doing that work as critical to their ability to stay current and credible. They took a "pracademic" (Wilson, 2015) or scholar-practitioner approach (Blimling, 2011; Komives, 1997). One participant stated:

> I sometimes refer to . . . student affairs educators as 'we' in the classroom because I don't know that I've fully made that transition. And in some ways, I hope that . . . I don't. I want to maintain my proximity because that's the importance of being an educator in a professional preparation program is to maintain that tie with the profession. (Kniess et al., in press)

Students also tend to value the experience the former administrator brings to the classroom, but fellow faculty members may not.

Once they have obtained a position, tenure-track faculty members must be self-directed and meet all the expectations and milestones or risk not receiving tenure, which would mean having to leave the position. They must create a research agenda and consider how they will achieve it over the course of their career, giving special attention to the first 3 to 5 years while they are pursuing tenure. Many institutions currently implement rigorous third-year reviews that limit the timeframe within which faculty must make meaningful progress toward tenure and promotion or face nonrenewal.

It is critical that new faculty members understand the research expectations of their institutions. Some institutions will provide tenure-track faculty with very specific expectations, in terms of numbers and types of publications expected, whereas other promotion and tenure expectations are less specific. At some campuses, faculty will be strongly encouraged or required to apply for grants, with the expectation that they will secure some level of funding.

Some programs and institutions also employ another type of faculty position within higher education programs: clinical faculty. Clinical faculty members typically enjoy tenure-like job protections and have similar responsibilities concerning teaching and program administration but different responsibilities regarding research and scholarship. There are a limited number of these positions, but the combination of teaching and administrative responsibilities may be particularly appealing to individuals who enjoyed similar elements in their practitioner roles.

PRACTICAL ADVICE

Moving from an administrative role to a faculty position is not a lateral move. Individuals who make this transition need to be prepared to start a new career. They may also need to be prepared to take a pay cut (McClusky-Titus & Cawthon, 2004; Benjamin, Kniess, & Boettcher, 2015), although sometimes they can make up the salary difference by teaching summer courses. On the other hand, those who complete full-time doctoral programs and immediately become tenure-track assistant professors typically enjoy an increase in salary.

Individuals who intend to make the transition from administrator to faculty member must be proactive in their efforts to prepare for the shift. Simply because they studied higher education does not mean that they will understand the expectations of the academy better than those who come from other disciplines, and they may be surprised by their lack of knowledge (see, e.g., Eddy & Gaston-Gayles, 2008). Student affairs professionals are certainly educators, but teaching at the graduate level is very different from working with undergraduate students outside the classroom.

Although exactly how administrators should prepare depends on the role they seek, some of the following strategies might be useful to anyone who wishes to make the transition from the role of administrator to the role of faculty member.

Talk with Current Faculty

Research suggests that the knowledge administrators have of higher education and how it works is not sufficient preparation and that they need focused opportunities to practice the skills required for faculty work (Eddy & Gaston-Gayles, 2008). Potential faculty members should observe and talk with those in the types of positions they are interested in to better understand the job. Discussing the faculty experience with individuals who share similar life circumstances (e.g., faculty members who have children) can help professionals determine how life as a faculty member will fit with their personal lives. Resources for connecting with faculty members and ascertaining what they are discussing include subscribing to the CSPTalk listserv, attending events and conference programs sponsored by the NASPA Faculty Council or the ACPA Commission on Professional Preparation, and attending ASHE or American Educational Research Association (AERA) conferences. At the local level, participating in departmental faculty meetings, sitting in on a faculty committee meeting, or attending faculty senate/faculty governance meetings can provide insight into some elements of faculty work (McCluskey-Titus & Cawthon, 2004).

Teach

Understanding pedagogy and having graduate teaching experience when entering the job market are valuable. However, most graduate students are not trained as teachers, and new faculty may feel that they have not been adequately prepared to teach (Eddy & Gaston-Gayles, 2008). As Gaff and Pruitt-Logan (1998) noted, "We have never really prepared graduate students to become college professors. Traditional doctoral study is designed to give graduate students the capacity to conduct original research.... Many graduate students, however, acquire no experience in the complex tasks of teaching" (p. 77). Offering to teach or co-teach a class, guest lecturing in a course, and participating in national faculty development programs, such as Preparing Future Faculty, are several ways to fill the gap (Gaff & Pruitt-Logan, 1998).

Research

Faculty search committees must consider whether candidates for faculty positions will be successful in earning tenure and promotion. As a result, applicants who have already published their research have a distinct advantage over others. Aspiring faculty members can demonstrate their interest in the scholarly role by engaging in research. They might work on an individual project related to their job or personal interests, or they might work on a joint project with a faculty member as a partner. In a recent study of administrators transitioning to faculty roles, one faculty member said that she tries to partner with higher education practitioners to enhance her credibility and improve her publishing opportunities (Kniess, Benjamin, & Boettcher, 2016). It can also be useful to present research papers at conferences, and ACPA, NASPA, ASHE, and AERA provide such opportunities.

Do What Faculty Do

Once administrators have observed and talked with faculty members and have a better sense of the work and how their time will be spent, they must prepare to make the transition. As noted in the literature, faculty work is solitary, isolated work (Tierney & Rhoads, 1994), and it is important for professionals to be aware of this. Conducting research, preparing courses, and grading are typically solitary activities that can be surprising experiences for higher education administrators who are accustomed to having a great deal of daily contact with many individuals and for whom there may be few independent projects. Full-time doctoral students may make the transition to faculty work more easily because faculty work overlaps with their own. Although the lack of research makes definitive statements impossible (Evans & Williams, 1997; Goodchild, 2013), informal analysis suggests that the majority of tenure-track higher education faculty were full-time doctoral students. When they become faculty members, they simply continue to do the same kind of full-time, self-directed, solitary work they did as doctoral students.

Administrators may want to make scholarly writing a priority if they want to transition to faculty roles. In a study of higher education faculty by Benjamin et al. (2015), one faculty participant recommended that administrators make writing a priority. She noted that although some may think that it is easier for faculty to find time for writing, it is equally challenging as a faculty member to set aside time for scholarship.

Another faculty participant in the study explained that he had isolated himself when writing his dissertation in order to simulate the experience of the self-directed and often solitary work of faculty members (Benjamin et al., 2015). Administrators who are most successful at making the transition will be those who know and understand how they work best and are self-directed and self-motivated, particularly in the area of scholarship.

Consider Institutional Type and Fit

Faculty members need to consider where opportunities exist and what types of institutions and programs match their interests and skills. McCluskey-Titus and Cawthon (2004) recommended "understanding the type of institution where the faculty position is listed, and the expectations of faculty at that type of institution" (p. 331). A candidate who has considered institutional type and culture can select institutions that are a "good fit." For example, a faculty member who enjoys research but is most passionate about teaching would likely not be happy at an institution that expects its faculty to devote the majority of their time to scholarship. Conversely, a faculty member who wishes to focus primarily on scholarship would likely not be satisfied at an institution that expects its faculty to carry a heavy teaching load. Wise candidates will also ask faculty members to explain the institution's requirements for obtaining tenure.

CHALLENGES AND RECOMMENDATIONS

It is important for faculty to stay current in higher education practice and to be "passionate about the *practice* of student affairs" (McCluskey-Titus & Cawthon, 2004, p. 318). Komives (1997) noted that the connection between practice and teaching benefited the field of higher education administration in general: "Linkages between practitioners and faculty and between practice and preparation are essential for the health and continued vitality of this complex field" (p. 199). Reybold (2008) found that faculty benefited professionally from participating in both the academic and occupational/practitioner communities by gaining in disciplinary expertise and credibility. The challenge for most faculty is how to stay current when they are no longer student affairs professionals.

To collect current information about the field and maintain a connection with current practice, new faculty members have employed a number of strategies, including collaborating on projects with student affairs professionals, attending local student affairs campus events, reading current literature on higher education practice, attending NASPA and ACPA professional meetings, and attending practitioner-focused sessions (Benjamin et al., 2015). Some faculty members coming from administrative positions and identifying themselves as practitioners–teachers have brought their understanding of administration with them (Benjamin et al., 2015) and intentionally talked *"from* practice" (Reybold, 2008, p. 141), but they must be able to talk about the current practice, not the practice that they once did.

Connecting with higher education administrators themselves is an important part of staying current and maintaining a connection, although faculty may need to overcome perceived status differences and reach out, since practitioners may assume that student affairs/ higher education faculty do not want to be actively involved in student affairs division work. As noted by one participant in a recent study:

> There's a perception that faculty members are aloof and think they're better than anybody else. I'm always very aware in situations with student affairs colleagues that I cannot act like that, not that I would, but I feel like I almost ... have to be the one that walks over and says "Hello" to them. (Kniess et al., in press)

Once faculty do reach out, they may realize many benefits to establishing a connection with their administrative colleagues. In McCluskey-Titus and Cawthon's (2004) study, participants cited their administrative colleagues' role in crafting meaningful courses.

Another challenge for faculty members is finding a mentor (McCluskey-Titus & Cawthon, 2004). Eddy and Gaston-Gayles' (2008) research suggested that "chosen" individuals in graduate programs (those groomed by faculty for faculty work) had advantages in the job search process, including the advantage of having advocates in the faculty members who had selected them. Graduate students who are not chosen should seek out mentors who can help prepare them for the faculty experience. Professional development opportunities, particularly those devised for new faculty members, such as the Preparing Future Faculty or similar programs (Gaff & Pruitt-Logan, 1998), may offer structured mentoring programs or, at a minimum, opportunities for new faculty to interact with experienced faculty who may be available as mentors.

CONCLUSION

Student affairs and higher education preparation programs and the graduate students enrolled in them greatly benefit from the experience and knowledge that administrators bring to the classroom as adjunct faculty members or full-time faculty members. Administrators who choose to transition into teaching must be prepared to start a new career, although they will want to bring their knowledge of the practice of administration with them into their new roles. They must adopt strategies to keep their knowledge of practice up-to-date, and they benefit by reaching out to their administrative colleagues and staying connected to student affairs practice. Professionals who seek faculty positions must be suited to solitary work and able to fulfill various faculty responsibilities, such as teaching, research, and service. Various faculty roles are currently obtainable, but some roles may be more suitable or accessible for certain individual. Those who decide to teach should select graduate preparation programs on the basis of program focus or emphasis and the types of degrees offered.

QUESTIONS FOR REFLECTION

- What elements of the core faculty roles (teaching, research, and service) hold the greatest and least appeal and interest for you?

- How well suited are you to the realities of faculty life, particularly the isolation that many faculty say is a feature of their work? Are you self-motivated and self-determining?

- What opportunities exist for you to demonstrate your ability to succeed as a teacher and scholar and gain experience? (Current doctoral students and student affairs professionals who have already earned a doctorate and are working full time will have different opportunities.)

- As a full-time faculty member, how will you stay current and connected to student affairs practice?

REFERENCES

American Personnel and Guidance Association. (1967). The role and preparation of student personnel workers in institutions of higher learning. *Journal of College Student Personnel, 8,* 62–65.

Anderson, G. V. (1948). Professional standards and training for college personnel workers. *Educational and Psychological Measurement,* 451–459. doi: 10.1177/001316444800800305

Association for Counselor Education and Accreditation. (1977). Standards for the preparation of counselors and other personnel services specialists. *Personnel and Guidance Journal, 55,* 596–601. doi: 10.1002/j.2164-4918.1977.tb04311.x

Benjamin, M., Kniess, D., & Boettcher, M. (2015, March). *Making the leap from administrator to faculty member: Stories of transition.* Presentation at the annual convention of ACPA–College Student Educators International, Tampa, FL.

Blimling, G. S. (2011). Developing professional judgment. In P. M. Magolda & M. B. Baxter Magolda (Eds.), *Contested issues in student affairs: Diverse perspectives and respectful dialogue* (pp. 42–53). Sterling, VA: Stylus.

Carnegie Classification of Institutions of Higher Education. (n.d.). About Carnegie Classification. Retrieved from http://carnegieclassifications.iu.edu

Commission on Professional Development. (1964). *A proposal for professional preparation in college student personnel work.* Indianapolis, IN: Council of Student Personnel Associations in Higher Education.

Coomes, M. (2013). [Grad prep program founding dates revised]. Unpublished raw data.

Coomes, M. D., Belch, H. A., & Saddlemire, G. L. (1991). Doctoral programs for student affairs: A status report. *Journal of College Student Development, 32,* 62–68.

Council for Accreditation of Counseling & Related Educational Programs. (2009). *2009 CACREP standards.* Retrieved from http://www.cacrep.org/wp-content/uploads/2013/12/2009-Standards.pdf

Council for Accreditation of Counseling & Related Educational Programs. (2015). *2016 CACREP standards.* Retrieved from http://www.cacrep.org/for-programs/2016-cacrep-standards

Council for the Advancement of Higher Education Programs. (2010). *A commitment to quality: Guidelines for higher education administration and leadership preparation programs at the masters degree level.* Retrieved from http://docplayer.net/1045871-A-commitment-to-quality-guidelines-for-higher-education-administration-and-leadership-preparation-programs-at-the-masters-degree-level.html

Council for the Advancement of Standards for Student Services/Development Programs. (1986). Preparation standards and guidelines at the master's level for student services/development professionals in post-secondary education. In *CAS standards and guidelines for student services/development programs* (pp. 101–109). Washington, DC: Author.

Council for the Advancement of Standards in Higher Education. (2012). *Master's-level student affairs professional preparation programs: CAS standards and guidelines.* Washington, DC: Author.

Council of Student Personnel Associations in Higher Education & American Personnel and Guidance Association. (1969). Guidelines for graduate programs in the preparation of student personnel workers in higher education. *Personnel and Guidance Journal, 47,* 493–498.

Eddy, P. L., & Gaston-Gayles, J. L. (2008). New faculty on the block: Issues of stress and support. *Journal of Human Behavior in the Social Environment, 17*(1), 89–106. doi: 10.1080/10911350802168878

Evans, N. J., & Williams, T. E. (1997). Student affairs faculty: Characteristics, qualifications and recommendations for future preparation. In N. J. Evans & C. E. Phelps Tobin (Eds.), *The state of the art of preparation and practice in student affairs: Another look* (pp. 105–123). Lanham, MD: University Press of America.

Gaff, J. G., & Pruitt-Logan, A. S. (1998). Preparing college faculty. In M. S. Anderson (Ed.), *The experience of being in graduate school: An exploration* (New Directions for Higher Education, No. 101, pp. 77–86). San Francisco, CA: Jossey-Bass.

Goodchild, L. F. (2013). Higher education as a field of study: Its history, degree programs, associations, and national guidelines. In S. Freeman, L. S. Hagedorn, L. F. Goodchild, & D. A. Wright (Eds.), *Advancing higher education as a field of study: In quest of doctoral degree guidelines—Commemorating 120 years of excellence* (pp. 21–44). Sterling, VA: Stylus.

Jones, A. J. (1948). Preparation of guidance and personnel workers. *Review of Educational Research, 15,* 205–213. doi: 10.2307/1168728

Kniess, D., Benjamin, M., & Boettcher, M. (in press). Negotiating faculty identity in the transition from student affairs practitioner to tenure-track faculty. *College Student Affairs Journal.*

Kniess, D., Benjamin, M., & Boettcher, M. (2016, March). *Administrator-faculty transitions: Common purposes, different paths.* Paper presented at the annual conference of NASPA–Student Affairs Administrators in Higher Education, Indianapolis, IN.

Koch, R. M. (1966). *The professional education of student personnel workers in higher education at Teachers College, Columbia University, 1913–1938* (Unpublished doctoral dissertation). Teachers College, Columbia University, New York, NY.

Komives, S. R. (1997). Linking preparation with practice. In N. J. Evans & C. E. Phelps Tobin (Eds.), *The state of the art of preparation and practice in student affairs: Another look* (pp. 177–200). Lanham, MD: University Press of America.

LaBarre, C. (1948). *Graduate training for educational personnel work* [Student Personnel Work Series, No. 11]. Washington, DC: American Council on Education.

Lloyd-Jones, E. (1949). The beginnings of our profession. In E. G. Williamson (Ed.), *Trends in student personnel work* (pp. 260–264). Minneapolis, MN: University of Minnesota Press.

Leonard, E. A. (1934). Student deans: Course for advisers of girls and deans of women at Syracuse University. *Bulletin of the Association of American Colleges, 20,* 546–551.

Mathews, L. K. (2015). *The dean of women.* New York, NY: Houghton Mifflin.

McCluskey-Titus, P., & Cawthon, T. W. (2004). The grass is always greener on the other side of the fence: Making a transition from student affairs administrator to full-time faculty. *NASPA Journal, 41,* 317–335. doi: 10.2202/0027-6014.1336

NASPA–Student Affairs Administrators in Higher Education. (n.d.) Graduate program directory. Retrieved from https://www.naspa.org/careers/graduate/graduate-program-directory

Reybold, L. E. (2008). Practitioner-faculty dialectic: Balancing professional identities in adult education. *Journal of Adult Development, 15,* 140–147. doi: 10.1007/s10804-008-9045-8

Robinson, D. F. (1966). Analysis of three statements relative to the preparation of college student personnel workers. *Journal of College Student Personnel, 7,* 254–256.

Saddlemire, G., & Knock, G. (1979). *Consider the college student development profession.* Washington, DC: American College Personnel Association.

Schwartz, R. (2010). *Deans of men and the shaping of modern college culture.* New York, NY: Palgrave Macmillan.

Sturtevant, S. M. (1928). What is a professional course for deans of women? *School and Society, 28,* 259–262.

Tierney, W. G., & Rhoads, R. A. (1994). *Faculty socialization as a cultural process: A mirror of institutional commitment* (ASHE–ERIC Higher Education Report No. 93-6). Washington, DC: The George Washington University, School of Education and Human Development.

Wilson, M. D. (2015). Pracademia: The future of the lifelong learner. *About Campus, 20*(2), 28–31. doi: 10.1002/abc.21189

12

STRATEGIES FOR EFFECTIVE SUPERVISION

Kelli Peck Parrott

SUPERVISORS CAN BE found at every level of higher education organizations, from the vice president for student affairs, who either directly or indirectly supervises the work of the entire division, to the newest graduate hall director, who is required to supervise the work of student staff. However, quality supervision is much rarer than it should be, and the lack of good supervision (Tull, 2006; Winston & Hirt, 2003) may partly explain the attrition of the newest in the field. Poor supervision can have many other far-reaching effects.

Why would good supervision be uncommon among a group of professionals whose primary calling is working to develop and educate students? Doesn't logic dictate that professionals who are skilled at working with students would excel at working with other staff members?

The problem of poor supervision among student affairs practitioners may be linked to a general misconception existing in the profession. Practitioners often confuse supervising with other functions common to the profession, such as advising, mentoring, and managing.

An advisor's role is to guide, counsel, and inform; and the advisor's chief goal is the student's education or learning processes—organizational outcomes come second. Advisors frequently counsel organizations in which students are volunteers, and the organization may have confusing position descriptions or no real mechanism for accountability. In academic advising, advisors' interactions with students are limited; their duty is to guide students in regard to degree plans, major selection, and corresponding regulations; but students make their own decisions and suffer the consequences of poor decisions, such as delayed graduation or holds on registration. In contrast, supervisors prioritize organizational outcomes and final products, and the learning, development, and personal goals of employees come second at best. The employee has a job description, accountability mechanisms are in place, and there are consequences if the employee fails to produce results.

Like advisors, mentors guide, counsel, challenge, and support. The best mentors are usually unbiased but knowledgeable confidants not involved in the mentee's day-to-day work. Although a supervisor may be a mentor, the mentor-mentee relationship works best if it involves informal relationships without formal accountability mechanisms. When supervisors do serve in a mentoring role, they typically focus on the individual's needs rather than the organization's needs.

Although positions that entail supervision are often referred to as management positions, management is not the same thing as supervision; management is more closely associated with task oversight and creating structure and consistency in organizations (Northouse, 2016). In her often-repeated quote, Rear Admiral Grace Hopper, co-inventor of the computer, argued that "you manage things, you lead people," and she noted that management efforts sometimes eclipse those of leadership (as cited in Schieber, 1987, p. 9).

The roles of advisor, mentor, and manager may support the role of a supervisor, but they are not identical to the role of a supervisor. A professional who is a good advisor, mentor, or manager is not necessarily a good supervisor. In fact, being a good supervisor is more complicated than people assume (Tull, 2009).

This chapter will discuss:

- the definition of supervision,
- the complexity of supervision,
- Winston and Creamer's (1997) synergistic supervision model,
- employees in a variety of career stages and generations,
- related legal issues, and
- best practices of good supervisees.

DEFINING SUPERVISION

Successful student affairs practitioners are rewarded by being required to supervise the work of others—often the newest professionals in the field, who need the most guidance. Unfortunately, practitioners often receive little direction in how to supervise the work of others successfully (Arminio & Creamer, 2001; Schuh & Carlisle, 1991; Tull, 2009). It is often presumed that student affairs practitioners who had previous success in other higher education roles will be effective supervisors as well. Since these professionals often lack experience and training in supervision, supervisors' first efforts are often based on trial and error methods, and the poor quality of their supervision negatively affects the commodity the field can least afford to affect negatively—the newest professionals, who are at the highest risk of leaving the field (Janosik et al., 2003).

In simple terms, a supervisor is a person "who has one or more staff members reporting to him or her and for whose performance the supervisor shares responsibility" (Scheuermann, 2011, pp. 5–6). Within an increasingly complex higher education environment, supervisors are being called upon to handle a great deal more: While trying to meet the mission and goals of the institution, they are expected to advise, guide, and counsel students; handle the complaints, questions, and expectations of parents, upper-level administrators, and faculty who often do not understand or value their positions; and manage the increasingly litigious environment in which they are expected to consistently do more with less (Scheuermann, 2011).

Common Approaches

Common approaches to supervision include the authoritarian, laissez-faire, and companionable approaches (Winston and Creamer, 1997). Authoritarian supervision presumes that employees require constant attention in order to meet the requirements of their positions. Authoritarian supervisors set goals, and they work to ensure that their employees are consistently meeting those goals. In contrast, laissez-faire supervisors provide employees with a great deal of freedom. They communicate goals and expect that their employees will accomplish these goals without much guidance or interference from the supervisor. As the name implies, laissez-faire supervisors are hands-off supervisors. Companionable supervisors prefer to form friendship-like relationships with their employees and try to motivate supervisees through these more personal relationships.

Preferred Styles

Most professionals have a preferred style of supervising and a preferred style of being supervised, or they view some styles as appropriate in some situations and not in others (Winston, 2006). Some professionals view authoritarian supervisors as micromanagers; however, new professionals may welcome or need, at least initially, the clear expectations and guidance they provide. Laissez-faire supervisors might leave new professionals feeling lost, whereas highly experienced, high-performing professionals in long-standing positions might find this style appropriate. Companionable supervisors may not provide enough structure for new professionals, who may wish to have a good relationship with their supervisors but need boundaries and not friendship (Winston, 2006); however, experienced, highly functioning teams may find that the companionable, relationship-based approach is very effective. As Winston (2006) noted, supervisors may supervise in the way they like to be supervised, but employees may not want or value the supervisor's preferred supervisory style. Some styles match particular types of work environment. For example, in a financial aid or international student services office, where ever-changing laws and paperwork call for strict guidelines and protocols, an authoritarian style may be best.

Since no single supervisory style fits all professionals and situations, it is not surprising that new student affairs professionals might be critical of the supervision they receive. Even if they do not know what good supervision is (Winston, 2006), new professionals may have unexplored expectations or needs concerning supervision that a single supervisor does not or cannot satisfy. Winston and Hirt (2003) surveyed new professionals on the supervision they were receiving. Respondents reported the following criticisms:

- ineffective communication,
- infrequent feedback concerning performance,
- insufficient professional sponsorship,
- a lack of structure,
- a lack of autonomy (micromanagement),
- a failure to recognize their limitations,
- a lack of emotional and material support,
- a lack of consistency in dealing with issues and people, and
- poor or negative role models.

Obviously, these new professionals did not believe they were receiving the supervision and leadership they had hoped to receive in their first position.

Models of Supervision

Most discussions of supervision and staffing have focused only on handling problem employees, but Winston and Creamer (1997) focused on the entirety of staffing as key to the successful leadership of higher education. Recognizing the need for a balanced approach to student affairs supervision, Winston and Creamer (1997) proposed both an integrated staffing model and a synergistic supervisory style.

Winston and Creamer's (1997) integrated staffing model focused on the idea that supervision is at the core of staffing but is only one of six key elements. According to Winston and Creamer (1997), supervisors need to dedicate time and resources to the following:

- recruiting and selecting staff,
- orienting staff to new positions and the institution,
- supervising,
- continually developing staff,
- appraising performance,
- and separating (added to the model in 2002).

In their integrated staffing model, Winston and Creamer (1997) described a new approach to supervision. *Synergistic supervision* is a cooperative effort between the supervisor and the employee, and the primary goal is to balance the mission and goals of the institution with the personal and professional goals of individual employees. Previous supervisory styles generally focused on either the goals of the organization or the well-being of employees, but this style focuses on both. Some of the key components of synergistic supervision include the following:

- developing an open and trusting relationship with employees;
- working with employees to identify personal and professional goals;
- identifying and promoting professional development opportunities for both supervisors and employees;
- discussing organizational attitudes and values;
- performing frequent, informal performance appraisals to provide on-going feedback and guidance; and
- discussing both exemplary and poor performance. (Saunders, Cooper, Winston, & Chernow, 2000)

Winston and Creamer's (1997) model of synergistic supervision is supported by other research. Arminio and Creamer (2001) found that high-quality supervisors keep a dual focus, balancing the needs of the institution and the needs of their employees. But when the needs of both conflict, high-quality supervisors first focus on the needs of their employees. High-quality supervisors use common supervisory skills such as motivating, listening, managing, and giving feedback and guidance, but they do so consistently. Winston (2006) found that high-quality supervisors always supervise and lead within the context of ethics and values.

THEORY TO PRACTICE

Orientation and Training

Initially, all new employees need to understand the organizational context in which they find themselves. To that end, supervisors should provide employees with on-going discussions about the history, values, culture, and dynamics of the institution and the department. Supervisors are the guides to the new territory, and they need to plan and prepare for these discussions, recognizing that new professionals will not know what they do not know and may not ask the right questions. Newly promoted professionals can also benefit from these discussions and explanations because although they may have been knowledgeable and highly skilled in their previous positions, upward movement changes their environment. The higher employees climb on the organizational ladder, the less protected they are from politics and power.

Next, train, train, and then train some more. New professionals (including millennials) tend to be highly educated but not necessarily highly skilled. In a study called the PreparedU project, Bentley University (2014) surveyed more than 3,000 business executives, recruiters, college students, college graduates, students' parents, and university administrators and found that although there was some disagreement as to what "preparedness" entailed, nearly all respondents—including millennials themselves—agreed that millennials were unprepared for the workplace. Determining why is a subject for future research; however, one explanation for millennials' unpreparedness might be their different experiences of work in childhood (Howe & Strauss, 2007). In prior generations, children commonly held some kind of part-time or seasonal employment. Baby boomers and Generation Xers often worked their first job (paid employment for someone other than parents) when they were young teens or preteens (e.g., delivering newspapers, mowing lawns, babysitting, etc.). In contrast, many millennials' first jobs were as resident advisors or graduate assistants. For some, their first professional position was their first job. As a result, millennial employees sometimes lack basic skills and knowledge about such things as arriving on time and appropriate professional attire (Bentley University, 2014). Supervisors need to ensure that even the basics of professional behavior are covered in orientation and training.

One way supervisors can develop new employees and help them understand the organizational culture and values is to explain, when ethically possible, why decisions are made; how a new employee's work fits into the larger context of the program, department, division, and university; and why specific processes and procedures exist. If new employees understand the reasons for decisions, processes, and procedures, they are better able to understand the culture, regulate their behavior, and make decisions within the expected parameters and context. More experienced professionals may view new employees' need to know why as disrespectful and the product of misplaced feelings of entitlement. However, explaining why serves the greater good as it helps to transmit organizational culture and knowledge and increases employee motivation and understanding.

Relationships

Trust is one of the most critical elements of the supervisor-supervisee relationship (Scheuermann, 2011). Although trust can only be established over time, supervisors can nurture its development by saying what they are going to do and doing what they say. The more employees can depend upon their supervisors' words and actions, the more likely they are to trust their supervisors. Supervisors also establish trust by modeling ethical behavior. Arminio and Creamer (2001) found that "quality supervision [is] an on-going process founded in ethics and values and applied through principled behaviors" (para. 21). Ethical behavior in turn engenders loyalty and respect. In the words of Rear Admiral Grace Hopper, "Leadership is a two-way street, loyalty up, loyalty down. Respect for one's superiors; care for one's crew" (CBS News, 1983). Employees tend to be loyal when they perceive that their supervisors promote employees' needs, defend employees when needed, and practice values-laden leadership. In short, in order to build the type of rapport that serves both the goals of the organization and the development of the individual, trust has to be developed in the supervisor-supervisee relationship.

Regularity and consistency are other important elements of the supervisor-supervisee relationship. When asked about the processes that exemplified high-quality supervision, several higher education professionals responded that great supervisors "hold regular meetings with individuals and groups; involve staff members in planning; utilize a great deal of face-to-face contact; communicate consistently, thoroughly, and often; and introduce challenges to staff members in timely portions" (Arminio & Creamer, 2001, para. 24).

As Winston and Creamer (1997) emphasized in the synergistic model, regular communication and meetings are key to effective supervision. Supervisors should regularly plan and schedule one-on-one meetings with supervisees to communicate the mission and goals of the institution and understand the personal and professional goals of the supervisee. Unfortunately, consistent communication is not the norm in many supervisory relationships. Although Arminio and Creamer (2001) explained that "supervisors must know enough about the staff member to understand their strengths, weaknesses, fears, joys, and dreams" (para. 27), in their study of higher education supervision, Saunders, Cooper, Winston, and Chernow (2000) found that 47% of the employees surveyed met with their supervisor individually less than once a month.

Supervisors should also be sensitive to generational differences in communication styles in the workplace. According to Twenge, Campbell, Hoffman, and Lance (2010), baby boomers, Generation Xers, and millennials differ in their communication styles, perhaps preferring or feeling more comfortable with the styles they grew up with or that were norms when they entered the workforce. Baby boomers tend to favor face-to-face communication over electronic or phone communication; they also appreciate a personal touch and understand the importance of hierarchy. They may appreciate or expect to be addressed by their name and title. On the other hand, independent Generation Xers tend to be more direct and blunt, particularly in e-mails, their preferred form of communication. They appreciate immediate communication, though their definition of immediate may be within 24 to 48 hours, whereas millennials expect instant responses. However, millennials tend to believe e-mail is antiquated and prefer texting or a variety of other forms of electronic communication; few actually use their phones to make phone calls—they prefer the newest forms of electronic communication. However, if supervisors need to communicate with millennials about something very important, constructive, or negative, they should communicate in person to ensure that millennials receive their message in the way they intend.

Staff Development

Employee development will look different depending on the individual's career stage (Marsh, 2001). Initially, a new professional will work on basic skills to be proficient in a position and may go to his or her supervisor frequently during this stage for answers to issues and concerns. Through regular developmental conversations that focus on the development of the employee and not simply the day-to-day operations of the department, the supervisor should begin asking the employee to design possible solutions before approaching the supervisor. After working with the supervisor to vet the pros and cons of possible solutions, the employee should have a deeper understanding of departmental and institutional cultures, processes, and norms as well as how his or her supervisor thinks and makes decisions. This learning process develops to the point where the employee goes to the supervisor only for approval of self-developed and self-analyzed solutions. The process culminates in the employee knowing how to independently handle issues and concerns and simply informing the supervisor of the steps the employee has taken to address new issues.

Once new professionals have developed proficiency and autonomy in their entry-level positions, they may look toward promotion.

Depending upon the size of the institution and division, opportunities for continued promotion may be limited—sometimes to move up, student affairs professionals have to move to other institutions (Marsh, 2001). If opportunities for promotion are not available, professionals can also further develop skills by moving to a lateral position, or they might choose to pursue a doctoral degree. (For more information about planning professional development, see Chapter 8.) Effective supervisors talk honestly with employees about their skills and abilities.

In mid-career, employees often move into middle-management positions requiring supervision skills and development (Marsh, 2001), but at the middle-management level, there can be a bottleneck, and employees can become frustrated about promotion opportunities. However, supervisors can look for ways to increase these employees' responsibilities and decision-making opportunities so that they continue to develop. In these cases, supervisors can encourage staff members to increase their leadership roles in professional organizations, publish and present at conferences, serve in other institutional roles, or even become adjunct faculty members. It is critical that supervisors know their employees' interests and desires.

For late career employees, the focus on work often shifts (Marsh, 2001). Employees may become less engaged in their work as they look toward retirement, whereas others may feel reluctant to retire. Supervisors can help these employees begin to develop other identities and thus smooth their transition. They can also encourage employees to advance the profession by taking upper-level leadership positions in professional organizations and mentoring or teaching less experienced professionals (Carpenter, 1991).

At every stage of career development, the lines of professional and personal development often blur. When employees are beginning their careers, they are often developing their personal lives as well, engaging in committed relationships and perhaps even having children (Marsh, 2001). Even today, women often still carry most of the day-to-day responsibilities of caring for children (Pew Research Center, 2015), and supervisors should be sensitive to their additional responsibilities and understand the affect those responsibilities can have on women's career development. However, all employees can benefit from information regarding childcare and insurance support.

In mid-career, professionals often have increasing family responsibilities. They may find that moving to achieve promotion can be more difficult, and they may become frustrated. Supervisors should give careful attention to the transition process. This might include offering dual-career resources, assisting with moving expenses, and helping to find schools in the local area.

Finally, in late career, employees may feel burdened by having to finance their adult children's college education or having to care for aging parents. Supervisors who highlight institutional policies or community resources that address these issues can help employees balance professional and personal demands. Although many people might consider these issues personal and unrelated to the workplace, high-quality supervisors wisely assist employees with such issues to ensure that the organization's needs are also met (Arminio and Creamer, 2001).

Generational differences exist in the role works plays in identity formation and in balancing personal life with professional life. Twenge et al. (2010) found that although baby boomers strongly identify with their work, tend to live to work, and value their work ethic above all else, Generation Xers work to live and place a premium on work–life balance. However, work–life balance has been elusive for this generation, and they are frustrated by millennials' reluctance to pay their dues at work. Twenge et al. (2010) explained that millennials definitely work to live and that for many, promotion is not worth what they would have to sacrifice. One study of millennials across the world found that "nearly half of respondents in every region said they *would* give up a well-paid and prestigious job to gain better work–life balance" (Bresman, 2015, para. 9).

In the United States, millennials are often perceived as lazy because they are reluctant to work 50 to 60 hours a week. However, most of the working world shares their perspective. In Marshall and Bonner's (2003) study of workers in Australia, New Zealand, the United States, Malaysia, South Africa, and the United Kingdom, lifestyle (work–life balance) was found to be the most important work anchor or the most important reason why workers choose to stay in their current position. If higher education is to maintain and develop the best employees, supervisors must also consider the work–life balance issues of employees.

Appraisal and Feedback

Although both formal and informal feedback is critical for all employees, Saunders et al. (2000) found that more than half (54%) of student affairs professionals stated that they had not received an informal work evaluation over the past year. These professionals were operating complex divisions of student affairs and affecting the lives of many students, all without knowing whether they were doing it well.

In regular meetings, supervisors should consistently review an employee's work and provide the employee with learning and improvement opportunities. Supervisors should give feedback in both formal and informal formats, and the feedback they provide should be direct, timely, and specific—that is, they should tie the feedback to behaviors, goals, and outcomes; they should explain thoroughly; and, when they are giving constructive feedback, they should offer clear guidance concerning what needs to improve and how to improve it. If supervisors schedule informal feedback and appraisals, then formal appraisals will contain no surprises and will not generate the fear or anxiety that they do when employees are unsure of their supervisor's views of their performance.

Millennials appear to want or need frequent feedback (Heathfield, 2016; Meister & Willyerd, 2010), and many businesses are finding new and creative means for generating it that could be useful in higher education as well. According to Meister and Willyerd (2010), some employers have established microfeedback, an online, on-demand feedback system in which millennials can request immediate electronic feedback in 140 characters or less. For millennials accustomed to instant messaging and Twitter, the brief feedback format is familiar, not curt or offensive.

For example, employees might request immediate feedback from all attendees concerning a meeting they ran or a program they offered. Their feedback request might focus on a specific issue, such as their organization of the agenda or their ability to facilitate dialogue, or it might address more broadly the outcomes of the meeting. Attendees provide the brief, 140-character feedback immediately and directly to the employee. Providing feedback takes little time, and attendees can complete it while the information is fresh in their minds. This approach could also be useful for the supervisor in that the feedback comes from multiple sources and provides documentation. Businesses are also successfully providing unique mentoring opportunities, such as anonymous electronic mentoring—millennials can request advice or insights in an anonymous, nonjudgmental environment. Although nothing can replace the benefits of the supervisor's direct feedback and guidance, such methods of meeting the feedback needs of this newest generation of employees are promising.

Separation

Separation is a natural component of higher education staffing and has both positive and negative aspects (Janosik et al., 2003). After developing professionally, talented student affairs practitioners may find that they are ready for the challenge of advanced positions but that promotion opportunities do not exist at their institution (Marsh, 2001). To advance, they must seek a position at another institution. Although such a move can disrupt the life of the employee, it can have positive outcomes for the institutions involved and the higher education field. The movement of professionals among institutions facilitates the sharing and development of knowledge and practices.

On the other hand, if employees are not meeting expectations, they may need to separate from the institution. Supervisors should have worked with employees to develop the knowledge, skills, and abilities they need to succeed in their positions, and when their performance declines, supervisors should develop a clear plan for improvement that includes support and training and that spells out expectations, consequences, and timelines. That is, supervisors should ensure that employees have been fully trained to perform their jobs well *before* they decide to separate employees from the organization. To fulfill this responsibility, supervisors must provide regular communication and feedback to their employees, to appropriate senior leaders who are in the employee's direct reporting lines, and to human resources offices, which provide oversight for separation procedures.

Supervisors are legally responsible for training and supervising their employees. The courts have established four common law duties for administrators: the duty to train, to supervise, to maintain equipment and property, and to warn of impending danger (Kaplin & Lee, 2014). Supervisors who do not train and supervise their employees effectively expose the university and themselves to liability claims.

To defend against claims of negligence, supervisors should provide reasonable care to prevent foreseeable harm caused by employees' poor work performance. By exercising due diligence, supervisors can meet all legal responsibilities concerning training and supervision. This includes providing tangible evidence that supervisors are meeting their duties to train and supervise. Therefore, supervisors should develop good documentation habits early.

Documentation is a necessary component of effective supervision, although requirements concerning documentation will vary among institutions and offices. Much of the tangible evidence for documentation already exists in the form of meeting minutes, attendance records, training agendas, and so on. However, supervisors should also regularly document their communication with employees, both positive and constructive. Supervisors can refer to these records when providing informal feedback as well as formal evaluations. Detailed records can be even more valuable when supervisors must handle an employee who is not meeting expectations. Without documentation and evidence of due diligence, institutions are often unable to terminate an individual's employment, and the supervisor must restart developmental steps to improve the employee's performance, often to the frustration of everyone involved. Supervisors should not delay documenting employee issues and their own developmental efforts until they are ready to terminate an individual's employment. Instead, they should develop early the habit of keeping records of supervision meetings to improve their effectiveness and save both time and frustration.

Documentation can take a variety of forms, depending on the style and preferences of the supervisor. Some supervisors prefer to keep physical files on each supervisee. The supervisor can collect any type of physical artifact of the supervisee's work, training, and supervision and include it in the file. Such artifacts might include meeting agendas and minutes, notes or letters written about the employee, copies of training agendas, previous performance reviews, and notes taken during meetings between the employee and the supervisor. Other supervisors prefer to use a personal journal, with a section for each responsibility area and each employee. After each meeting, the supervisor might make brief notes about what was discussed, what feedback or direction was given, and the goals to be accomplished before the next meeting and in the long term. For others, electronic journals or files are more convenient, though the content may be similar. Regardless of the documentation method used, supervisors should intentionally communicate with employees and document communication in a consistent manner; the documentation should be easily accessible, and documenting should become part of the supervisor's routine.

Legal Issues

Supervisors must be aware of the legal implications of supervision. The law is constantly evolving, and supervisors who keep up-to-date with laws concerning employment can more easily identify and avoid negative situations. Most important, supervisors need to know that the law usually defines minimum expectations or the minimal level of behavior that must occur; it usually does not identify best practices or aspirational behavior. This may sound like an exercise in semantics, but it is an important distinction. Good supervisors use the law to identify minimal requirements while at the same time aspiring to greatly exceed the minimum in their practice. In simple terms, the best higher education professionals aspire to always do the right thing, not just to avoid lawsuits.

Most employment-related law tries to establish fairness in hiring practices and in the workplace. Several laws exist to protect employees or potential employees, including Title VII of the Civil Rights Act of 1964, Title IX of the Education Amendments of 1972, the Equal Pay Act of 1963, the Age Discrimination in Employment Act of 1967, the Americans with Disabilities Act of 1990, the Rehabilitation Act of 1973, and others. Kaplin and Lee (2014) explained:

The rationale for laws prohibiting discrimination in employment decisions is that characteristics such as race, sex, religion, or age (among others) are irrelevant for employment decisions. In debates prior to the passage of the Civil Rights Act of 1964, the first comprehensive federal law prohibiting employment discrimination, congressional leaders stressed the financial cost to both business and members of the minority groups of employment decisions based not on individual qualifications or merit, but on "immutable" characteristics such as sex or race. (p. 159)

Perhaps the most widely utilized federal employment law is Title VII of the Civil Rights Act of 1964 (Kaplan & Lee, 2014). Title VII prohibits discrimination in employment based on race, color, religion, sex, or national origin, establishing these classifications as protected. Prior to the passage of the Civil Rights Act, though employment discrimination was considered reprehensible, it was not illegal. Title VII established that hiring, promotion, or other employment decisions based on race, color, religion, sex, or national origin were illegal unless the employer could clearly establish the classification as a bona fide occupational qualification, or "BFOQ." For instance, when hiring employees to work in a woman's locker room, the employer might argue that the sex of the employees supervising the locker room must be restricted (Kaplin and Lee, 2014).

Title IX was not expressly written as employment law, but it prohibits sex discrimination in educational institutions that receive federal funding. It can therefore be applied with regard to sexual discrimination in employment at colleges and universities receiving federal funds. The Equal Pay Act also applies to sexual discrimination in regard to pay; it ensures that individuals are not paid less for equal work because of their sex. Other laws, such as the Age Discrimination in Employment Act, the Americans with Disabilities Act, and the Rehabilitation Act, prohibit discrimination against classifications not protected by Title

VII. The Americans with Disabilities Act and the Rehabilitation Act specifically prohibit discrimination against otherwise qualified individuals who have a disability.

Student affairs professionals should have a solid understanding of the legal parameters involved in employment. Institutional human resources offices and professional organizations provide relevant training materials, and numerous books and articles on employment law offer additional knowledge on the topic.

ADVICE FOR SUPERVISEES

Although not all higher education positions require professionals to supervise the work of others, all positions require professionals to be supervisees. The goal of supervisees should be to serve students and the university and make the work of supervisors easier. The following are suggestions for being a successful supervisee.

- **Bring solutions, not just problems.** In any new position, employees experience a learning curve. At first, as they become accustomed to the position, organizational culture, and institution, they have many questions for their supervisor. However, supervisees should strive to bring solutions as well as problems to their supervisor and to one day be able to report to their supervisor what the problem was and how they handled it.
- **Keep supervisors informed.** Supervisees should be diligent about communicating with their supervisor. Early in the relationship, supervisees should ask about communication preferences (e.g., phone, e-mail, text, etc.), and which types of issues require immediate communication and which ones can wait. Individual communication preferences differ, so each time a supervisee gets a new supervisor, communication styles and methods may

have to be adjusted. For example, one vice president for student affairs preferred that everything be presented to him in a one-page memo of bulleted statements. Regardless of the complexity of the issue, he preferred to have everything on a single-page document. He had to digest a large amount of information daily in a very large division, and the one-page memo allowed him to process information quickly. This method also required all who worked for him to focus on what was most salient.

- **Recognize that supervision is difficult.** One of the most predictable mistakes new employees make is to assume that their boss is not really working, only supervising the work of others. Overseeing the work of others is complex and often difficult. A supervisor may work with several employees, all with different challenges, skill sets, and levels of experience and expertise. A supervisor's work may appear to be simple, but what appears to be simple seldom is. The following story illustrates this concept.

> *The new owner of a factory decided to conduct an audit; he reviewed the responsibilities and salaries of each factory worker. Although the responsibilities and salaries of most of the factory workers seemed reasonable, he found it difficult to understand the role of one employee who sat in a special office overlooking the factory. This employee's sole responsibility was to watch over the operation of the factory and, when needed, to press a large button that would immediately stop the operations of the factory. The employee seemed to have a simple job and yet was paid more than every other employee. The owner confronted the employee. "Why is it that I pay you more money than I pay any other employee to simply press a button?" The employee calmly responded, "You do not pay me more money than every other employee to press a button; you pay me more money than anyone else to know **when** to press the button."*

The employee understood that halting the operations of the factory for even a few moments could be costly to the company, but not halting the operations in certain situations could be even more costly in terms of revenue or even lives. Supervisors often understand the complexity of work operations at a level their employees do not.

- **Recognize that supervisors have a bigger picture.** Supervisors and employees often have very different views of operations. Their perspectives can be compared to views of a pond's ecosystem. Employees are often fish in the pond. Depending on their level of experience and their position in the organization, they might be big fish that patrol and are familiar with the entire pond, or they might be very small minnows that attempt to stay in a smaller section of the pond. Supervisors are the birds in the nearby trees whose limbs extend over the pond. What each of the animals sees and knows as reality is quite different. The minnows know only their small section of the pond. The larger fish know the entire pond, but only from below the water's surface—the surface of the water distorts their view of the sky and the nearby trees. However, the birds can see the entire pond clearly through the water, and they can see the insects flitting across the pond's surface, the other animals coming to drink, and the changes in the weather and seasons.

Supervisees should recognize that their view of an organization is often limited by virtue of their position, and that supervisors and leaders have the big picture view. Some decisions may not make sense from a supervisee's perspective. However, it is wise for supervisees to give their supervisors the benefit of the doubt, especially when supervisors make sound decisions and have the employees' best interests at heart. Supervisors will view this trust and support as maturity and will often reward employees.

- **When asking for something, use the two times rule.** Employees who want to ask their supervisor for something or want to disagree with a decision should raise the subject with their supervisor only twice. If the supervisor denies the request at first, the subject may be broached once more. However, if the supervisor denies the second request, the employee should drop the subject and find a way to move on. Continuing to raise the subject after the second attempt may be perceived by the supervisor as annoying and could create ill will.
- **Recognize that supervisors are often caught in the middle.** Supervisees should understand that not all of the decisions that affect their organization are made by their supervisor. In fact, a supervisor may not fully support some decisions. Supervisees should recognize that supervisors may be modeling professionalism when supporting their boss's decision. Employee grousing may only make the supervisor's work that much more difficult. Although it may be acceptable to express disagreement initially, if the decision does not require the supervisee or the organization to adopt illegal or unethical positions or practices, the supervisee should let the issue go.
- **Be a team player and offer to help.** Supervisees should keep in mind that they are not the only ones who work hard and want to succeed. Supervisors will appreciate a supervisee who offers assistance when they have a lull in their workload. Offering assistance helps the supervisor and affords the supervisee additional experience.
- **Remember that the supervisee is 50% of the relationship.** Whether a supervisor–supervisee relationship works or not, the supervisee is 50% of the equation and has at least 50% of the responsibility. Supervisees should do everything possible

to make the relationship successful. It is not necessary for the supervisee to like the supervisor and vice versa. What is necessary is that both individuals work well together.

- **Try to keep things off the supervisor's plate.** Supervisees should try to prevent problems from occurring or solve problems before they reach the boss's level. This will earn the supervisee the respect and gratitude of the supervisor. Believe it or not, supervisors recognize who creates problems and who fixes them. Supervisees should strive to be problem solvers.
- **Play nice with others.** Unfortunately, too much of administrators' time can be monopolized by personnel issues and petty conflicts instead of the important work of supporting students and the educational mission of the institution. Supervisees should develop good working relationships with their colleagues and try to handle any conflict that arises directly, personally, and professionally. (For more information about handling conflict, see Chapter 6). Employees should help their supervisors focus on the real work at hand.

CONCLUSION

Of all the critical skill sets that student affairs practitioners need to master, supervisory skills are perhaps the most difficult to develop. Other skills have a clearly defined knowledge base that can be taught, but supervision is as much an art as it is a set of skills. Some professionals never master supervisory skills or the art of supervision, which is detrimental to their careers. Student affairs professionals can master the art of supervision by balancing the needs and goals of the institution with the needs and goals of employees, while working diligently to train employees and communicate clearly with them.

> **QUESTIONS FOR REFLECTION**
>
> ❓ What type of supervisory style do you prefer? Has it always been your preference, or has your preference changed over the course of your career?
>
> ❓ What type of supervisory style feels most comfortable to you as a supervisor? Which is most difficult? Why?
>
> ❓ In what ways do you practice due diligence in relation to training and supervision? How do you document your efforts?
>
> ❓ How can you be a better supervisee for your supervisor?

REFERENCES

Arminio, J., & Creamer, D. G. (2001). What supervisors say about quality supervision. *College Student Affairs Journal, 21*(1), 35–44. Retrieved from https://sacsa.site-ym.com/page/CSAJ

Bentley University. (2014). The PreparedU project: An in-depth look at Millennial preparedness for today's workforce [Web slideshow]. Retrieved from http://www.slideshare.net/BentleyU/prepared-u-project-on-millennial-preparedness

Bresman, H. (2015, February). What millennials want from work, charted across the world. *Harvard Business Review.* Retrieved from https://hbr.org/2015/02/what-millennials-want-fromwork-charted-across-the-world

Carpenter, D. S. (1991). Student affairs profession: A developmental prospective. In T. K. Miller & R. B. Winston, Jr. (Eds.), *Administration and leadership in student affairs: Actualizing student development in higher education* (2nd ed.). Muncie, IN: Accelerated Development.

CBS News. (Producer). (1983, March 6). *The captain is a lady* [Video file]. Retrieved from http://www.cbsnews.com/videos/the-captain-is-a-lady

Heathfield, S. (2016, September 23). 11 tips for managing millennials. *The Balance.* Retrieved from http://humanresources.about.com/od/managementtips/a/millenials.htm

Howe, N., & Strauss, W. (2007, July/August). The next 20 years: How customer and workforce attitudes will evolve. *Harvard Business Review, 85*(7–8), 41–42.

Janosik, S., Creamer, D., Hirt, J., Winston, R. B., Jr., Saunders, S., & Cooper, D. (2003). *Supervising new professionals in student affairs: A guide for practitioners.* New York, NY: Brunner-Routledge.

Kaplin, W. A., & Lee, B. A. (2014). *The law of higher education* (5th ed.) San Francisco, CA: Jossey-Bass.

Marsh, S. R. (2001). Using adult development theory to inform staff supervision in student affairs. *College Student Affairs Journal, 21*(1), 45–56. Retrieved from https://sacsa.site-ym.com/page/CSAJ

Marshall, V., & Bonner, D. (2003). Career anchors and the effects of downsizing: Implications for generations and cultures at work. *Journal of European Industrial Training, 27*(6), 281–291. doi: 10.1108/03090590310479911

Meister, J. C., & Willyerd, K. (2010, May). Mentoring millennials. *Harvard Business Review, 88*(5), 68–72.

Northouse, P. G. (2016). *Leadership: Theory and practice* (7th ed.). Los Angeles, CA: Sage.

Pew Research Center. (2015, November 4). *Raising kids and running a household: How working parents share the load*. Retrieved from http://www.pewsocialtrends.org/2015/11/04/raising-kids-and-running-a-household-how-working-parents-share-the-load

Saunders, S., Cooper, D., Winston, R. B., Jr., & Chernow, E. (2000). Supervising staff in student affairs: Exploration of the synergistic approach. *Journal of College Student Development, 41*(2), 181–192. Retrieved from http://www.myacpa.org/journal-college-student-development

Scheuermann, T. (2011). Dynamics of supervision. In L. D. Roper (Ed.), *Special issue: Supporting and supervising mid-level professionals* (New Directions for Student Services, No. 136, pp. 5–16). San Francisco, CA: Jossey-Bass.

Schieber, P. (1987, March/April). The wit and wisdom of Grace Hopper. *OCLC Newsletter, 167,* 9. Retrieved from http://library.oclc.org/cdm/ref/collection/p267701coll28/id/1007

Schuh, J. H., & Carlisle, W. (1991). Supervision and evaluation: Selected topics for emerging professionals. In T. K. Miller & R. B. Winston, Jr. (Eds.), *Administration and leadership in student affairs: Actualizing student development in higher education* (2nd ed.). Muncie, IN: Accelerated Development.

Tull, A. (2006). Synergistic supervision, job satisfaction, and intention to turnover of new professionals in student affairs. *Journal of College Student Development, 47*(4), 465–480. doi: 10.1353/csd.2006.0053

Tull, A. (2009). Supervision and mentorship in the socialization process. In A. Tull, J. B. Hirt, & S. A. Saunders (Eds.), *Becoming socialized in student affairs: A guide for new professionals and their supervisors*. Sterling, VA: Stylus.

Twenge, J., Campbell, S., Hoffman, B., & Lance, C. (2010). Generational differences in work values: Leisure and extrinsic values increasing, social and intrinsic values decreasing. *Journal of Management, 36,* 1117–1133. doi: 10.1177/0149206309352246

Winston, R. B., Jr. (2006). Supervision of new professionals in student affairs: Assessing and addressing needs. *College Student Affairs Journal, 26*(1), 64–89.

Winston, R. B., Jr., & Creamer, D. G. (1997). *Improving staffing practices in student affairs*. San Francisco, CA: Jossey-Bass.

Winston, R. B., Jr., & Hirt, J. B. (2003). Activating synergistic supervision approaches: Practical suggestions. In S. M. Janosik, D. G. Creamer, J. B. Hirt, R. B. Winston, Jr., S. A. Saunders, & D. L. Cooper (Eds.), *Supervising new professionals in student affairs: A guide for practitioners*. New York, NY: Brunner-Routledge.

13

ADVANCING TO LEADERSHIP LEVELS
Changing Rules

Dean Bresciani

MUCH HAS BEEN written, both in scholarly and public media forums, about the increasing pressures on all levels of higher education leadership fueled by growing levels of public visibility and scrutiny (Acker & Wechsler, 2006; Eckel & Hartley, 2011; Gunsalus, 2006; Hendrickson, Lane, Harris, & Doorman, 2013; McKenna, 2015; Mendan, 2010). Pressures on leadership have increased in large part because of the economic downturn affecting colleges across the country, and levels of public visibility and scrutiny have risen because of the very public and immediate nature of emerging communication tools such as social media and cell phone-based camera and video. This technology allows immediate eyewitness reporting by anyone present. Even the smallest decisions, actions, and incidents are exposed to public review and evaluation, often with incomplete or selective information provided to the public.

As the demand for public accountability, the challenges of working with multiple functions, and the constant burdens of responding to critical issues such as dwindling resources and growing regulations has put leaders under increasing pressure, the attrition rate for leaders at the senior (vice presidents, deans) and executive (presidents, chancellors) levels has increased. Leaders are less likely to stay in their positions either because they choose not to or because the institution has made a decision to remove them (Cook, 2012; Hempsall, 2014). At the executive level, leaders may serve 5 to 7 years (Cook & Kim, 2012). At the senior level, leaders may serve a longer term, but the length of the term is dependent on the desires of executive leaders. When executive leaders have a different vision or want to select their own administrative teams, senior-level leaders can find themselves out of a job with little or no warning (Kuk, King, & Forrest, 2012).

As the attrition rate among upper-level leaders rises, traditions concerning the preparation of upper-level leaders and leadership expectations are changing (Eddy & Rao, 2009). Historically, the promotion pattern was vertical and straight. But length of service, experience in specific administrative positions, and quality performance within one functional role no longer translate into predictable advancement. Rather, to advance in higher education in the contemporary era, student affairs professionals who aspire to upper-level leadership or who are open to such roles must have a broad range of experiences and competencies, and they must carefully plan for leadership roles.

This chapter will discuss:

- current trends in higher education leadership,
- how those trends influence the developmental needs of student affairs professionals seeking leadership positions,
- what leadership looks like in an increasingly complex environment,
- how student affairs professionals can prepare for advancement to these levels, and
- the competencies student affairs professionals need for upper-level positions.

CURRENT TRENDS IN HIGHER EDUCATION LEADERSHIP

Advancement in higher education leadership has historically been based on holding institutional positions in divisions such as academic affairs or student affairs and then rising incrementally through the professional ranks, as culturally expected in each division. Some division cultures prefer leaders with specialized knowledge of the targeted division, whereas other division cultures prefer a leader with the greatest possible breadth of experience. Cultural expectations can steer professionals toward focused experiences at one institution or a broader set of experiences acquired through regular moves to different institutions.

The culture of higher education still influences individuals' decisions regarding leadership advancement, but the fundamental rules of leadership in the field have changed as demands on leaders have increased, as individuals have become reluctant to seek upper-level positions, and as institutions choose to select executive leaders from private and political sectors to fill immediate needs. These changes suggest that traditional paths of preparation and advancement within higher education may be failing to provide an adequate foundation for leadership, including socialization support and a definition of successful performance. Traditional paths are also failing to provide a robust candidate pool that can meet the needs of contemporary higher education institutions.

Leader Recruitment

Oversight groups have become increasingly desperate to find a "magic bullet" leadership solution to meet contemporary demands (Shaw, 1999). Despite having qualified individuals already within the higher education environment, the trend is to look past traditional preparation (Bresciani, 2014; Cook, 2012; Hendrickson, et al., 2013;

McKenna, 2015). Institutions looking for outside-of-the-box solutions to contemporary challenges have chosen to recruit leaders from other types of large, complex organizations rather than to develop leaders from within. Historically, presidents commonly held the chief academic officer role prior to advancement. Today, a third of modern presidents still ascend to the executive level from this academic position, but the number is declining as institutions look outside of the academy for leaders. Presidents coming from industry or government now represent a fifth of today's college presidents (Cook & Kim, 2012).

Recruiting leaders from business, military, and federal and state government is seen as a quick way to address the demands and pressures of modern higher education, and hiring executive leaders from these organizations has, in many ways, proven successful. However, there are as many examples of failure as there are of success (McKenna, 2015). Business and military leaders bring resource and organizational management skills to the higher education environment, but they meet with unfamiliar challenges when they find that they cannot direct and control individuals working within higher education. Internal constituencies often compete and are sometimes openly at odds with each other, and the insulated perspective of presidential leadership can perplex even the most successful business and military leaders. A common phrase likening higher education leadership to "herding cats" suggests that even the most perfunctory leadership directives can fail to produce intended effects and often lead to a political quagmire instead. The public nature of their leadership and the institution's performance also catches many of these leaders off guard.

Presidents coming from political sectors may be perceived as good leadership choices because they are experienced with settings in which they are unable to wrangle direct administrative control. There are few other environments in which individual leaders have less direct control of their organizations than political environments; yet many of these leaders are successful at guiding their organizations in desired directions. However, when they move into higher education settings, they must try to understand the complex and unique political culture of higher education in which leadership roles do not have internal majority support nor the external political capital needed to gain favorable treatment. Even individuals who have some political leverage tend to expend that leverage much faster than those in broader and less transparent environments. As a result, these leaders with political experience are ineffective at building political support throughout the institution. Although they can have an effect on specific issues plaguing higher education such as revenue streams and government oversight, their lack of understanding of the core activities and norms of the academy makes it difficult for them to be effective leaders in the higher education environment.

Yet the trend of looking outside of higher education for presidential candidates continues, and its persistence may point to problems *inside* the academy. One contributing problem is that individuals following traditional career development paths to dean and provost positions lack interest in advancing to the presidency or lack the relevant skill sets to do so (Cook, 2012; Eckel & Hartley, 2011). The segment of higher education leaders interested in subjecting themselves to the demands of the position is declining (Eckel & Hartley, 2011) even as the pool of candidates with the needed skills and competencies to assume these positions is shrinking (McDade, Dowdall, Marchese, & Polonio, 2009).

Another contributing problem is that candidates are often measured by subjective optics rather than objective priorities for political reasons. If a competing institution chooses to pursue presidents outside of higher education, other institutions may consider doing so as well even if there is no clear reason to do so other than a desire to remain competitive (DiMaggio & Powell, 1983; Fennell, 1980; Meyer, 1979).

One could argue that the "professionalization" of higher education leadership is not so different from the professionalization of leadership in most fields. Student affairs as a profession emerged in colleges in the mid-20th century in response to the need to manage student behavior, uphold professional standards, and provide students with career paths (Cohen & Kisker, 2010). The profession has barely moved through two generations of leadership and is still adapting and evolving to meet needs. Fields such as business and engineering went through similar transitions and over time developed clear paths toward leadership, so it is safe to assume that student affairs will do the same.

Current challenges in presidential leadership suggest that there may be a need to reframe the academic mission of institutions to meet economic, societal, and political demands. Leaders who can leverage all perspectives may need to be enlisted (Acker & Wechsler, 2006; Budig, 2002; Gunsalus, 2006; Shaw, 2005). This need to reframe comes with a need for both senior- and executive-level leaders to have substantially different skill sets.

Pipeline and Candidate Pool Limitations

Despite the significant change in upper-level leadership preparation backgrounds, presidential demographics remain unchanged. The typical college president is a Caucasian male who holds a doctoral degree and is in his early sixties. This profile has not changed in almost three decades (Cook & Kim, 2012; Freeman & Kochan, 2012), and it is unlikely to change significantly, even when these leaders begin to retire in a few years because barriers in the pipeline to the presidency prevent other demographic groups from ascending to that level.

Although the contemporary era has seen a substantial increase in the number of those entering higher education administrative ranks

(Bresciani, 2014), barriers in the pipeline to the presidency limit other groups but especially women and people of color. At the mid-level ranks, women are well represented in numbers, but their experience is often overlooked during leadership searches, which limits their forward progression toward senior-level roles (Cox & Salsberry, 2012). Women account for almost half of senior-level leaders, but their positions often include a wide variety of responsibilities, and they may not have access to the level of authority and decision-making abilities needed for leadership advancement. This limitation becomes a clear problem considering that women represent less than half of the chief academic officer positions, which is a traditional pathway to the presidency, and only a quarter of women actually hold presidential positions.

People of color have a more challenging situation. Only 13% reach the college presidency rank, mostly at institutions below the doctoral classification such as regional institutions, community colleges, and historically Black colleges and universities (Cook & Kim, 2012), and the rate of growth of this group's advancement to the presidency has stalled and even declined in recent years. Gasman, Abiola, and Travers (2015) explained that more people of color could ascend into senior and executive leadership positions if those in higher education paid more attention to where the career pipeline begins. People of color are often admitted in limited numbers to doctoral programs and may not persist through completion; only a fifth finish their degrees.

To compensate for barriers in the pipeline that limit the available pool of candidates, Gasman et al. (2015) recommended that institutions hire outside evaluators trained in minority recruitment and retention efforts to conduct a review of hiring policies and processes. Institutions could use reviews to identify systemic problems that limit candidate pools. Gasman et al. (2015) also recommended that institutions create task forces to address diversity issues in upper-level positions and develop mentoring programs to identify and support promising professionals. Researchers have found that professionals—particularly women and people of color—who receive support and recognition for strong work performance and who are guided toward relevant leadership experiences are more likely to be more motivated to ascend to senior and executive leadership (Cox & Salsberry, 2012; Hannum, Muhly, Shockley-Zalabek, & White, 2014; Hempsall, 2014; McNair, 2015).

LEADERSHIP IN A COMPLEX ENVIRONMENT

Jones, Lefore, Harvey, and Ryland (2012) explained that although no single approach to leadership can meet all the needs of higher education, leaders already inside the academy can improve their leadership if they take a broader, or distributed, view of resolving complex problems.

Distributed leadership engages stakeholders across the institutional environment and emphasizes cross-functional collaborations for problem-solving using five dimensions:

- The *context* dimension refers to external and internal influences on the environment and their impact on both the problem and possible solutions.
- The *culture* dimension focuses on recruiting individuals for the collaborative effort based on personal interest or expertise rather than position in the institution.
- The *change* dimension refers to gathering perspectives on problems and possible solutions from across a wide range of units and constituents.
- The *relationship* dimension highlights the ability of those involved in the collaborative effort to identify and resolve conflicts between individual members early in the process.

- The *activity* dimension addresses how to prepare for and implement change at the institution as well as how to secure the needed resources to support change. (Jones et al., 2012)

Building cross-functional collaborative teams can be difficult because of the organizational culture differences found in higher education (Jones et al., 2012). Academic and student affairs representatives often have diverse values and priorities and varying degrees of authority or ability to promote change. Before teams can address the complex issues that form their mission, they must first develop trusting relationships with each other and be trained in effective collaboration practices such as engaging in respectful dialogue, reflection, and interaction. Once trust and collaboration practices are established, collaborative teams need the support of existing leadership in the form of resources, infrastructure, and time to conduct their work.

In order to excel in leadership, professionals at executive and senior leadership levels need to know how to participate in, facilitate, and support this distributed approach to problem-solving. Schexnider (2008) called for visionary leaders who can address these challenges through the "ability to muster a broad array of professional skills and talents in order to advance the mission or goals" (p. 497). Professionals working in various student affairs and academic support roles are well positioned to meet these needs, as they regularly work with diverse populations and facilitate collaborative efforts to influence change.

Professionals who intend to advance from early and mid-career roles into senior- and executive-level leadership must go beyond initial training and preparation and expand their competencies and experiences. They should plan for and intentionally seek additional development to position themselves for leadership opportunities.

ADVANCEMENT TO UPPER LEVELS

When developing career goals, student affairs professionals may have general ideas about advancing to upper-level positions but not plan for what that may look like (Cox & Salsberry, 2012; McNair, 2015). The conundrum seems to revolve around understanding the implications of advancing and succeeding in these roles and weighing the rewards and liabilities that come with them. Many professionals tend to equate success with promotion, whereas the two may not have any relationship at all; and they may rationalize that a promotion, title, or higher level of compensation will provide job satisfaction, whereas a promotion may actually result in dissatisfaction and unhappiness in the work environment. Professionals should instead consider senior- and executive-level positions as potential outcomes to explore rather than required steps, and they should understand the demands on leaders within the field of higher education before choosing a career path.

To determine whether success means progressive ascension into more demanding positions, student affairs professionals must find the optimal intersection of their skills, abilities, interests, and quality-of-life preferences with job demands and expectations. They must carefully analyze the advantages and disadvantages of promotion opportunities, required skills, and the sacrifices they must make to be successful in such roles. They should also consider whether they have a need to control performance outcomes or if they are comfortable being evaluated in terms of factors they have little control over that commonly come with promotion and higher-level responsibilities.

In addition, professionals who plan to advance to leadership roles must consistently review their successes and their suboptimal efforts or results as well as other professionals' evaluation of their successes and suboptimal efforts. They must dispassionately measure their abilities, aptitudes, and performance and compare those with the abilities, aptitudes, and performance that would be expected of them in higher-level leadership positions. They must also have a thoughtful, long-term agenda that includes academic preparation and professional development experiences because they will need time to develop their natural and learned leadership proclivities and technical skills (McNair, 2015). Those who can blend these self-evaluations, abilities, skills, preparation, and experiences together, or have the conviction to do so purposefully and mechanically, can position themselves for success.

Preparation and Development Needs

To be eligible for senior- or executive-level leadership positions in virtually any unit or division in higher education institutions, student affairs professionals now must have a graduate or terminal degree; this graduate preparation is critical, if not obligatory, to understanding scholarship and its application in and outside of higher education. A terminal degree is necessary for senior and executive leadership levels. It gives professionals more credibility with faculty and prepares them to understand leadership requirements and new career possibilities in the field (Eddy & Rao, 2009). It also provides foundational knowledge and opportunities for professionals to enhance their skills in integrating complex ideas, communicating, managing interpersonal relationships, and managing tasks (Freeman & Kochan, 2012).

Most doctoral programs do not offer leadership courses for senior and executive levels, but they do offer a course or two on leadership theory to help professionals shape their leadership skills (Eddy and Rao, 2009). However, Hempsall (2014) has argued that traditional leadership skills taught by and practiced in doctoral programs are no longer effective in higher education administration environments because demands on leadership have changed. Hempsall (2014) claimed that preparation programs should adopt the distributed leadership approach and train professionals to:

- communicate well,
- collaborate effectively, and
- manage perceptions across all constituent groups.

Researchers (American Association of Community Colleges, 2005; Cook & Kim, 2012; Cox & Salsberry, 2012; Freeman & Kochan, 2012; Hempsall, 2014; Schexnider, 2008) have reported that professionals in executive leadership positions must have competencies in and an understanding of other essential leadership practices and processes. These include:

- fundraising,
- resource management,
- organizational management,
- retention strategies, and
- university processes.

Upper-level leaders also need to be able to read well and quickly, skimming over the details and focusing on the main points (Cox & Salsberry, 2012).

McDade et al. (2009) noted that the strongest candidates in upper-level leadership searches are those who can:

- grow new revenue streams,
- work well with faculty, and
- connect with industry.

They also noted that many potential candidates had incomplete preparation in required areas, including:

- financial management,
- fundraising, and
- advanced leadership experience.

McDade et al. (2009) advised professionals interested in leadership to do the following:

- be good at their jobs,
- be recognized for it,
- learn as much as possible about all aspects of the institution,
- take risks at mid-career, and
- volunteer for experiences in other areas of campus.

McNair (2015) encouraged professionals to gain additional experience and suggested that they:

- act in place of the senior or executive leader at public events, fundraisers, and board meetings; or
- serve as an interim leader in another campus unit.

Professionals should express their desire to seek these types of opportunities. They can then be on the short list of candidates when the experiences arise. Professionals should also regularly participate in workshops, webinars, and other development activities to help prepare for upper-level roles (McNair, 2015).

Mentors and Mentoring

Mentors can help student affairs professionals learn more about organizational and political influences in the higher education environment and develop an action-oriented plan for leadership advancement (Cox & Salsberry, 2012; McNair, 2015). They can also introduce professionals to a broader network of administrators (Cox & Salsberry, 2012; McNair, 2015). In addition, mentors can provide a safe place for professionals to challenge comfort zones, discuss fears, and obtain honest feedback about job performance and abilities (McNair, 2015).

Those ascending to or already holding senior- and executive-level leadership positions have a responsibility to identify promising professionals in the institution and mentor them toward advancement (McNair, 2015). Rosser (2004) found that aspiring leaders desire opportunities to develop competencies and experiences necessary to obtain senior and executive leadership. When supported in this endeavor, these professionals are more likely to be satisfied in their positions and persist into advancement opportunities.

Women and people of color should specifically seek mentors as a way to aid in leadership preparation. Researchers have demonstrated that the support, advisement, and encouragement provided by mentors can help women and people of color overcome some of the challenges of navigating the system and help them maintain a clear sense of self during the process (Cox & Salsberry, 2012; Hannum et al., 2014).

All aspiring leaders should be aware of the transitional nature of upper-level positions (Kuk et al., 2012). Since leaders can be removed unexpectedly as the result of changes in governing board perceptions, influence from constituents, or natural adjustments in the institution's direction, professionals need to put "financial, emotional, and career safety nets into place" (Kuk et al., 2012, p. 188) before they apply for advanced positions. By understanding the political nature of employment at the upper levels, they can plan for outcomes and ask for what they need when negotiating benefits for a new role.

Search Firms

After student affairs professionals have developed a broad range of experiences and competencies to supplement their individual job roles, a last step in planning for leadership advancement is to consider registering with search firms. (See Chapter 9 for more information regarding the registration process.) Almost half of the searches conducted by search firms are for professionals who qualify for senior-level positions, so even professionals who wish to advance from mid-level leadership can use these firms (McDade et al., 2009). Higher education institutions are increasingly using search firms because search firms are able to recruit from established networks of professionals and verify references and backgrounds. Search firms can also provide an impartial perspective on candidates and help manage the overall process, which can last from 3 to 4 months and include 30 or more candidates. As more institutions turn to search firms to manage upper-level leadership searches, professionals considering advancement should become part of these networks and be ready for the opportunities firms identify.

"IF I HAD IT TO DO ALL OVER AGAIN"

Much can be learned from informal discussions with a broad range of higher education leaders. The material presented in this section is informed by such discussions. Upper-level leaders were asked to reflect on the early, middle, and later years of their careers and to consider lessons they would offer individuals aspiring to leadership roles in higher education. Several broad themes emerged.

Understand the Institution's Culture

Leaders who wish to successfully direct an organization at all levels must try to understand the culture of the organization. Although anything they have learned from similar or disparate organizations or settings may help them navigate challenges, leaders should recognize that no two organizations are the same. Even subtle differences can become substantial roadblocks if leaders do not approach those differences in a nuanced way after giving thoughtful consideration to the institution's culture.

Leaders face the reciprocal risk of being handcuffed by the culture of an organization. Although they must understand, appreciate, and respect culture, leaders must also subtly and at times overtly promote change. They should do so thoughtfully and strategically, without taking shortcuts or reacting emotionally. The best leaders understand methods of managing culture and combine those methods to improve organizational performance. Key elements of their success are understanding, balance, and timing.

Add Value

To advance, and to succeed after advancement, leaders must provide demonstrable "value added" to an institution. Leaders must balance strength of personality and skill sets that result in measurable organizational success. Leaders who do not are likely to provide suboptimal leadership. With traits such as graciousness, approachability, and respectfulness, leaders with the necessary skills are often able to succeed even in the face of antagonistic pressures.

Consider Quality of Life

Leaders are successful in their roles in proportion to the time and energy they put into them—up to a point. Any professional can reach a point of exhaustion beyond which he or she cannot recover or continue. Identifying that point is an individual concern and should not be a matter of competing with others. Intentional professionals will understand personal limits concerning workloads, pressures, and demands, and they will pursue roles and responsibilities that align with their capacities.

Those who work longer, harder, and better than others do tend to succeed in leadership advancement, but there is an obvious quality-of-life exchange that can only be assessed on an individual basis. Two very different individual assessments are evident in the following descriptions of executive leadership in higher education.

One provost, responding in an ironic manner to the lack of interest among higher education professionals in pursuing a presidential role, said:

> If you're interested in professional roles that are incredibly demanding, high stress, terribly politicized, demand long hours,

are often—if not constantly—in the public eye for criticism, allow little if any "life balance," require an ability to respond to crisis on an extemporaneous basis both in terms of the event and its political and media implications, and are willing to be compensated at a level well below private-sector roles with similar financial, personnel, and technical expertise demands . . . a career in higher education leadership may be for you!

But a president who ascended to the position after an extensive career in student affairs had a very different perspective; he found the demands that the provost had derided to be challenging and rewarding parts of the job.

There have been few times that I've doubted my decision to devote a lifelong career to higher education. Although it's doggedly demanding and often exhausting, it is also incredibly rewarding beyond anything I can describe.

Another particularly successful president explained the situation in this way: "I'll have plenty of time to sleep when I'm dead."

Consider Fit

The preceding observations from upper-level leaders suggest that matching the individual and the leadership role drives success. A good fit can be defined by the extent to which an individual's personality, motivations, energies, intuitive and technical skills, and ability to grasp and incorporate institutional cultures match the demands of the role. If professionals are to achieve success as leaders, all fit factors need to be present and consistently honed to meet the needs of the position. Mentors and other leadership role models can assist professionals to evaluate fit and develop skills that relate to fit. Professionals should make it a priority to focus on fit as part of their development.

CONCLUSION

This chapter reviewed the complex higher education environment, the ways in which societal conditions affect leadership preparation pipelines and programs, and the competencies and skills required of senior and executive leaders. Student affairs professionals who wish to advance to leadership roles from current positions on college and university campuses can overcome current challenges through intentional planning. To prepare themselves for the requirements of leadership, professionals should obtain a broad spectrum of experience, develop competencies required for distributed leadership, pay attention to necessary tasks such as fundraising and resource management, and be alert and open to possibilities for advancement.

> **QUESTIONS FOR REFLECTION**
>
> ❓ What leadership responsibilities in higher education are you open to pursuing, and what positions do you need to focus on to exercise those responsibilities?
>
> ❓ What is the political climate for upper-level leadership at your institution?
>
> ❓ What competencies and experiences do you need to obtain to align with the requirements of the distributed leadership model?
>
> ❓ Which mentors can help you prepare for leadership advancement, and what do you expect to learn from those relationships?
>
> ❓ What aspects of the trends in higher education leadership do you feel most uncomfortable about, and what can be done to alleviate your fears?

REFERENCES

Acker, D., & Wechsler, H. S. (2006). *Can state universities be managed? A primer for presidents and management teams*. Westport, CT: Praeger.

American Association of Community Colleges. (2005). *Competencies for community college leaders*. Washington, DC: Author.

Bresciani, D. (2014). The future of university leadership starts here. *Leadership Exchange, 12*(3), 24.

Budig, G. A. (2002). *A game of uncommon skill: Leading the modern college and university*. Westport, CT: Oryx Press.

Cohen, A. M., & Kisker, C. B. (2010). *The shaping of American higher education: Emergence and growth of the contemporary system* (2nd ed.). San Francisco, CA: Jossey-Bass.

Cook, B. J. (2012). *The American college president study: Key findings and takeaways, 1–6*. Washington, DC: American Council on Education.

Cook, B., & Kim, Y. (2012). *The American college president 2012*. Washington, DC: American Council on Education.

Cox, K. S., & Salsberry, T. (2012). Motivational factors influencing women's decisions to pursue upper-level administrative positions at land grant institutions. *Advancing Women in Leadership, 32*(1), 1–34.

DiMaggio, P. J., & Powell, W. W. (1983). The iron cage revisited: Institutional isomorphism and collective rationality in organizational fields. *American Sociological Review, 48,* 147–159. doi: 10.2307/2095101

Eckel, P., & Hartley, M. (2011). *Presidential leadership in an age of transition: Dynamic responses for a turbulent time.* Washington, DC: American Council on Education.

Eddy, P., & Rao, M. (2009). Leadership development in higher education programs. *The Community College Enterprise, 15*(2), 7–26.

Fennell, M. L. (1980). The effects of environmental characteristics on the of hospital clusters. *Administrative Science Quarterly, 23,* 484–510. doi: 10.2307/2392265

Freeman, S., & Kochan, F. K. (2012). Academic pathways to university leadership: Presidents' descriptions of their doctoral education. *International Journal of Doctoral Studies, 7*(1), 93–124.

Gasman, M., Abiola, U., & Travers, C. (2015). Diversity and senior leadership at elite institutions of higher education. *Journal of Diversity in Higher Education, 8*(1), 1–14. doi: 10.1037/a0038872

Gunsalus, C. K. (2006). *The college administrator's survival guide.* Cambridge, MA: Harvard University Press.

Hannum, K. M., Muhly, S. M., Shockley-Zalabek, P. S., & White, J. S. (2014). Women leaders within higher education in the United States: Supports, barriers, and experiences of being a senior leader. *Advancing Women in Leadership, 35,* 65–76.

Hempsall, K. (2014). Developing leadership in higher education: Perspectives from the USA, the UK and Australia. *Journal of Higher Education Policy and Management, 36*(4), 383–394. doi: 10.1080/1360080X.2014.916468

Hendrickson, R. M., Lane, J. E., Harris, J. T., & Dorman, R. H. (2013). *Academic leadership and governance of higher education.* Sterling, VA: Stylus.

Jones, S., Lefore, G., Harvey, M., & Ryland, K. (2012). Distributed leadership: A collaborative framework for academics, executives and professionals in higher education. *Journal of Higher Education Policy and Management, 34*(1), 67–78. doi: 10.1080/1360080X.2012.642334

Kuk, L., King, M., & Forrest, C. (2012). The lived transitions of senior student affairs leadership. *Journal of Student Affairs Research and Practice, 49*(2), 175–191.

McDade, S. A., Dowdall, J. A., Marchese, T. J., & Polonio, N. A. (2009). Preparing leaders for colleges and universities: The view from search firms. *Change: The Magazine of Higher Learning, 41*(5), 46–53. doi: 10.3200/CHNG.41.5.46-54

McKenna, L. (2015, December). Why are fewer college presidents academics? *The Atlantic.* Retrieved from http://www.theatlantic.com/education/archive/2015/12/college-president-mizzou-tim-wolfe/418599

McNair, D. E. (2015). Deliberate disequilibrium: Preparing for a community college presidency. *Community College Review, 43*(1), 72–88. doi: 10.1177/0091552114554831

Mendan, L. (2010). *The marketplace of ideas: Reform and resistance in the American university.* New York, NY: W. W. Norton.

Meyer, J. W. (1979). *The impact of the centralization of educational funding and control on state and local organizational governance* (Program Report No. 79–120). Stanford, CA: Stanford University Institute for Research on Educational Finance and Governance.

Rosser, V. J. (2004). A national study on midlevel leaders in higher education: The unsung professionals in the academy. *Higher Education, 48,* 317–337. doi: 10.1023/B:HIGH.00000 35543.58672.52

Schexnider, A. J. (2008). Executive leadership: Securing the future of black colleges and universities. *International Journal of Organization Theory and Behavior, 11*(4), 496–517.

Shaw, K. A. (1999). *The successful president: "Buzzwords" on leadership.* Phoenix, AZ: Oryx Press.

Shaw, K. A. (2005). *The intentional leader.* Syracuse, NY: Syracuse University Press.

14

THE KEEPERS OF THE PROFESSION

Donald D. Gehring

THE PURPOSE OF this chapter is to encourage student affairs professionals to fulfill their responsibility to maintain and *grow* the student affairs and higher education professions, whose mission is to help students learn and develop. Like those in ancient clans who were keepers of the flame, student affairs practitioners are the keepers of the profession. In his book *Russell Rules*, basketball player Bill Russell (2002) referred to a sign in his locker room that said, "If you have to play the game, you might as well play to win." As engaged professionals, student affairs practitioners have the opportunity to accomplish extraordinary things in and for the profession and the organizations with which they work.

This chapter will review how to accomplish extraordinary things through:

- using the five commitments of leadership as a guide,
- conducting research and publishing findings,
- presenting sessions at conferences,

This chapter is a modification and expansion of Donald Gehring's address at the 2015 Southern Association for College Student Affairs (SACSA) conference in Greenville, South Carolina, on the responsibilities of higher education administrators to grow the profession.

- mentoring other professionals, and
- inspiring a team.

A CHANGING PROFESSION

In day-to-day work life, student affairs professionals tend to focus on the immediate, but they should also think of the long term. New professionals or middle managers will likely spend the next 30 to 35 years in higher education. The future is uncertain, and it is not necessary to have all the answers; but it is necessary to learn to live with the questions. Student affairs professionals should ask themselves questions such as, What challenges will I face in those years? What new edicts will the courts produce that will affect my work? What new regulations will the Department of Education issue that will affect my work? What will new students be like in the next 30 years? What new theories will evolve, and how will they change the way I work with students? How will my professional associations respond to these challenges? The point is this: student affairs professionals should think strategically.

During my 39 years in higher education, I lived with many questions, such as:

- When would students' due process and First Amendment rights finally evolve?
- What were the implications of the Civil Rights Act of 1964?
- Would the Higher Education Act of 1965 mean more than money?
- How would we implement Title IX in 1972? (We still had curfew for women at the little Baptist College where I was the dean of students.)
- Did we really have to reconfigure all of our buildings to comply with the Rehabilitation Act of 1973? How could we afford it?

- Did the Family Educational Rights and Privacy Act (FERPA) in 1974 really mean we could not send grades home or send copies of disciplinary letters to parents?
- What were the implications of the Civil Rights Restoration Act of 1987?
- How were we going to notify every student of student rights under the Drug Free Schools and Communities Act of 1989?
- Who was going to collect the information required by the Campus Security Act of 1990, and how were we going to provide that information to students?

The Sexual Assault Victims Bill of Rights of 1992 made the previous questions even more complex, and a series of Amendments to the Higher Education Act of 1965 raised many more.

Today, we have all these legal issues and the Dear Colleague letters explaining expectations for implementing federal policies, and as if that were not complex enough, the federal government continues to issue more than 3,000 regulations a year (Levin, 2013). In March 2013, Congress passed the Violence Against Women Act (VAWA) and made several changes to the Annual Security Reports and the Clery Act, including additional crime statistics, two new categories of hate crimes, a refined definition of "Timely Warnings," additional program requirements and policy statements, and specific elements for the student conduct process. Congress has also considered legislation requiring a Clery Act coordinator, increased fines for violations, and a plethora of other requirements, and it is considering a Concealed Carry on Campus Act, a Campus Safety Act, and the Taylor Clemente Higher Education Act, recognizing cyber bullying or harassment. Try to imagine how many regulations these laws will spawn.

The future of higher education and of student affairs—in an environment in which legislation proliferates and the accelerating rate of change is forcing everyone to become "frantic learners" (De Pree, 2008, p. 66)—is at best uncertain. The amount of leadership needed is in direct proportion to that uncertainty (De Pree, 2008).

FIVE COMMITMENTS OF LEADERSHIP

Kouzes and Posner (2012) developed five commitments of leadership. These commitments form the basis of our work in higher education and can guide those who wish to exercise leadership to advance the field and the profession.

- The first commitment, *model the way*, encourages leaders to establish expectations of others and then to live up to those standards in their own behavior.
- The second commitment, *inspire a shared vision*, promotes the art of persuasion to motivate others toward accomplishments.
- The third commitment, *challenge the process*, inspires leaders to look for ways to innovate, take risks, and engender change in organizations.
- The fourth commitment, *enable others to act*, emphasizes teaching the skills necessary to accomplish tasks and encouraging everyone to work together toward goals.
- The final commitment, *encourage the heart*, reminds leaders that individuals need support, guidance, recognition, care, and kindness in order to accomplish great things.

HOW TO ACCOMPLISH EXTRAORDINARY THINGS

After I spoke to a group of student affairs practitioners on one occasion about professionalism, several members of the audience asked, "How am I supposed to read journal articles, take part in professional organizations, and contribute to the research while doing my job and taking care of my family and myself?" I responded by saying, "Yes, you do need to take of yourself and your family, and that alone is not easy, but if you're not consistently reading the latest research, developing the profession, and contributing to the literature, maybe you need to be in another profession." There are many ways in which to contribute to the student affairs profession, including conducting research, writing, volunteering for jobs in professional organizations, and mentoring others to fulfill the responsibilities of the profession.

Conduct Research

As a young professional, I thought that I could never contribute to the profession—that was for the older men and women who were more experienced and knowledgeable. I was wrong! We all exist in a state of relative ignorance. Others know things I do not know, and I know things they do not know. We can all learn from each other. One of the best ways to contribute to the knowledge base of the profession is to conduct research and publish it for others to critique.

Student affairs professionals most likely had a research or assessment class in their graduate preparation programs, so they know *how* to conduct research. The question is *what* to research. One of my professors once told me, "Research informs practice, but practice informs research." He meant that what a student affairs professional does in his or her administrative position should spark ideas and questions to ask. An example from my own experience may illustrate this point.

As a supervisor of men's housing at Emory University, I was tired of having to resolve roommate conflicts. The question occurred to me, "Why don't these roommates get along?" Were there factors they could be matched on that would make them more compatible? I was the person who assigned roommates, so I decided to try an experiment. I matched one group of roommates on five factors discovered in the literature (Gehring, 1970). Previous studies showed that roommates who were compatible had one or more of these factors in common, but the research did not show whether roommates assigned on these factors would be compatible. I set out to match one group of roommates on the five factors and another group on a random basis to see if there would be any significant differences in the two groups. As it turned out, there were no significant differences between the matched groups and the random groups in the number of roommate problems. Whether there were roommate problems was simply a matter of chance. My practice informed the research, and the research informed my practice. From then on, I assigned students on a random basis and began to think of other ways to help students solve their roommate conflicts.

The literature is also full of researchable ideas. Practitioners should be reading professional journals and publications regularly and with pencil in hand. In reading, thoughts will occur to practitioners such as, "I wonder if . . ." or "What if I were to do it this way?" Practitioners should jot down questions for later reference. When an epiphany occurs, practitioners should see if they can engage a colleague to discuss the idea. Good colleagues will ask questions that will help practitioners refine their ideas. Some colleagues may even want to work on the project. Including others who have more experience or who can help in planning is never a bad idea.

Whatever practitioners decide to research, they should be sure they can access the data necessary to conduct the study and obtain the appropriate approval from an Institutional Review Board (IRB). IRBs ensure that research is ethically conducted and that proper protections are in place for the researchers and the research subjects. While IRBs are sometimes viewed as a hassle and a lot of red tape, they are there to guide professionals in conducting quality research.

Publish

Practitioners should submit their research to professional journals. At one end of the spectrum, there are peer-reviewed journals. Editors of these journals receive the manuscript and then send it out to reviewers in a blind review process. In a single blind review, the names of the reviewers are kept from the author. In a double blind review, which is more common among research journals, neither do the reviewers know the identity of the author, nor does the author know the identity of the reviewers. These journals tend to be a little more selective and may have a low acceptance rate. Other journals without a blind review process rely on the discretion of the editor or invite authors to write.

Regardless of the type of publication, once an article is submitted, the editor will have it reviewed and return it to the author with comments or criticisms. The editor may decline the article outright; however, the editor usually gives critical feedback that helps an author revise the manuscript. Editors seldom accept first drafts as is for publication, even those written by the most experienced researchers and writers in the field.

Receiving criticism is a difficult part of the process, and authors need a thick skin to accept the editor's suggestions. Although it can be difficult to hear any criticism, authors should not be discouraged. Authors must remember that the editor is trying to help them. They should take the criticism and revise the piece. In some instances, the editor will respond with very specific feedback and instructions to "revise and resubmit" the article. These are often referred to as "R&Rs" among faculty and are highly sought after. Although there is still no guarantee the editor will publish the piece, it is presumed that if the author makes the suggested revisions, the piece will be suitable for publication. If an article is rejected, the author may wish to make changes and submit the piece to another publication. It is good for authors to become accustomed to criticism, as it serves to improve their writing and increases their chances of receiving R&Rs.

Present at Conferences

Practitioners who do not wish to submit their research to professional journals can share their findings with others in the profession by presenting at conferences. To begin the process, practitioners should create a proposal, which is a brief description of the presentation. The proposal should focus on the data that will be shared, learning outcomes for participants, and any existing scholarly literature that informs the topic. Guidelines and instructions for writing a successful proposal are posted by most national organizations, and following these can be very helpful. Practitioners can gain an informed perspective on what makes proposals stand out from others by volunteering to become a reviewer of conference proposals. Associations often have calls for programs/proposals far in advance of the conference, and proposals are usually submitted anywhere from 3 to 9 months ahead of the conference.

Presentation formats can vary. They are usually short breakout sessions of approximately 50 to 60 minutes, but they can be longer, such as preconference workshops lasting several hours. There are also more research-based formats available, such as poster sessions and paper presentations.

In a poster session, research project details are displayed during the conference on large professional posters like those displayed in grade school science fairs, but they are much better posters! There are usually one or two formally scheduled opportunities during the conference for presenters to stand by their posters and answer questions from attendees.

Paper presentations usually involve presenting a research paper during a shared session with other paper presenters. For instance, in a 1-hour conference session, there may be three research papers being presented, and each presentation lasts 15 minutes. A discussant, usually an advanced professional or faculty member, facilitates the session and provides feedback on each research paper. The goal is to share the most important aspects of the research, observe reactions to the findings, and receive critique for the purposes of improvement.

The type of conference a practitioner selects to share his or her research at matters as well. On the national level, associations such as NASPA–Student Affairs Administration in Higher Education and ACPA–College Student Educators International tend to focus on traditional 1-hour sessions, preconference workshops, and paper presentations. Paper and poster formats are often the methods used by other associations such as the Association for the Study of Higher Education and the American Educational Research Association. There is often significant competition for all formats at these national conferences, so practitioners would be wise to check out regional and state associations as well. The conferences for these organizations are smaller and may focus on one or two types of presentation formats, and the competition is not as heavy for many of them, so it is easier for presenters to have their proposals accepted and share their research with a more intimate audience.

The format in which presenters share their research does not matter as much as finding a way to share it. A regional housing conference accepted my roommate study as a presentation, and the questions attendees asked after the conclusion of the presentation helped me refine the presentation for submission to a journal. The editor then suggested changes, and after making those, my article was accepted for publication (Gehring, 1970). I still have the postcard informing me that the article had been accepted! Once the first hurdle is cleared, practitioners will have the confidence to try again.

Serve the Profession

Another way to contribute to the profession is through service, which might involve helping others in large or small ways. Practitioners can seek out opportunities to serve by talking to association leaders, committee chairs, and conference chairs. Associations are always looking for help, so practitioners should not turn down any chance to serve, no matter how minor. In order to serve effectively, practitioners should be mindful to meet deadlines and use resources wisely and conservatively. Practitioners should look for ways to improve their little corner of the organization or the organization as a whole. Good work will be recognized, and additional opportunities will open up for dedicated volunteers to advance their careers and the profession.

Some people serve by challenging the status quo for the sake of needed reform. Kouzes and Posner (2012) explained that people do their best when they have an opportunity to change the way things are. That can mean doing things differently or doing some things that have never been done before. As Ralph Waldo Emerson said, "Do not go where the path may lead; go instead where there is no path and leave a trail" (Graham, 2014, p. 7). However, practitioners need to understand that challenging the status quo is risky, and there will always be those in every organization who want to throw cold water on any new idea. This should not deter practitioners from challenging the status quo. Practitioners should be ready to address concerns, for there is no question that institutions and professional associations can do many things differently or do things they have never done before. For example, years ago, Commission XV in ACPA was charged with supporting the field of judicial affairs, but I did not think it was providing enough support for student conduct administrators given the changing environment of laws and federal regulations. As a result, I challenged the process and took the risk of creating a new organization devoted entirely to student conduct. The naysayers claimed that we did not need another major national organization and that existing associations were meeting those needs. I did not let them stop me; I continued to challenge the process.

The Association for Student Conduct Administrators (ASCA) now has more than 1,700 members at more than 850 colleges and universities and is the leading organization in student conduct administration.

Practitioners who challenge the process will go far by enlisting others to help. Kouzes and Posner (2012) explained that one enlists others by inspiring a shared vision. People follow those who know where they are going. Student affairs leaders need to have a vision of where an organization is going, whether serving as a member of a committee, chairing a committee, or sitting on the board. Leaders should ask themselves questions such as, What am I trying to accomplish? What are the steps along the way? How will what I am doing be different from what everyone else is doing? Developing a clear plan can help leaders inspire others to support the idea and become involved in the process.

No matter how a student affairs practitioner serves, if the practitioner wishes to exercise leadership and accomplish extraordinary things for the profession, he or she must foster collaboration and strengthen others; in this way, everyone wins (Kouzes & Posner, 2012). This philosophy guided former Los Angeles Lakers basketball coach Phil Jackson (1995), who said that the Hopi expression "You cannot lift a pebble with one finger" was part of a winning strategy. The team members knew it took cooperation to accomplish their goals. This idea is also expressed in Rudyard Kipling's (1895) poem "The Law of the Jungle":

> Now this is the Law of the Jungle—as old and as true as the sky;
> And the Wolf that shall keep it may prosper, but the Wolf that shall break it must die.
> As the creeper that girdles the tree-trunk, the Law runneth forward and back—
> For the strength of the Pack is the Wolf, and the strength of the Wolf is the Pack. (Stanzas 1–2)

Student affairs leaders must give their groups or committees the power to accomplish goals, and this is risky, as leaders have to give up some of their own power and share it with others. But by sharing power, leaders model the way for those who aspire to leadership (Kouzes & Posner, 2012). This behavior influences everyone who observes a leader's performance. Leaders also influence others with their attitude. By exuding an enthusiastic and optimistic attitude, leaders can positively affect others around them.

Time is the one commodity none of us can create or replenish. How practitioners spend their time sends a clear message of what they value and think is important. There are many ways to engage in the profession, such as by attending professional conferences or staying abreast of current higher education administration research and case law. The 11th century Persian poet Omar Khayyam warned, "The Moving Finger writes: and having writ, moves on: nor all thy piety nor wit shall lure it back to cancel half a line nor all thy tears wash out a word of it" (Fitzgerald, 1992, p. 25). Practitioners should think carefully and be intentional about how they spend their time. Students and colleagues notice these things and will copy professional behavior in ways that practitioners cannot even imagine.

Mentoring is another activity through which practitioners can help to advance the profession. Practitioners may be thinking to themselves, "I can't mentor someone. I don't have enough experience. I am still depending on someone to mentor me." It is easy for practitioners to think they do not have enough experience or know enough, but the truth is that each individual has something to contribute to others. Practitioners can model the behavior of their own mentors in order to help rising professionals. For example, a practitioner may follow in his or her mentor's footsteps by critiquing a newer staff member's presentation or introducing the staff member to another professional. (See Chapter 4 for more guidance on mentoring).

Regardless of how practitioners serve the profession, they should be sure to heed Kouzes and Posner's (2012) advice about planning and ensuring the success of small efforts. Practitioners who are realistic and take small steps will be successful. Success gives organizations and individuals pride in accomplishments and the courage to take the next step.

Kouzes and Posner's (2012) last commitment for those who want to accomplish extraordinary things in organizations is to encourage the heart. Student affairs practitioners should recognize contributions and celebrate accomplishments. There is a basic psychological principle in this practice. People tend to repeat behavior that is rewarded. Practitioners should always keep in mind that praise and expressions of thanks are significant forms of reward. Robert Townsend (1971), former president of Avis Car Rental, authored the book *Up the Organization*. The chapter on "Thanks" consisted of just one very short sentence—"A word too seldom used." Gratitude does not cost anything, and yet it is greatly appreciated. Celebrations create positive interactions and provide concrete evidence that people genuinely care about each other—after all, they invested time in the celebration.

CONCLUSION

Higher education has faced many challenges, and there are even more on the horizon. The field of student affairs needs dedicated practitioners to be the keepers of the profession—to provide leadership, inspiration, research, solutions to challenges, and individual and group contributions. As practitioners persevere and contemplate how to give back, they should keep in mind this story of an old, holy hermit who lived in the forest:

Two boys were endeavoring to play a joke on a hermit. One intended to hold a bird in his hand behind his back and ask the hermit if the bird was dead or alive. If the hermit said the bird was dead, the boy intended to open his hand and let the bird fly up to the sky. If the hermit said it was alive, the boy planned to crush the bird in his hand to prove that the wise old man was wrong. "Father," said one of the lads, "I have a small bird in my hand. Is it alive or dead?" There was silence. The old man noticed a feather floating down behind the youngster's back. He fixed the boy with a gaze. Eventually, he chuckled and said: "Well, boys, it all depends on you!"

To the keepers of the profession, I ask: How will the student affairs profession develop? My answer: "It all depends on you."

REFERENCES

De Pree, M. (2008). *Leadership jazz: The essential elements of a great leader.* New York, NY: Crown Business.
Fitzgerald, E. (1992). *Rubaiyat of Omar Khayyam.* Boston, MA: Branden Publishing.
Gehring, D. D. (1970). Prediction of roommate compatibility. *Journal of College Student Personnel, 11*(1), 58–61.
Graham, D. (2014). *The very best of Ralph Waldo Emerson.* United States of America: Createspace.
Jackson, P. (1995). *Sacred hoops: Spiritual lessons from a hardwood warrior.* New York, NY: Hachette Books.
Kipling, R. (1895). *The second jungle book.* London, UK: Macmillan.
Kouzes, J. M., & Posner, B. Z. (2012). *The leadership challenge: How to make extraordinary things happen in organizations* (5th ed.). San Francisco, CA: Jossey-Bass.
Levin, M. R. (2013). *The liberty amendments: Restoring the American republic.* New York, NY: Threshold Editions.
Russell, B. (2002). *Russell rules: 11 lessons on leadership from the twentieth century's greatest winner.* New York, NY: NAL Trade.
Townsend, R. (1971). *Up the organization: How to stop the corporation from stifling people and strangling profits.* New York, NY: Fawcett.

THE AUTHORS

Kevin W. Bailey, PhD, is vice president of student affairs at the University of West Florida. In 25 years of experience in higher education, he has served the profession in a variety of state, regional, and national organizations and has contributed book chapters on topics such as African American men, campus crisis management, and professional development for new student affairs educators.

Mimi Benjamin, PhD, is an assistant professor in the Student Affairs in Higher Education Department at Indiana University of Pennsylvania. Before joining the faculty, she held positions in residence life and academic services and served as assistant to the vice president of student affairs and interim dean of students. She earned her doctorate from Iowa State University in educational leadership and policy studies with a focus on higher education.

Dean Bresciani, PhD, is president of North Dakota State University. Before assuming that position, he served as both vice president for student affairs and as an adjunct full professor in educational administration at Texas A&M University. He held similar positions at the University of North Carolina at Chapel Hill and North Carolina State University. He has a doctorate in higher education finance with a doctoral minor in economics from the University of Arizona, a master's in college student personnel from Bowling Green State University, and a bachelor's in sociology from Humboldt State University.

Lesley-Ann Brown-Henderson, PhD, is the executive director of the Department of Campus Inclusion and Community at Northwestern University. In this role, she oversees three units: multicultural student affairs, student enrichment services, and social justice education. Prior to arriving at Northwestern, she worked in the counseling center at Michigan State University and in the Department of Multicultural Services at Texas A&M University. She has also been heavily involved with NASPA, working with The Placement Exchange and the NASPA Undergraduate Fellows Program.

Shelia Higgs Burkhalter, MBA, is vice president for student affairs at the University of Baltimore. In more than 20 years of experience in higher education, she has served as the chair of The Placement Exchange, the NASPA Undergraduate Fellows Program, and the Alice Manicur Symposium for Women Aspiring to Become VPSAs. She earned an MBA in management from the University of Arkansas at Fayetteville along with a master's in higher education and student affairs from Indiana University–Bloomington.

Rebecca McBride Bustamante, PhD, is an associate professor of educational leadership at Sam Houston State University, where she teaches courses in leadership, organizational behavior, and research methods. She has extensive administrative experience in higher education, both in the United States and in Latin America. Her research interests center on assessing organizational culture and developing culturally responsive leaders.

Mikia Carter, MEd, is an experiential learning coordinator at the University of West Florida. She received her bachelor's degree in graphic design with a minor in public relations at the University of Montevallo and her master's degree in college student affairs administration from the University of West Florida. Her research interests include mentorship, leadership, and first-generation college students. She previously served as a NASPA Graduate Associate Program member.

Peggy A. Crowe, PhD, is director of the Counseling and Testing Center at Western Kentucky University. She earned a BS in sociology from the University of Wisconsin–Stevens Point, an MAE in higher education in student affairs at Western Kentucky University, and a PhD in higher education administration from Bowling Green State University. She is an active member in professional and service organizations such as NASPA Region III; the Southern Association for College Student Affairs; Delta Sigma Theta Sorority, Inc., Bowling Green Alumnae Chapter; and the Association for University and College Counseling Center Directors.

Donald D. Gehring, EdD, is professor emeritus and past director of the Higher Education Administration Doctoral Program at Bowling Green State University. In 1988, he founded the Association for Student Judicial Affairs and served as its first president. In honor of his expertise and service, the association renamed its judicial training seminar as the Donald D. Gehring Academy. He serves as a consultant for higher education issues and was recognized by NASPA as a Pillar of the Profession.

Peggy C. Holzweiss, PhD, is an assistant professor in higher education administration at Sam Houston State University, where she teaches courses across the curriculum, including courses in resource management, assessment, research, and advising. She has administrative experience in higher education for areas such as academic programs, student life assessment, and student organization advising.

Her research interests are broadly focused on professional development in higher education, distance education student needs, teaching, and learning.

Merna Jacobsen, PhD, is director of organizational and employee development at the University of Colorado at Boulder. She has worked in the field of conflict resolution for more than 25 years and is a certified mediator. In addition to conducting mediations, she instructs others in mediation, facilitation, and conflict resolution. She conducts research and is published in the field of crisis leadership in higher education.

John Wesley Lowery, PhD, is a professor and department chair in the Student Affairs in Higher Education Department at Indiana University of Pennsylvania. He previously held administrative roles in residence life and student conduct. He earned his doctorate at Bowling Green State University in higher education administration. He has served as a faculty member and coordinated graduate programs at Oklahoma State University and the University of South Carolina.

Amelia Noël-Elkins, PhD, is the director of University College at Illinois State University. She previously served as an associate athletics director and academic advisor at Indiana University Bloomington. She holds a bachelor's degree from Harvard and Radcliffe Colleges with a concentration in history. She holds a master's degree in college student personnel administration and a doctoral degree in educational policy from Indiana University Bloomington.

David W. Parrott, EdD, is vice president for student affairs at the University of Florida. In his 35 years of working in higher education, he has worked in or supervised almost every area of student affairs, including residence life, student discipline, veterans' services, student health services, and counseling services. He has served as president for the Association for Student Conduct Administrators (ASCA) and as the chair for the ASCA Foundation. He has also served as an adjunct professor at Western Kentucky University, Western Michigan University, and Texas A&M University, teaching higher education law.

Kelli Peck Parrott, PhD, is a clinical professor at the University of Florida in the Student Personnel in Higher Education and Higher Education Administration Programs. She began her career in student affairs in 1992, working in a variety of areas, including residence life, student conduct, student disability services, and student activities. Since 2000, she has served as a faculty member at Western Michigan University, Grand Valley State University, and directed the master's program at Texas A&M University for 15 years.

William Smedick, EdD, is a full-time senior lecturer in the Center for Leadership Education in the Whiting School of Engineering at Johns Hopkins University. His previous positions at Johns Hopkins University include director of leadership programs and assessment, and director of student activities/union. He is a former chair of the board of directors for the National Association for Campus Activities and has served that association for many years in a variety of leadership and programmatic positions.

INDEX

Figures are indicated by "f" following the page number.

A

Abiola, U., 299–300
Academic360.com, 209
Academic affairs
   academic advising, 250, 268
   adjunct faculty positions and, 254
   culture of, 33
   international job opportunities and, 217
   student affairs merging with, 8–9
Acceptance of employment, xi, 225–243
   culture of institutions and, 232–235
   decline of other offers, 230–232
   negotiations and, 226–232
   response time, 226
   supervisors and, 239–241
   transitions, planning for, 235–241
Accountability, 19–20, 267–268, 293
Accountability partners, 186–187, 238
Accreditation organizations, 20, 248
ACE (American Council on Education), 5–6
ACES (Association for Counselor Education and Accreditation), 247
ACPA. *See* American College Personnel Association
Adjunct faculty positions, 250, 253–254
Adjustment to new institutions, 228, 235–241
Administrative assistants, 99–101
Administrators. *See also* Executive leadership positions
   adjunct faculty positions and, 253–254
   faculty, collaboration with, 261–262
   professionalism and, 46–47
   salaries of, 3
   subculture and, 33
   tenure-track faculty transition and, 255–261
Advanced degrees
   challenges of, 186–187
   characteristics of, 249–250, 249f
   history of, 246–248
   for leadership positions, 303
   organizations and guidelines for, 246–248
   process for obtaining, 184–186
   student diversity and, 299
   timing of, 182–183
   types of, 181–182
ADVANCE Working Group Dual-Career Studies, 214
Advisors, 250, 267–268
AERA (American Educational Research Association), 258–259
Age. *See* Generational differences
Age Discrimination in Employment Act, 285–286
Airport interviews, 212
Alcohol, 213
All-but-dissertation (ABD) status, 184

333

Allen, W., 234–235
Alternative dispute resolution, 126
American Arbitration Association, 134
American College Personnel
   Association (ACPA)
   Commission on Professional
      Preparation, 258
   competencies for professionals,
      47–48, 143, 167, 174, 236
   conference presentation
      opportunities and, 259, 321
   education guidelines, 246–247
   history of, 5
   *Professional Competency Areas for
   Student Affairs Educators*, 12, 52
American College President
   Study of ACE, 6
American Council on
   Education (ACE), 5–6
American Educational Research
   Association (AERA), 258–259, 321
American Personnel and Guidance
   Association (APGA), 246–247
Americans with Disabilities
   Act (1990), 285–286
Anarchical institutions, 30,
   94–96, 233
Anderson, M. L., 196
Anthropological approach to
   culture, 26–27, 30
Appraisal. *See* Feedback
Arbitration, 126, 132
Arminio, J., 273, 275
Artifacts in organizational culture,
   28–29, 29f, 35, 37
Assessments for campus
   climate, 233–235, 241
Association for Conflict Resolution, 134
Association for Counselor Education
   and Accreditation (ACES), 247
Association for Student Conduct
   Administrators (ASCA), 322–323
Association for the Study of Higher
   Education (ASHE), 258, 259, 321
Attendance records, 283
Attire, professional, 213, 274
Attrition rates, 293–294
Authoritarian supervision, 270–271
Azakasi, S. J., 119

B

Baby boomer generation, 81–83,
   274, 276–277, 279
Background searches, 210
Bagunu, G. A., 71
Bailey, Kevin W., 67
Balancing work and life. *See*
   Work–life balance
Baltimore, Maryland, 214–215
Baxter Magolda, M. B., 149,
   152, 169–171, 236
Bazron, B. J., 34
Beer, L. E., 187, 189
Behavior. *See also* Etiquette
   best practices and, 284
   codes of conduct, 144–146.
      See also Ethics
   conflict management,
      skills for, 135–136
   conflict resolution and, 128
   culture and, 27, 37–38, 59–60
   happenstance learning theory and, 16
   modeling, 135, 189–190,
      275, 289, 316, 324
   politics of institutions and, 110–111
   professional, 45–65. *See
      also* Professionalism
   relationship conflicts and, 121–122
   of supervisors, inappropriate, 155–157
   for support networks, 69–70
   workaholic, 172–173
Behavioral interview questions, 211
Benefits, 11–12
Benjamin, Mimi, 245, 256, 260
Bensimon, E. M., 35–36
Bentley University, 274
Bess, J. L., 34
Best practices, 284. *See also*
   Professional standards
Biddix, J. P., 175–176, 179, 181
Birnbaum, Robert, 30, 94, 233
Blimling, G. S., 148
Body language, 83
Boettcher, M., 256

Bolman, L. G., 27
Bona fide occupational qualification (BFOQ), 285
Bonner, D., 280
Boredom, 180–181
Boulding, K., 119
Boundaries, 59–60
Brack, J., 82
Branham, L., 38
Bresciani, Dean, 293
Brown-Henderson, Lesley-Ann, 195
Budget cuts at institutions, 11, 15, 20–21
Bureaucratic institutions, 30, 94–95, 233
Burkard, A., 52
Burkhalter, Shelia Higgs, 195
Burnout, 173, 180, 308
Business cards, 72
Business leaders, 6–8, 296
Bustamante, Rebecca McBride, 25, 34–36

C

CACREP (Council for Accreditation of Counseling and Related Educational Programs), 247–248
CAHEP (Council for the Advancement of Higher Education Programs), 248
Cameron, K. S., 234
Campbell, S., 276
Campus experts, 61
Campus interviews, 212–213
Campus security, 315
Candidate pools for leadership positions, 298–300
Cardon, P. W., 72
Career paths. *See also* Faculty positions; Job searches
 advanced degrees and, 181–187
 gender and, 279
 lateral moves and, 201–202, 278
 leadership positions and, 179, 297, 302–307
 mentors and, 76, 78–79
 natural transitions in, 178–181
 nontraditional, 18–20
 personal priorities and, 16–17
 politics of institutions and, 106
 staff development and, 277–279
 supervisors and, 87–88, 241
 types, 17–18
Carnaghi, J. E., 235
Carpenter, D. S., 63–64
Carter, Mikia, 67
CAS. *See* Council for the Advancement of Standards in Higher Education
Cawthon, T. W., 260, 262
Cell phones, 277, 293
Chain of command, 61. *See also* Organizational hierarchy
Challenges, ethical, 146–148, 152–157. *See also* Ethics
Change leadership, 41
Characterizations, 123
Chernow, E., 178, 276
Child care, 279
The Chronicle of Higher Education, 176, 204, 215
Circle of conflict model (Moore), 121–122, 127, 130–131
Civil Rights Act (1964), 285–286
Clark University, 246
Clayton-Pederson, A., 234–235
Climate, organizational, 28, 35
Clinical faculty, 257
Coaches, 82–83
Cobb, B., 142
Codes of conduct, 144–146. *See also* Ethics
Cognitive–epistemological domain of development, 236
Cognitive skills for conflict management, 134
Cohen, M., 30
Cole, D. C., 52
Collaboration. *See also* Meetings
 accountability partners and, 186–187, 238
 with campus experts, 61
 conflict resolution and, 126
 with faculty, 33, 261
 in job searches, 213–215
 leadership skills and, 300–301, 323–324
 as marketable job skill, 203
 mentors and, 79

networks and, 178
politics of institutions and, 98, 100, 104–105, 112
in research, 214, 259, 318
self-authorship and, 170
Colleagues. *See also* Staff; Support networks
cuts in employment of, 4, 8–9, 11
ethical decision-making with, 153–155
international employment and, 218
professional development and, 15–16
relationships with, 58–60, 62, 180, 290
research partnerships with, 259, 318
search firms, nominations for, 210
subcultures of, 32–34
transitions to new jobs and, 236, 241
College committees, 252
Colleges. *See* Institutions
Collegial institutions, 30, 94–95, 233
Collins, D., 187
Colonial colleges, 4
Columbia University, 246
Communication. *See also* Face-to-face communication; Meetings; Technology
campus culture and, 40
chain of command and, 61
for conflict resolution, 132, 136
conversation skills, 70, 84–85
cultural differences and, 59–60
to decline job offers, 231–232
documentation of, 283–284
generational differences in, 72, 82, 276–277
listening skills and, 113, 273
nonverbal, 83
during off-work hours, 188–189
professionalism in, 54–58
with stakeholders, 107–110
supervisor–employee relationships and, 40, 61–62, 219, 239, 276, 286–287
Communities of practice model (Wenger), 48–52
Community colleges, 14. *See also* Institutions
Community connections, 69, 189, 228
Companionable supervision, 270–271

Competencies
in conflict resolution, 132–134
cultural, 34–39
in ethics, 142–143, 158–160
for executive leadership positions, 175–176, 301–305
gaps in, 12–13
job searches and, 202
politics of institutions and, 107–110
professional, 12–13, 63, 143, 167, 174, 236
professional development and, 16
professionalism and, 47–48, 50–52
self-assessment for, 143, 174, 236
for supervisors, 284–286
in technology, 7, 12
transitions to new jobs and, 236
Competition
for conference presentation opportunities, 321
conflict resolution and, 119–120, 126
for faculty positions, 253
leadership positions and, 297–298
politics of institutions and, 98, 104–105
for students, 8
Compliance-based groups, 20
Conferences
current practices and, 49, 261
ethics competencies and, 160
faculty experience, researching, 258
job searches and, 216
for placement, 207–208
presentation opportunities at, 259, 278, 320–321
professional development opportunities, 15, 176
search firms attending, 209
support networks and, 87
Confidants, 153–156
Confidentiality, 83, 154–156, 206. *See also* Privacy
Conflict analysis skills, 132–133
Conflict management, 119
Conflict resolution, x, 117–139
application of, 124–127
competencies for, 132–134

INDEX **337**

culture and, 117–118
defined, 119
examples, 127–131
politics of institutions
  and, 93, 104–107
supervisors and, 134–136
theories and models of, 120–124
Conflict Resolution Toolkit (Furlong), 121
Connectors, 67, 99–101
Consistency, supervisor
  relationships and, 275–276
Constantine, M. G., 34
Constructive conflict, 124–125
Consulting careers, 19–20
Continuing education. *See*
  Professional development
Conversation skills, 70, 84–85
Cooper, D., 276
Cooperation, conflict and, 120
Corporate culture, 29–30
Co-teaching classes, 259
Cotton, J. L., 86
Council for Accreditation of Counseling
  and Related Educational Programs
  (CACREP), 247–248
Council for the Advancement of Higher
  Education Programs (CAHEP), 248
Council for the Advancement
  of Standards in Higher
  Education (CAS), 46–47,
  144, 174, 202, 247–248
Council of Student Personnel
  Associations in Higher Education
  (COSPA), 246–247
Counseling
  academic, 250, 267–268
  graduate programs and, 247–249, 249*f*
  mentors and, 84
  supervision and, 267–268
Cover letters, 202, 207, 216
Creamer, D. G., 272–273, 275, 276
Credibility, 112, 123, 259, 303
Credit checks, 210
Crenshaw, K., 27
Crime, 315
Crises, 62, 68
Criticism. *See* Feedback

Cross, T. L., 34
Cross-functional collaborative
  teams, 300–301
Crowe, Peggy A., 225
CSPTalk listserv, 258
Cultural wealth model, 197
Culture. *See also* Culture of institutions
  communication styles and
    expectations, 59–60
  conflict resolution and, 117–118
  defined, 26–27, 27*f*
  ethical decisions and, 149–151
  international employment and, 216–218
  organizational, 27–31, 29*f*,
    34–35, 40–41, 96
  problem solving and, 300
Culture audits, 34–39
Culture of institutions, x, 25–44
  assessments and frameworks
    for, 233–235, 241
  classifications of, 94–95, 232–233
  conflict resolution and, 135–136
  cross-functional collaborative
    teams and, 300–301
  cultural competence and audits, 34–39
  culture definition and, 26–27, 27*f*
  ethics and, 145–146, 160
  job searches and, 198
  leadership positions and, 307–308
  negotiations for new jobs and, 226
  organizational culture and, 27–30, 29*f*
  organizational fit and, 260–261
  professional competencies and, 50–51
  subcultures, 27, 31–34, 40
  supervisors and, 39–41, 240
  theories of, 30–31
  training new-hires and, 274–275
Culture reviews, 38–39
Curriculum for graduate
  programs, 247–249

D

Dalton, J. C., 144, 147, 148
Data conflicts, 121–122, 131
Deal, T. E., 27, 28
The Dean of Women (Mathews), 246
Debt, 183

Decision-making processes
  challenges of, 289
  ethics and, 141, 148–157
  politics of institutions and,
    96–101, 106–112
  staff development and, 277–278
  training new-hires and, 274–275
Decline of job offers, 230–232
De Dreu, C., 118, 127
Dee, J. R., 34
Dennis, K. W., 34
Departmental committees, 252, 254
Departmental faculty meetings, 258
Destructive conflict, 124–125
Dilemmas, ethical, 146–148,
  152–157. *See also* Ethics
Disabilities, employment and, 285–286
Disciplinary actions, 171, 282–283
Discrimination, 197, 284–286
Disengagement, 38
Dispute resolution. *See*
  Conflict resolution
Dissertations, 184–186, 260
Diversity
  discrimination and, 284–286
  leadership positions and, 298–300, 306
  mentoring and, 86
  subcultures and, 32–33
Division subcultures, 32
Doctoral degrees. *See* Advanced degrees
Doctoral Universities, 251
Documentation responsibilities
  of supervisors, 283–284
Domains of development
  (Baxter Magolda), 236
Doubt, 172–173
Dougharty, W. H., 233, 235
Dougherty, T. W., 69
Downtime, 189
Dress, professional, 213, 274
Driver's license checks, 210
Dual job searches, 213–215
Due diligence, 282–283
Dulworth, M., 73–74
Duration of job searches, 199

E

Eddy, P. L., 262
Eells, Walter Crosby, 3
Electronic identity, 58. *See
  also* Social media
Elliott, M., 123
E-mail communication, 54–55, 57,
  176, 188–189, 276–277
E-mentoring, 83–84
Emergencies, 62, 68
Emerson, Ralph Waldo, 322
Emotional intelligence, 73–74
Emotions. *See also* Stress
  burnout and, 173, 180
  career transitions and, 180–181
  conflict management and,
    125, 134–135
  ethical decision-making
    and, 152–153, 159
  relationship conflicts and, 121–122
  unemployment and, 204
Employees. *See* Staff
Employers, needs of, 7. *See also*
  Expectations of employers
Employment. *See* Job changes;
  Job searches; *specific types*
Ensher, E. A., 84
Environmental scans, 36–37, 211
Equity scorecards (Bensimon), 35–36
Ethics, x, 141–164
  codes of conduct and, 144–146
  conflict resolution and, 132
  decisions based on, 148–157
  defined, 142
  ethical dilemmas, 146–148, 152–157
  in higher education, 142–143
  job searches and, 205–207
  model for decision-making, 152–157
  modeling behavior for, 275
  nontraditional careers and, 19–20
  principles of, 144
  supervision and, 273
  supervisors and, 157–159
Ethnicity. *See* Diversity
Etiquette
  for communication methods, 54–58

INDEX

for e-mail, 55
in meetings, 53–54
for offices, 60–62
for social media, 55–58
for work relationships, 58–60
Evenings, working, 172–173,
    187–188, 308–309
Exams for advanced degrees, 184
Executive leadership positions,
    xi, 293–312
  adding value to institutions and, 308
  advancement to, 302–307
  attrition rates for, 293–294
  communication preferences for, 61–62
  competencies for, 175–176, 301–305
  complex environments and, 300–301
  cultural models and, 31
  culture of institutions and, 307–308
  decision-making process
    and, 96–99, 151
  experience needed for, 175–176, 179
  higher education trends for, 295–300
  organizational culture and, 29
  organizational fit and, 309
  pipeline and candidate pool
    limitations for, 298–300
  power centers and players, 99–101
  quality-of-life considerations
    and, 308–309
  recruitment for, 6–8, 295–299
  student affairs professionals,
    effect on, 11
Expectations of employers
  culture of institutions and, 38–40
  ethics and, 158
  job terminations and, 282–283
  legal minimums for, 284
  networking and, 68
  new jobs, transition to, 225, 234–239
  office etiquette and, 60–62
  professionalism and, 49, 52–55
  social media use and, 56–58
  supervisors and, 61–63, 190
  for teaching positions, 250–251
  for tenure-track faculty, 256–257
  training for. *See* Training
  work relationships and, 58–60

Experience
  of administrators in teaching
    positions, 256
  for employment, 274
  functional area job changes
    and, 202–203
  with job searches, 199, 220
  lack of, 50–51, 148–149
  leadership positions and,
    175–176, 182–183, 305
  mission and service, 216–217
  professional behavior and, 45–46
  professional development and,
    170, 172, 177, 181
  promotions and, 294
  for supervision, 269
  in teaching, 258–259
Experts on campuses, 61
Eye contact, 59

F

Facebook, 56, 71. *See also* Social media
Face-to-face communication
  generational preferences and, 72, 276
  networking and. *See* Support networks
  professionalism and, 55, 58–60
  with students, 9–10
  supervision and, 277
Faculty development programs, 259
Faculty positions, xi, 245–266
  adjunct, 253–254
  advice regarding, 257–261
  challenges in, 261–263
  preparation programs for,
    181–187, 246–250, 249f
  research responsibilities, 251–252
  roles overview, 252–253
  service responsibilities, 252
  subcultures of, 33–34
  teaching responsibilities, 250–251
  tenure-track, 255–257
  visiting, 255
Family. *See also* Work–life balance
  career advancement and, 279
  dual-career couples, 213–215
  international employment
    and, 218–219

Family Educational Rights and
    Privacy Act (FERPA, 2015), 50
Family leave policies, 188
Favors, 110–111
Federal funding, 128, 285
Federal policies, 50, 314–315,
    322. *See also specific acts*
Feedback
    conflict resolution and, 134
    culture of institutions and, 40–41
    ethical behavior and, 160
    for journal articles, 319
    in meetings, 53
    from mentors, 35
    professionalism and, 51, 62–63
    for publications, 319–321
    from stakeholders, 108
    from supervisors, 63, 180,
        190, 240, 280–284
Field observations, 35
Fight-or-flight response, 101–102
Finances, personal, 180, 183,
    230, 256–257, 279
Finances of institutions
    budget cuts, 11, 15, 20–21
    employment discrimination and, 285
    federal and state funding, 13, 128, 285
    job negotiations and, 230–231
    leadership pressures and, 293
    power centers and, 99
    transitions to new jobs and, 239
Fischler, L. A., 75
Fisher, R., 120–121
Five commitments of leadership
    (Kouzes & Posner), 316
Flexible scheduling, 188
Focus group interviews, 35
Force and power, 93
Formal conflict resolution, 126–127, 136
Formal vs. informal language, 59–60
Forrest, C., 142
Forret, M. L., 69
Frames of conflict, 123–124, 132
Friendships. *See also* Support networks
    with mentors, 78–80
    outside profession, 189
    with students, 56–57, 236

Functional résumés, 202
Furlong, G. T., 119, 121
Furlough days, 11

G

Gaff, J. G., 258–259
Gasman, M., 299–300
Gaston-Gayles, J. L., 262
Gatekeepers, 99–101
Gehring, Donald D., 313
Gelberg, W., 70
Gender. *See also* Diversity
    imposter syndrome and, 172
    leadership positions and, 298–300, 306
    work–life balance and, 188, 279
Generalization vs. specialization, 14–15
Generational differences
    in communication preferences,
        72, 82, 276–277
    in feedback preferences, 281
    mentoring relationships and, 81–83
    in work ethic, 279–280
    in work experience, 274
    work–life balance and, 188, 279–280
Generation X and Y, 72, 81–83,
    274, 276–277, 279
Geographic considerations in
    employment, 200–201, 228–230
Getting to Yes (Fisher & Ury), 120
Gladwell, Malcolm, 67–68
Goals
    authoritarian supervision and, 270
    career, 87–88, 241. *See
        also* Career paths
    conflict resolution and, 120
    for ethics competencies, 143
    of institutions, 30
    job searches and, 198, 220
    for meetings, 253
    for mentoring relationships, 84
    transitions to new jobs and, 236
Goleman, D., 73
Goodman, J., 196
Gordon, S. A., 80
Graduate degrees. *See* Advanced degrees
Grants, 256–257
Gratitude, 325

Grenny, J., 125
Grief, stages of, 204
Grievance processes, 126–127, 132, 254
Group identity subcultures, 32–34
Group interviews, 212
Guest lecturers, 259
"Guidelines for Graduate Programs in the Preparation of Student Personnel Workers in Higher Education" (COSPA & APGA), 247

H

Haley, K., 62–63
Hamel, V., 134
Happenstance learning theory (Krumboltz), 16
Harassment, 128
Harvey, M., 300
Hawes, C., 62–63
Hempsall, K., 303–304
Heraclitus of Ephesus, 107
Heywood, Andrew, 93–94
Hierarchy, 276. *See also* Organizational hierarchy
HigherEdJobs.com, 204, 215
Higher education organizations. *See* Institutions
Higher education trends, x, 3–24
  career paths, 17–18
  competition for students, 8
  daily e-mails about, 176
  ethics and, 142–143
  executive leadership, recruiting, 6–8
  institutional types, 13
  job searches and, 201
  for leadership, 295–300
  new technologies, 9–10
  nontraditional careers, 18–20
  organizational structures, 8–9
  personal priorities, 16–17
  professional competencies and, 12–13, 175
  professional development, 15–16
  professional relevance, 10–20
  specialization vs. generalization, 14–15
  student affairs profession and, 4–6
  supervisors and, 20–21

Hill, K., 134
Hiring process, 284–285. *See also* Acceptance of employment
Hirt, J. B., 187, 271
Hoffman, B., 276
Holzweiss, Peggy C., 141, 167
Hopper, Grace, 268
Horizontal career moves, 201–202, 278
Hostile environments, 128
Housing options, 230
How Colleges Work (Birnbaum), 94
Humility, 113
Hurtado, S., 234–235
Hybrid course delivery, 9

I

Identity
  career, 78
  in communities of practice, 51
  conflict resolution and, 123
  culture and, 27
  electronic, 58. *See also* Social media
  group identity subcultures, 32–34
  job searches and, 197
  professional, 15, 18, 178
  racial and gender issues and, 86
  retirement and, 278
  self-authorship and, 168–172
  subcultures and, 31–34
  tenure-track faculty transition and, 255–256
Illinois Policy Institute, 3
Immersive international experiences, 216–217
Imposter syndrome, 172–173, 190–191
Incompatibility, 119–120
Indeed.com, 204
Industry, executive leadership from, 6–8, 296
Informal conflict resolution, 126–127, 136
Informal vs. formal language, 59–60
Inside Higher Ed, 176
Institute of Cultural Affairs, 134
Institutional Review Boards (IRBs), 318
Institutions
  budget cuts at, 11, 15, 20–21

career paths and, 17–18
change establishment at, 41
climate of, 28, 35
codes of conduct and, 145
conflict resolution methods
  for, 126, 132, 136
culture of, 25–44. *See also*
  Culture of institutions
employment cuts at, 4, 13
ethical dilemmas, 147
faculty positions at, 245–266.
  See also Faculty positions
finances. *See* Finances of institutions
legal regulations for, 314–315
mission of, 227, 298
organizational fit and, 232, 260–261,
  309. *See also* Work environment
organizational models of,
  30–31, 94–96, 232–233
organization of. *See*
  Organizational hierarchy
politics of, 91–116. *See also*
  Politics of institutions
processes and procedures of, 126–127,
  136, 171, 178, 188, 274–275
public scrutiny of, 293
reorganizations of, 16
retirement investment in, 11–12
student affairs positions and, 14–15
subcultures within, 31–34
support networks within, 69
trends for. *See* Higher education trends
types of, 13, 251
values of, 28–29, 29*f*, 96, 149,
  158–161, 234, 274–275
Integrity, 206–207
Interest-based conflicts, 120–123
Interim leaders, 305
International Association for
  Conflict Management, 134
International Association of
  Facilitators, 134
International job searches, 215–219
International Symposium of NASPA, 216
International work–life balance, 280
Internships, 217
Interpersonal domain of
  development, 236
Intersectionality, 27, 33, 40
Interviews for culture audits, 35, 38
Interviews for employment
  asking questions during, 161
  ethics and, 205–206
  for international opportunities, 216
  lateral career moves and, 202
  marginalized identities and, 197
  at placement conferences, 207–208
  preparation for, 211–212
  with search firms, 210–211
  types, 211–213, 216
  unemployed time and, 203
Intrapersonal domain of
  development, 236
Introverts, 54, 70, 83–86
IRBs (Institutional Review Boards), 318
Isaacs, M. R., 34

J

Jackson, Phil, 323
Jacobsen, Merna, 117
Jaeger, A., 62–63
Jakeman, R. C., 180
Janosik, S. M., 147
Javinar, J. M., 179–180
Job applications. *See* Cover
  letters; Résumés
Job changes. *See also* Acceptance
    of employment
  ethics of institutions and, 160–161
  faculty positions. *See* Faculty positions
  institutional budget issues and, 11–12
  natural transitions and, 178–181
  politics of institutions and, 106
  preplanned. *See* Career paths
  for promotion opportunities, 278, 282
  pros and cons of, 18
  seeking employment. *See* Job searches
  support networks and, 75
Job expectations. *See* Expectations
    of employers
Job satisfaction, 118, 179, 188, 302
Job searches, xi, 195–223. *See also*
    Acceptance of employment
  with doctoral degrees, 182

dual-career couples and, 213–215
employment during, 255
ethics and, 160–161, 205–207
factors in transition process, 196–200
functional area job changes, 202–203
geographic-specific, 200–201
international, 215–219
lateral job changes, 201–202
leadership positions, 306–307
mid-level placement and, 207–209
as professional development practice, 177
search firms for, 209–213, 306–307
supervisors and, 219–220
unemployment during, 203–205
Job security, 4, 11–12, 294, 306
Johnson, J., 62–63
Jones, S., 300
Jones, S. J., 188
Journal publications, 319. *See also* Publications

K

Kaufman, S., 123
Keeling, R. P., 47
Kelly, K. E., 76–77
Kennedy, A. A., 28
Khayyam, Omar, 324
King, P. M., 169–171
Kipling, Rudyard, 323
Kitchener, K. S., 144
Kniess, D., 256
Knight, A., 174–175, 189–190
Knowledge gaps, 12–13, 16, 158–159, 240–241, 274
Komives, S. R., 261
Kouzes, J. M., 316, 322–323, 325
Kram, K. E., 78–80
Krumboltz, J. A., 16
Kuk, L., 142

L

Laissez-faire supervision, 270–271
Lance, D., 276
Langdon, E. A., 80
Late-career employees, 278

Lateral career moves, 201–202, 278
"The Law of the Jungle" (Kipling), 323
Law school, 181
Laziness, 280
Leadership activities
  to advance to leadership positions, 303–305
  collaboration and, 300–301, 323–324
  for conflict resolution, 132–133
  decision-making, 96–97
  five commitments of leadership and, 316
  institutional committee participation and, 252
  in meetings, 53–54
  organizational change and, 41
  problem-solving, 301
Leadership positions. *See* Executive leadership positions; Supervisors and supervision
Leadership theory, 303
Learning Reconsidered (Keeling), 47
Lefore, G., 300
Legal issues
  conflict resolution and, 126, 132
  for institutions, 314–315
  for supervisors, 282–286
Leist, J., 182
Lencioni, P., 125
LGBTQ (lesbian, gay, bisexual, transgender, and queer), 128, 218
Listening skills, 113, 273
Litigation, 126, 132
Loneliness, 218, 259–260
Lowery, John Wesley, 245
Loyalty of employees, 275

M

Magolda, P. M., 149, 152, 235
Managers, 268
Manning, K., 29–30, 33, 97, 99, 104
March, J., 30
Marginalized identities, 197
Marshall, B., 72
Marshall, V., 280
Martin, J., 31
Massive Open Online Courses

(MOOCs), 9
Master's degrees. *See* Advanced degrees
"Master's-Level Student Affairs Professional Preparation Programs Standards and Guidelines" (CAS), 247–248
Mathews, Lois Kimball, 246
Mayer, R. J., 119
McCluskey-Titus, P., 260, 262
McDade, S. A., 304–305
McMillan, R., 125
McNair, D. E., 305
Mediation, 126, 132, 134–135
Meetings
  for appraisal and feedback, 280–281
  connectors and gatekeepers and, 100–101
  documentation for, 283–284
  ethics training in, 157
  for faculty, 53–54
  politics of institutions and, 98
  professionalism for, 53–54
  supervisors and, 276
Meister, J. C., 281
Mentors and mentoring
  career development of, 278
  conflict resolution and, 134
  defined, 75
  diversity and, 86
  e-mentoring, 83–84
  for faculty members, 262–263
  functions and phases of relationship, 78–80
  identifying, 77–78
  introverts and, 84–86
  leadership positions and, 299–300, 305–306, 309
  for millennials, 81–83
  professional development and, 63
  sponsor relationships, 80–81
  stress management and, 173
  student affairs professionals as, 324–325
  supervisors as, 87, 268
  support networks and, 75–78
  transitions to new jobs and, 238
  types of, 75–76

Microfeedback, 281
Micromanagement, 270–271
Mid-career professionals, 17, 278–279, 305
Mid-level positions, 207–209, 306
Milem, J., 234–235
Milieu, 94. *See also* Politics of institutions
Military, leadership recruitment from, 296
Millennial generation
  communication styles, 276–277
  feedback, need for, 281
  mentors for, 81–83
  networking and, 72, 82
  training and orientation for, 274
  work ethic of, 280
  work–life balance and, 279–280
Minorities. *See* Diversity; Gender
Miscommunications, 83
Mission of institutions, 227, 298
Mission/service experiences, 216–217
Models of supervision, 272–273
MOOCs (Massive Open Online Courses), 9
Moore, Christopher, 121–122, 127–128, 130–131
Morton, D., 120
Motivational skills, 273

N

Name preferences, 59–60
National Association for Community Mediation, 134
National Association of Colleges and Employers, 8
National Association of Student Personnel Administrators (NASPA)
  competencies for professionals, 47–48, 143, 167, 174, 236
  conference presentation opportunities and, 259, 321
  Faculty Council, 258
  history of, 5
  International Symposium, 216
  Professional Competency Areas for Student Affairs Educators, 12, 52
National Education Association, 46

Negligence, 282–283
Negotiation. *See* Conflict resolution
Negotiations for job offers, 226–232
Nelson, J. A., 34–35
Networking. *See* Support networks
Networking quotient (NQ), 73–74
Network mentoring, 83–84
Noël-Elkins, Amelia, 3
Nonprofit groups, 69
Nontraditional careers, 18–20
Nonverbal communication, 59–60, 83
Note-taking of supervisors, 283–284

O

Office etiquette, 60–62
Office politics. *See* Politics of institutions
Online feedback systems, 281
Online instruction, 9–10, 251, 253
Onwuegbuzie, A. J., 34–35
Organizational climate, 28, 35
Organizational culture, 27–31, 29f, 34–35, 40–41. *See also* Culture of institutions
Organizational Culture and Leadership (Schein), 28
Organizational fit, 232, 260–261, 309. *See also* Work environment
Organizational hierarchy
  acceptance of new job and, 227
  chain of command and, 61
  changes in, 8–9, 11, 16, 20–21, 106–107
  conflict resolution and, 128–131
  interdepartmental relations and, 228–229
  political functioning and, 94–96
  power centers and players, 99–101
  support networks and, 69, 73, 78
Orientation
  legal responsibility for, 282–283
  for new hires, 236
  supervisors and, 273–275
Ott, M., 52
Outreach, job searches and, 201
Overcoming the Five Dysfunctions of a Team (Lencioni), 125
Overqualification, 202

P

Pacing, politics of institutions and, 107–110, 112
Panel interviews, 212
Paper files, 283–284
Paper presentations, 320–321
Parrott, David, W., 91
Parrott, Kelli Peck, 267
Partnerships. *See* Collaboration
Part-time advanced degree programs, 183
Part-time employment, 19–20, 203
Patterson, K., 125
Peddy, S., 75
Peer-reviewed journals, 319
Pellegrini, E. K., 83
Pelletier, F., 134
Perfectionism, 172–173, 191
Personal culture audits, 36–38
Personal finances, 180, 183, 230, 256–257, 279
Personal journals for documentation, 156, 284
Personal narratives, 197
Personal priorities, 16–17, 228–229
Personal values
  culture of institutions and, 38–39
  ethics and, 149–151, 160
  international employment and, 218
  job searches and, 198, 214
Persuasiveness, 112–113
Photographs, social media and, 56–57
Physical files, 283–284
Pipelines for leadership positions, 298–300
Placement conferences, 207–208
The Placement Exchange, job postings on, 215
Pluri-identities, 27, 33, 40
Poitras, J., 134
Political institutions, 30, 94–96, 233
Political sectors, leadership recruitment from, 296–297
Politics of institutions, x, 91–116
  advice on, 106
  defined, 92–94
  ethics and, 149–150, 158

leadership positions and, 296–297
organizational models and, 94–96
players vs. victims, 101–103
positive view of, 91–92
power centers and players, 99–101
reciprocation and, 110–111
stakeholders and, 107–110
tensions caused by, 96–99
tips for, 111–114
transitions to new jobs and, 240
Porter, J., 80–81
Positive outlook, 16, 113–114
Posner, B. Z., 316, 322–323, 325
Poster sessions, 320
Power, 93, 99–101, 124
Preconference workshops, 320
Prejudice, 197, 284–286
"Preparation Standards and Guidelines at the Master's Degree Level for Student Services/Development Professionals in Postsecondary Education" (CAS), 247
PreparedU project, Bentley University, 274
Preparing Future Faculty, 259
Presentations
  at conferences, 259, 278, 320–321
  for dissertations, 186
  for employment interviews, 211–213
  introverts and, 84
Presidents. *See* Executive leadership positions
Privacy
  e-mail communication and, 57
  e-mentoring and, 83
  ethical decision-making and, 150, 154–156
  job offers and, 231
  job searches and, 206
  social media and, 57, 71
Problem solving, 96–97, 300–301.
  See also Conflict resolution
Professional associations. *See also specific associations*
  as communities of practice, 49
  for conflict resolution, 134
  for environmental scans
    of institutions, 36
  ethics competencies and, 160
  history of, 5–6
  participation in, 252, 278, 322
  professional development and, 15–16, 178
  search firms, nominations for, 210
Professional competencies.
  See Competencies
Professional Competency Areas for Student Affairs Educators (ACPA & NASPA), 12, 52
Professional courtesy, 231–232
Professional development, xi, 167–194
  activities for, 174–175. *See also* Conferences
  advanced degrees for, 181–187
  in conflict resolution, 133–134
  ethics and, 145, 149–151
  for faculty members, 259, 262
  feedback from supervisors and, 63
  funding for, 230–231
  imposter syndrome and, 172–173
  for leadership positions, 303–305
  mentors and, 80
  natural transitions, 178–181
  opportunities, preparation for, 177–178
  professional needs, assessing, 173–177
  professional relevance and, 15–16
  self-authorship, 168–172
  for specific functional areas, 202–203
  supervisors and, 189–191, 240–241
  transitions to new jobs and, 236
  work–life integration and, 187–189
Professional identity, 15, 18
Professionalism, x, 45–65.
  See also Reputations
  acquisition of, 48–52
  basics of, 274
  in communication, 54–58
  defined, 46–48
  maintenance of, 316–317
  in meetings, 53–54
  office etiquette and, 60–62
  practice of, 52–62
  reciprocation and, 110–111

INDEX **347**

respectful relationships and, 58–60
supervisors and, 61–63, 289
Professional journals, 319.
  See also Publications
Professional judgment, 105–106
Professional networks. *See*
  Support networks
Professional relevance
  career paths, 17–18
  competencies and, 12–13
  higher education trends and, 10–20
  knowledge of institutional types, 13
  nontraditional careers, 18–20
  personal priorities, 16–17
  professional development
    opportunities, 15–16
  specialization vs. generalization, 14–15
  of student affairs, 298
Professional standards, 46, 132, 247–248.
  See also Council for the Advancement
    of Standards in Higher Education
Professors. *See* Faculty positions
Promotion committees, 252
Promotions, 277–280, 282, 285
  to leadership positions, 294–295, 302
Provost appointments, 253. *See also*
  Executive leadership positions
Pruitt-Logan, A. S., 258–259
Publications
  faculty positions and, 251–253, 259
  staff development and, 278
  student affairs professionals
    and, 319–320
Public speaking
  at conferences, 259, 278, 320–321
  for dissertations, 186
  employment interviews and, 211–213
  introverts and, 84

Q

Qualifications. *See* Advanced
  degrees; Experience
Quality-of-life issues, 180, 214, 217–219,
  308–309. *See also* Work–life balance
Questions in interviews, 211
Quinn, R. E., 234
Quiñones-Ortega, D. N., 71

R

Race. *See* Diversity
Ragins, B. R., 86
Rankin, S. R., 233
Rapport, 275. *See also* Trust
Reading skills, 304
Reason, R. D., 233
Reciprocation, 110–111
Records in supervision, 283–284
Recruitment for leadership
  positions, 295–299
Reesor, L., 69–70
References, 204, 211, 216
Reframing of conflict, 123–124, 132
Regularity, supervisor relationships
  and, 275–276
Rehabilitation Act (1973), 285–286
Relationships. *See also* Mentors
  accountability partners, 186–187, 238
  conflicts in, 121–122, 127, 131
  ethical principles for, 144
  generational preferences for, 72
  meetings and, 54
  politics of institutions and, 94
  problem solving collaborations,
    300–301
  professionalism and, 58–60, 62
  research partnerships and,
    214, 259, 318
  sponsors, 80–81
  supervisors and, 271,
    275–277, 289–290
  for support. *See* Support networks
Religious beliefs, 128, 218
Relocation for employment, 200–201,
  215–219, 228–230, 279
Reputations
  acceptance of new job and, 225
  decline of new job and, 231
  electronic identities and, 58
  job searches and, 206–207
  meetings and, 53
  office etiquette and, 61–62
  social media and, 56, 72
Research
  collaboration in, 214, 259, 318

conference presentations on, 320–321
faculty responsibilities for, 251–253, 256, 259
keeping current with, 316–318
of student affairs professionals, 317–318
Research universities, 13, 251
Résumés
  campus interviews and, 213
  honesty in, 205
  for international opportunities, 216
  job searches and, 202
  for mid-level placements, 207–209
  networking and, 75
  skills and knowledge gaps, 12–13
Retirement, 11–12, 278
Revise and resubmit (R&Rs) publications, 319–320
Reward, 325
Reybold, L. E., 151, 261
Risk, conflict and, 124
Role changes, 198–199
Role models, 113, 133, 135–136. *See also* Mentors and mentoring
Roles of faculty, 252–253
Rosser, V. J., 179–180, 306
Rowney, J., 59
R&Rs (revise and resubmit), 319–320
Rudolph, F., 4
Russell, Bill, 313
Russell Rules (Russell), 313
Ryland, K., 300

S

Salaries
  faculty positions and, 257
  job searches and, 211
  leadership positions and, 309
  negotiation process for, 229–230
  tuition prices and, 3
Salimbene, S., 75
Sandberg, Sheryl, 13
Saunders, S., 276, 280
Scandura, T. A., 83
Scheduling issues, 187–188
Schein, Edgar, 28–29, 29*f*
Schexnider, A. J., 301

Schlossberg, N. K., 195, 196, 200, 220
Scholarly writing, 260
Scott, J. A., 182
Search firms for employment, 209–213, 306–307
Self-advocacy, 177
Self-assessment for competencies, 143, 174, 236
Self-authorship, 168–172, 179
Self-awareness, 134, 189
Self-concept theory (Super), 16
Self-esteem, 85, 204, 241
Self-mastery skills, 47
Self-negotiation, 136
Self-talk, 84
Senior leadership, 293–294. *See also* Executive leadership positions
Sequencing, politics of institutions and, 107–110, 112
Service responsibilities of faculty, 252, 254
The 7 Hidden Reasons Employees Leave (Branham), 38
Sexual discrimination, 285
Shapiro, J. P., 146
Shmueli, D., 123
Shy people, 54, 70, 84–86
Silver, B. R., 180
Situational interview questions, 211
Skills. *See* Competencies; Experience
Skills gaps, 12–13, 16, 158–159, 240–241, 274
Skills résumés, 202
Smedick, William, 45
Social activities, 85, 189, 228. *See also* Friendships
Social constructivism, 30
Social identities, 197
Socialization to new institutions, 228, 235–241
Social media
  culture audits of institutions and, 36, 38
  dangers of, 10
  generational preferences for, 72
  job searches and, 206, 210
  personal policy for, 57–58
  professionalism and, 54–58

INDEX

public scrutiny of institutions and, 293
support networks and, 67, 71–72
Specialization vs. generalization, 14–15
Sponsor relationships, 80–81
Staff
  campus culture and, 40
  employment discrimination and, 284–286
  higher education trends and, 20–21
  issues for supervisors and, 281–284
  loyalty of, 275
  meetings with, 276
  power of, 99–101
  professional development of, 277–280. *See also* Professional development
  respectful relationships and, 40, 59
  as supervisees, advice for, 286–290
  supervisor communications with, 40, 61–62, 219, 239, 276, 286–287
  termination of, 282–283
  training and orientation for, 273–275
  workaholic behaviors and, 172–173
  work evaluations for, 280–281
Staffing model, 272–273
Stakeholders, 6–7, 35, 107–110, 300. *See also specific groups*
Standard interview questions, 211
"Standards for the Preparation of Counselors and Other Personnel Services Specialists" (ACEA), 247
Stanford University, 214
State funding, 13
Status quo, challenging, 322
Steele, C., 197
Stefkovich, J. A., 146
Steinfeld, T., 231
Stenken, J. A., 68
Stereotypes, 121, 123, 197
Sternberg, R. J., 161
Stimpson, M. T., 63–64
Stoflet, T., 52
Stress
  burnout and, 173
  conflict and, 118
  introverts and, 84
  job changes and, 180
  leadership positions and, 308–309

living abroad and, 217–218
  management of, 189, 191, 199, 209
  transitions to new jobs and, 238
  unemployment and, 204
Structural conflicts, 121–122, 131
Student affairs profession, xi, 313–326
  academic affairs, merging with, 8–9
  acceptable behavior for. *See* Etiquette
  advanced degrees for, 181–187
  changing nature of, 314–316
  conference presentations and, 320–321
  culture of, 33
  disengagement and, 38
  ethics in, 141–164. *See also* Ethics
  faculty, collaboration with, 261–262
  five commitments of leadership and, 316
  history of, 4–6, 246–248
  international, 217
  philosophy of, 5
  politics of institutions and, 91–116. *See also* Politics of institutions
  professional development for, 167–194. *See also* Professional development
  professional relevance and, 10–20, 298
  publication contributions to, 319–320
  research contributions to, 317–318
  service to the profession and, 321–325
  specialization vs. generalization, 14–15
  trends higher education and, 3–24. *See also* Higher education trends
  value of, 7–8
The Student Personnel Point of View (ACE), 5
Students
  accountability for, 267–268
  adjunct faculty roles and, 254
  competition for, 8
  conflict resolution and, 317–318
  face-to-face communication with, 9–10
  retention programs for, 108–110
  services for, 6–7
  social connections with, 56–57, 236
  working with, 180
Study abroad, 216–217
Styles of supervision, 270–272
Subcultures, 27, 31–34, 40

Success
  celebrating, 85–86, 325
  generational differences in, 82
  imposter syndrome and, 172–173
  leadership positions and, 302, 309
  politics of institutions and, 107–110
Sue, D. W., 34
Super, D. E., 16
Supervisors and supervision, xi, 267–293
  advice for, 286–290
  campus culture and, 39–41
  challenges for, 287–288
  common approaches for, 270
  communication and, 54–55, 61–62, 219, 239, 286–287
  conflict resolution and, 134–136
  criticisms of, 271–272
  defined, 269–273
  ethics and, 157–159
  feedback from, 63, 180, 190, 240, 280–284
  higher education trends and, 20–21
  hiring process and, 239–241
  inappropriate behavior and, 155–157
  job searches of employees and, 219–220
  legal issues for, 284–286
  as mentors, 87, 268
  models of, 272–273
  orientation and training from, 273–275, 282–283
  professional development and, 189–191, 240–241
  professionalism and, 61–63, 289
  relationships and, 271, 275–277, 289–290
  separation from staff, 281–284
  skills for, 273, 276
  staff development, 277–280
  styles of, 270–272
  support networks and mentoring, 76, 86–88
  transitions to new jobs and, 236, 238
  trust and, 39, 239, 275
Support networks, x, 67–90
  advanced degrees and, 186–187
  behavior needed for, 69–70
  coalitions, 112
  connectors and, 67, 99–101
  diversity and, 86
  e-mentoring, 83–84
  generational differences in, 72
  introverts and, 84–86
  for job searches, 200–201
  maintenance and growth of, 73–75
  meetings and, 54
  mentors, 75–86. *See also* Mentors
  for millennials, 81–83
  politics of institutions and, 112
  professional development and, 178
  purpose of, 68–69
  social media and, 71–72
  sponsor relationships, 80–81
  stress management and, 173
  supervisors and, 76, 86–88
  transitions to new jobs and, 238
  types of, 74
Switzler, A., 125
Synergistic supervision model (Winston & Creamer), 239–241, 272–273, 276
Syracuse University, 246

T

Taras, V., 59
Taylor, C. M., 188
Teaching load, 251, 254
Teaching positions. *See* Faculty positions
Technology. *See also* Social media
  cell phones, 277, 293
  competence in, 12
  e-mail communication and, 54–55, 57, 176, 188–189, 276–277
  e-mentoring, 83–84
  employment interviews and, 212, 216
  millennials and, 81–82
  online feedback systems, 281
  online instruction and, 9–10, 251, 253
  students' competency in, 7
Telecommuting, 188
Telephone communication, 83–84, 231–232, 276–277
Telephone interviews, 212, 216
Temporary faculty positions, 255
Tenure-track faculty positions,

250–253, 255–261
Terminal degrees, 181
Termination of employees, 282–283
Texas Tech University, 9
Text messaging, 83, 277
Thomas–Kilmann conflict mode instrument, 125–126
Tierney, W. G., 31, 35, 228
Time management, 324
Timing
 of job searches, 198
 politics of institutions and, 107–110, 112
The Tipping Point (Gladwell), 67
Title VII of Civil Rights Act (1964), 285–286
Town hall meetings, 35
Townsend, Robert, 325
Training, 236, 273–275, 282–283. *See also* Professional development
Transition documents, 62
Transition model (Schlossberg), 195–200
Transitions to new jobs, 228, 235–241
Transparency, 113
Travers, C., 299–300
Trends. *See* Higher education trends
Triggers for job searches, 198
Trust
 conflict resolution and, 127
 ethical decision-making and, 153–156
 mentors and, 82–83
 politics of institutions and, 103, 113
 professionalism and, 59–60
 sponsor relationships and, 81
 supervisors and, 39, 239, 275
Tuition costs, 3, 7, 13
Tull, A., 239
Twenge, J., 276, 279–280
Twitter, 71–72. *See also* Social media

U

Underlying assumptions in organizational culture, 28–29, 29f
Unemployment, 203–205
Unethical behavior. *See* Ethics
Unionized institutions, 253
Universities. *See* Institutions

University committees, 252
Up the Organization (Townsend), 325
Ury, W., 120–121

V

Values. *See also* Personal values
 codes of conduct and, 145–146
 competing, political conflict and, 96
 conflict resolution and, 121–122, 127–128
 institutional, 96, 149, 158–161, 234
 organizational culture and, 28–29, 29f
 professional, 227
 religious beliefs and, 128, 218
 self-authorship and, 168–172
 subcultures and, 32
 supervision and, 273
VanHecke, J. R., 233, 235
Victims of institutional politics, 101–103
Video interviews, 212, 216
Visiting faculty positions, 255
Volunteer opportunities, 17, 69, 204, 268, 305

W

Weekends, working, 172–173, 187–188, 308–309
Wenger, E., 48–52
Whitt, E. J., 47
Willyerd, K., 281
Wilson, A., 45
Winston, R. B., Jr., 271, 272–273, 276
Women. *See* Gender
Workaholic behavior, 172–173
Work environment. *See also* Culture of institutions; Politics of institutions
 adjustment to, 228, 235–241
 ethical decision-making and, 156–157
 faculty positions and, 260–261
 hostile, 128
 job changes and, 11–12, 179–180
 job searches and, 206
 negotiations for new jobs and, 226–227
 unemployment and, 204
Work ethic, 279
Work evaluations, 280–281, 283

Work–life balance
  advanced degrees and, 187, 258
  generational differences in, 279–280
  international preferences in, 280
  job changes and, 179–180
  job searches and, 199
  leadership positions and, 308–309
  professional development and, 187–189, 278–279
  supervisors and, 190–191
Work relationships, 58–60.
  See also Colleagues

Writing, scholarly, 260. *See also* Publications

Y

Yosso, T., 197
Young, R. B., 147

Z

Zachary, L. J., 75
Zack, D., 70
Zajicek, A. M., 68